An Introduction to the Study of Ezekiel

Other titles in the T&T Clark Approaches to
Biblical Studies series include:

An Introduction to Revelation, Gilbert Desrosiers
The Pentateuch: A Story of Beginnings, Paula Gooder
An Introduction to the Study of Paul (Third Edition), David G. Horrell
An Introduction to the Psalms, Alistair G. Hunter
Jesus and the Gospels (Second Edition), Clive Marsh and Steve Moyise
Joshua to Kings, Mary E. Mills
Introduction to Biblical Studies (Third Edition), Steve Moyise
The Old Testament in the New, Steve Moyise
An Introduction to the Study of Luke–Acts, V. George Shillington
An Introduction to the Study of Isaiah, Jacob Stromberg
An Introduction to the Study of Wisdom Literature, Stuart Weeks

An Introduction to the Study of Ezekiel

Michael A. Lyons

Bloomsbury T&T Clark
An imprint of Bloomsbury Publishing Plc

B L O O M S B U R Y
LONDON • NEW DELHI • NEW YORK • SYDNEY

Bloomsbury T&T Clark

An imprint of Bloomsbury Publishing Plc

Imprint previously known as T&T Clark

50 Bedford Square 1385 Broadway
London New York
WC1B 3DP NY 10018
UK USA

www.bloomsbury.com

BLOOMSBURY, T&T CLARK and the Diana logo are trademarks of Bloomsbury Publishing Plc

First published 2015

© Michael A. Lyons, 2015

Michael A. Lyons has asserted his right under the Copyright, Designs and Patents Act, 1988, to be identified as Author of this work.

All rights reserved. No part of this publication may be reproduced or transmitted in any form or by any means, electronic or mechanical, including photocopying, recording, or any information storage or retrieval system, without prior permission in writing from the publishers.

No responsibility for loss caused to any individual or organization acting on or refraining from action as a result of the material in this publication can be accepted by Bloomsbury or the author.

British Library Cataloguing-in-Publication Data
A catalogue record for this book is available from the British Library.

ISBN: HB: 978-0-56711-046-6
PB: 978-0-56730-422-3
ePDF: 978-0-56766-309-2
ePub: 978-0-56766-310-8

Library of Congress Cataloging-in-Publication Data
Lyons, Michael A.
An introduction to the study of Ezekiel / Michael A. Lyons.
pages cm
ISBN 978-0-567-30422-3 (pbk) — ISBN 978-0-567-11046-6 (hbk) — ISBN 978-0-567-66309-2 (epdf) — ISBN 978-0-567-66310-8 (epub)
1. Bible. Ezekiel—Criticism, interpretation, etc. I. Title.
BS1545.52.L965 2015
224'.406—dc23
2014038603

Typeset by RefineCatch Limited, Bungay, Suffolk

For Rianne

Contents

Abbreviations ix

	Introduction	1
1	The Prophet Ezekiel and the Book of Ezekiel	7
2	From Prophetic Speech to Prophetic Book	49
3	Israel, Yhwh, Land, and Temple	115
4	From Problem to Solution	165

Bibliography 187
Index of Scriptural References 197
Index of Authors 213

Abbreviations

AB	Anchor Bible
ATD	Das Alte Testament Deutsch
BBB	Bonner Biblische Beiträge
BETL	Bibliotheca ephemeridum theologicarum lovaniensium
BHT	Beiträge zur historischen Theologie
BibOr	Biblica et orientalia
BKAT	Biblischer Kommentar, Altes Testament
BWANT	Beiträge zur Wissenschaft vom Alten und Neuen Testament
BZAW	Beihefte zur Zeitschrift für die alttestamentliche Wissenschaft
CBQ	*Catholic Biblical Quarterly*
CBR	*Currents in Biblical Research*
CHANE	Culture and History of the Ancient Near East
CR:BS	*Currents in Research: Biblical Studies*
EH	Europäische Hochschulschriften
ExpTim	*Expository Times*
FAT	Forschungen zum Alten Testament
HSM	Harvard Semitic Monograph
HUCA	*Hebrew Union College Annual*
ICC	International Critical Commentary

JBL	Journal of Biblical Literature
JSOT	Journal for the Study of the Old Testament
JSOTSup	Journal for the Study of the Old Testament Supplement Series
JTS	Journal of Theological Studies
LHBOTS	Library of Hebrew Bible/Old Testament Studies
LSTS	Library of Second Temple Studies
NBBC	New Beacon Bible Commentary
NICOT	New International Commentary on the Old Testament
OBO	Orbis biblicus et orientalis
PTMS	Princeton Theological Monograph Series
SBB	Stuttgarter Biblische Beiträge
SBLDS	Society of Biblical Literature Dissertation Series
SBLSCS	Society of Biblical Literature Septuagint and Cognate Series
SBLSS	Society of Biblical Literature Symposium Series
SBS	Stuttgarter Bibelstudien
SJOT	Scandinavian Journal of the Old Testament
ThLZ	Theologische Literaturzeitung
TR	Theologische Rundschau
TynBul	Tyndale Bulletin
VT	Vetus Testamentum
VTSup	Supplements to Vetus Testamentum
ZAW	Zeitschrift für die alttestamentliche Wissenschaft

Introduction

The book of Ezekiel strikes the modern reader as one of the strangest texts in the Bible. Its imagery is baffling and grotesque, and its language is repetitive, violent, and hyper-sexualized. It tells us next to nothing about the prophet Ezekiel, other than that he had disturbing visionary experiences and was told to perform unusual actions in public. But the book of Ezekiel was not composed in order to baffle its readers. Rather, it should be understood as an example of trauma literature: it was written for an audience who had undergone forced deportation to another land, whose city and temple had been destroyed by the Babylonian empire, and whose religious and political institutions had come to a devastating end. The book of Ezekiel was composed to interpret this disaster and offer an almost unimaginable hope for the deportees' future. To be sure, the book is ancient literature—and is therefore inevitably somewhat foreign to us. But the traumatic experiences it grapples with are all too common even today, and are felt around the world by groups of displaced peoples. Perhaps, then, the book is not as strange as we might think.

Those who are unfamiliar with the Bible are likely to know parts of the book of Ezekiel only as they have been appropriated and refracted through popular culture. For example, one might remember the American Negro Spiritual "Ezekiel Saw the Wheel" (or the song by the Grateful Dead containing similar imagery, titled "The Wheel"). A more recent reference to the book can be seen in the 1994 film *Pulp Fiction*, in which the character played by Samuel L. Jackson delivers an ominous tirade of Ezekielian-sounding judgment language (purportedly quoted from "Ezekiel 25:17") before repeatedly shooting another character at close range. And there is a line of whole-grain health foods marketed under the label "Ezekiel 4:9" (which, ironically, misses the point of the verse; Ezekiel is not attempting here to provide the secrets of a healthy diet!). But there is far more to the history of the book's use than the occasional nod it receives in popular culture.

The history of the book's reception actually begins *within* the book of Ezekiel itself, with editorial attempts to explain its contents and coordinate it with other books (see Chapter 2 of this volume for examples). The book of Ezekiel quickly began to exercise an influence on other texts as well. For example, Zech 10.2b-3; 11.16 (describing people as sheep afflicted by bad shepherds) alludes to Ezek 34.4-5, 10, 17. The passage about the shepherds and sheep in the "Animal Apocalypse" of 1 Enoch (1 Enoch 89.59-77) draws on both Ezek 34 and Zech 11. And the New Testament passages describing Jesus as the "good shepherd" who seeks out and cares for his flock (Matt 9.36; 18.12-14 [// Lk 15.1-7]; Jn 10.7-16) draw on the image of the sheep and the Davidic shepherd in Ezek 34.1-16, 23.

Early readers of the book of Ezekiel took its arguments to heart and longed for the restoration that it describes: spiritual transformation, peace and security from enemies, and a fertile land. Among the scrolls discovered at Qumran were fragments of a composition that is a rewritten form of the book of Ezekiel—a sort of commentary where the author puts into Ezekiel's mouth the questions of his own day. After the author lists several of Ezekiel's prophecies of restoration, he makes the prophet ask God when these hopes would be realized (4Q385 2.9; 4Q386 1.ii.2-3). Texts like these allow us to as it were "peer over the shoulder" of early readers of Ezekiel and see how they appropriated the book.

Ezekiel's arguments about spiritual transformation had a powerful impact on both Second Temple-period Jewish and early Christian communities: his language of iniquities cleansed with pure water and of obedience guaranteed by the gift of God's Spirit (Ezek 36.25-37, 33) can be found in 1QS 3.7-9; 4.21-22 and in Jn 3.5; Titus 2.14; 3.5-6; Heb 10.22. The language of Ezekiel's hope for the transformation and fertility of the land (Ezek 34.25-30) was turned into a prayer of blessing by the author of 11Q14 1.ii.7-10, 13-14. And while the modern reader may find the architectural details of Ezekiel's restored temple vision (Ezek 40-48) to be somewhat tedious, this was not true for the ancient Jewish author of the Temple Scroll (11QT), who drew on this vision to depict his own hopes for ideal temple service. The vision of the restored temple also contains a description of a reformed temple personnel (Ezek 44.15), a passage that was expounded allegorically in a text known as the Damascus Covenant (CD-A 3.20–4.4) in order to create a priestly identity for a later Jewish community. Ezekiel's temple imagery found a home in early Christian thought as well: Paul's argument in 2 Cor 6.16–18 that the Christian community metaphorically functions as God's temple is supported by a quotation of Ezek 37.27. And the features of Ezekiel's vision of a very high mountain with a restored temple and city—a site containing life-giving water and trees for healing, where God himself dwells with his people—appear in Rev 21.3, 10–21; 22.1–2 (cf. Ezek 37.27; 40.2–3; 47.1, 12; 48.15–16).

The tension between the harsh realities of living under empire and Ezekiel's promises of future divine protection and safety gave rise to the material in Ezek 38–39. These chapters draw on the rest of Ezekiel and on other biblical texts to envision a battle at the end of days, a battle in which Israel's enemies are vanquished and the promised security is finally realized. In these chapters, the enemy armies are led by "Gog," a shadowy eschatological foe who reappears in other early Jewish and Christian texts: LXX Num 24.7; LXX Amos 7.1 (where an army of locusts is led by "Gog the king"); 1Q33 (1QWar Scroll) 11.15–16; Rev 20.7–10. It is not difficult to see how the hope for security expressed in Ezekiel would have been immediately relevant to later communities who treasured this book as scripture.

It is scarcely an exaggeration to claim that Jewish and Christian fascination with the mysteries of the divine presence, the heavenly realm, and angelic entities would have alone been sufficient to guarantee the popularity of the book of Ezekiel for centuries. The book seems to have prompted early readers to attempt to see what Ezekiel saw: not surprisingly, accounts of visionary ascent into the heavenly realm are attested in both early Christianity and Rabbinic Judaism. For example, the apostle Paul mentions his experience of being "caught up to the third heaven" (2 Cor 12.1–6), and the vision of the divine throne room and its occupants in John's Apocalypse (Rev 4) seems to have been taken almost verbatim from the book of Ezekiel. Rabbinic Jewish sources reflect an ambivalence toward Ezekiel's visions of the divine: on the one hand, Rabbi Joshua is praised for his mastery of the "matters of the Chariot" (b. Ḥag. 14b); on the other hand, we find attempts in the Talmud to restrict discussion about what Ezekiel saw and about other "dangerous" topics. Particularly notable are the stories of the child who read the book of Ezekiel, perceived the nature of the mysterious *ḥashmal* (Ezek 1.4) and was consumed by fire (b. Ḥag. 13a), and of the four rabbis who "entered the Garden"—only one of whom "ascended and descended safely" (b. Ḥag. 14b; 15b).

Ezekiel's visions of the enthroned deity accompanied by angelic attendants in chapters 1 and 10 generated an intense interest in readers. This is reflected already in the early scribal tradition: MT Ezek 10.14 interprets the "wheels" seen by Ezekiel as angelic beings, and LXX Ezek 43.3 refers to God's throne-platform borne by the cherubim as "the Chariot" (cf. 1 Chr 28.18; Ben Sira 49.8). We have examples of early Jewish prayers (such as the "Songs of the Sabbath Sacrifice," 4Q403 1. ii.3–15; 4Q 405 20.ii, 21–22.1–4) and apocalyptic treatises (such as 1 Enoch 70.1–7) that draw upon Ezekiel in order to envision the heavenly realm and describe it as populated with angelic "chariots," "wheels," and "living beings." This imagery is preserved even in modern Jewish liturgical practice; the morning Sabbath prayer mentions the same angelic entities (the "wheels" and "living beings") described in Ezek 1 and 10.

The book of Ezekiel has played a notable role in speculation about another sort of angelic being—namely, Satan. Many are familiar with the story of the "Fall of Satan" (in which God's beautiful chief angel Satan was consumed with pride, attempted to take over heaven, and was cast down to earth in disgrace); a version of the story even appears in Milton's *Paradise Lost*. But this storyline was not invented by Milton. We can, for example, find it in the writings of the third century Christian theologian Origen (*On First Principles*, 1.5.4–5). Unable to account for the Adamic and priestly imagery in Ezek 28 (and the Mesopotamian mythic imagery in Isa 14), and seeing a parallel to Jesus' words about Satan's fall in Luke 10.18, Origen concluded that Ezek 28 was not speaking about the king of Tyre, but about Satan. Unaware of the origins of this misreading, many Bible readers are convinced that the story of Satan's fall is clearly taught by the Bible itself in Ezek 28!

The book of Ezekiel, then, has lost none of its power to intrigue, disturb, and offer hope. What I am attempting to do in this volume is not to offer the reader a history of research on Ezekiel (although I have included some of the most recent scholarship on the book), but to provide an explanation of the book that simultaneously functions as a guide to how biblical scholars read prophetic literature. This volume presumes an audience that is familiar with the Bible and in need of a resource more detailed than an encyclopedia entry but less detailed than a full commentary. The readers envisioned are graduate students (or advanced undergraduates) and teachers of biblical literature. Those who are looking for additional resources are encouraged to consult the sections titled "Further reading" at the end of each chapter as well as the bibliography.

In Chapter 1 of this volume, I examine the historical setting and literary presentation of the prophet Ezekiel, and discuss how these are significant for reading the book. I also discuss the literary features of the book— its structure, genres, distinctive language, and imagery. In Chapter 2, I examine critical models for understanding how the book of Ezekiel was composed, edited, and copied. In doing so I hope to show the reader how it is possible to move from observations about literary *strata* to questions about literary *strategy*, thereby sharpening our understanding of the arguments in the book. In Chapter 3, I discuss the main themes and arguments of the book of Ezekiel under the four topics of Israel, Yhwh, land, and temple. In Chapter 4, I attempt to synthesize the material in the book and show how it represents a deliberate attempt to offer solutions to the problems of Israel's deportation and exile in the sixth century.

1

The Prophet Ezekiel and the Book of Ezekiel

How is the depiction of Ezekiel the man (as exile, as prophet, as belonging to a priestly family) important for how we read the book? What do we know about the book's setting—both the setting in the book, and the setting of the book? What are the literary features of the book, including its structure, genres, and distinctive language and imagery? It is with these introductory questions that this chapter is concerned.

1. Ezekiel the prophet

There are two equally problematic approaches to a study of Ezekiel. The first can be seen when readers—perhaps under the influence of older models of historiography as "lives of great men"—attempt to reconstruct the personality of the prophet and treat the book more or less as an autobiography. The problem here is that we have no information about a prophet named Ezekiel other than what is presented in the book, and the limited information that we do have is selected and presented for the rhetorical purposes of the book. The second problematic approach can be seen when readers conclude that, since the book is not a detailed autobiography or history of the prophet, the prophet Ezekiel must therefore be a purely fictional character. But if we do not have enough information to reconstruct a detailed portrait of the prophet, neither do we have enough information to conclude that he did not exist. After all, there is nothing inherently improbable about the depiction of a priest-turned-prophet among the Jewish exiles in Babylon. But if these two approaches are problematic, how then should we approach this book?

A number of scholars (e.g., de Jong 2007; Patton 2004) have pointed out that we have no sure way of getting behind the book to recover "what really happened" in the life of the prophet. What we have in the book is a *literary depiction* of a prophet. It is instructive to consider the case of the famous surrealist René Magritte, who produced a work of art titled *The Treachery of Images*. It is a painting of a pipe with a statement underneath proclaiming, "*Ceci n'est pas une pipe*" ("This is not a pipe"). And indeed, the painting is not a pipe—it is simply a representation of a pipe. In a similar way, the book of Ezekiel offers a presentation of the prophet Ezekiel. As Corrine Patton (2004: 73) remarks, "Ezekiel is a character within the prophetic narrative, through whom the reader experiences the exile."

Reading the book as the presentation of the prophet will shape the expectations we bring to the text and the kinds of questions we ask. As *readers* of the book, we must ask: how is the prophet presented, and in what way is the presentation of the prophet relevant to the argument of the book? For example, Ezekiel the prophet is presented as a watchman who gives warning (Ezek 3.16–21; 33.1–9), as a spokesman for the deity Yhwh (Ezek 2.4), and as one who serves as evidence of the certainty of the divine word (Ezek 2.5; 33.33). This presentation of the prophet suggests that the book functions as a justification for interpreting the destruction of Jerusalem and deportation of its citizens as divine punishment. But Ezekiel is also presented as a priest—not just as one who acknowledges and interprets the profanation of temple and people, but as one who hopes for the restoration of temple and people. These two depictions relate to each other as part of a larger argument strategy that moves from problem to solution.

As *historians* who encounter the book, we may investigate the extent to which the depictions in the book of Ezekiel correspond to those in other ancient texts and to our interpretations of material evidence, and then draw conclusions about the historical plausibility or implausibility of these depictions. For example, we might on the one hand conclude with Moshe Greenberg (1983: 171, 201–2) that Ezekiel's visionary description of "abominations" in the temple (Ezek 8) is not a precise account of what was taking place on the fifth day of the sixth month in 592 BCE, but a telescoping and interpretation of Judah's religious history. On the other hand, we might conclude that the overall depiction of the prophet in the book is plausible, and that most of the accusations and oracles of judgment make best sense as an exilic-period attempt to explain why the disaster of exile occurred. We might also discover linguistic or sociological evidence that suggests a Babylonian provenance for some of the material in the book. But we should not be surprised when the book does not provide the information to reconstruct the life of the prophet, or to answer all our questions about the social conditions of Judean deportees in Babylon.

a. Ezekiel as an exiled Israelite and the setting of the book

According to the information in Ezek 1.1–3, Ezekiel son of Buzi was a priest who—along with other citizens of Jerusalem—was deported to Babylon in 597 BCE. The deportees were settled by the River Chebar, close to Nippur. He was (possibly; see the discussion below) thirty years old when he had his first visionary experience. According to Ezek 24.18, he was married, but became a widower while in Babylon. His wife's name is unrecorded; the statement that he was married is only significant for the sign act (his lack of public mourning at his wife's death) described in 24.15–18. Ezekiel's own name, which means "God strengthens" or "May God strengthen," seems to be the subject of wordplay in Ezek 3.7–9, where Ezekiel is told that God will make his face and forehead "strong" in order to stand up to his stubborn audience. The book describes him functioning as a "prophet"—that is, he has visionary experiences and begins to speak messages from Israel's deity YHWH to his community. While the community elders are described as occasionally consulting him for oracles (Ezek 14.1; 20.1), Ezekiel feels that no one takes him seriously (Ezek 21.5 [ET 20.49]; 33.30–32). In fact, the contents of the book suggest considerable tension between Ezekiel and his community. Beyond this, however, the book does not supply any other personal information.

To understand what Ezekiel is doing in Babylon, we must recall the larger historical and political context. At the end of the seventh century the Babylonian empire, led by King Nabopolassar (625–605), was rising to prominence. Assyria was in decline, having been decisively defeated by Babylon at the siege and destruction of the cities of Asshur (614 BCE) and Nineveh (612 BCE), and at the battle of Carchemish (605 BCE). Egypt's influence was also severely curtailed by the rise of Babylon. Although King Jehoiakim of Judah was originally installed on the throne as an Egyptian vassal, he became a vassal of Babylon for three years as Babylonian power grew in the west. His son King Jehoiachin was also a vassal of Babylon, but reigned only a few months before the Babylonian King Nebuchadnezzar II (605–562) invaded in 597 BCE and deported him along with the other elites of Jerusalem, including Ezekiel, to Babylon. Nebuchadnezzar then set Zedekiah, Jehoiachin's uncle, on the throne of Judah as a vassal. When King Zedekiah joined neighboring countries in revolting against Babylon, Nebuchadnezzar swiftly responded with military campaigns in the west. After a lengthy siege, the city of Jerusalem fell to the Babylonian army in 587 BCE, and both city and temple were burned. Captives from Judah were taken and resettled in Babylon.

The book of Ezekiel references the Babylonian invasions and ensuing forcible displacements of Jerusalem's citizens in 597 (Ezek 1.1–3) and 587 (Ezek 25.3; 33.21), as well as the downfall of the Judean monarchy (Ezek 19). It also references Babylonian actions towards surrounding countries, such as Ammon (Ezek 21.23–25 [ET vv. 18–20]), Tyre (Ezek 29.18), and Egypt (Ezek 30.21). What is significant for the understanding of the book is that the prophet responds to and offers an interpretation of these events: according to Ezekiel, the destruction of Jerusalem and its temple and the exile of its citizens was intended and facilitated by Israel's own deity YHWH as punishment (Ezek 5.11–12; 7.20–24; 17.11–21; 24.1–14, 21; 36.16–19). The hoped-for downfall of surrounding countries is depicted as an appropriate response to their mockery of and hostility to Jerusalem at its fall (e.g., Ezek 25.2–7; 35.2–15).

What were conditions initially like for the Judahite exiles in Babylon? Babylonian sources are scanty, and Ezekiel does not explicitly address this issue. But the information we do have is suggestive (cf. Albertz 2003: 98–111). On the one hand, what we see in the book of Ezekiel indicates that the exiles were not prisoners, but lived in their own community. Moreover, the book makes no reference to hostile actions by the Babylonians towards the community. After all, the purpose of deporting the elites of a vassal nation was not only to prevent further rebellion, but also to integrate them into the fabric of Babylonian society, thereby strengthening it. The letter to the exiles described in Jer 29.1–7 presumes that it was possible for the exiles to thrive in Babylon. And we do have data indicating that by the end of the exilic period, the Judeans enjoyed the same economic and legal rights as Babylonians (Albertz 2003: 101–2). On the other hand, those who underwent forcible displacement and resettlement would have experienced the loss of social ties and religious structures as well as the challenge of adjusting to a new geographical and cultural setting. Ezekiel speaks repeatedly about the shame of defeat and deportation exacerbated by the derision of surrounding nations (Ezek 5.14–15; 7.18; 22.4; 25.3, 8; 36.3–4, 6, 15). He also claims that the exiles of 597 were being marginalized with respect to their heritage by the residents of Jerusalem (Ezek 11.15). Finally, the deportees who survived the destruction of Jerusalem in 587 would have been subjected to humiliation and physical abuse after having undergone the horrors of siege warfare and captivity. A number of commentators have shown how these traumatic experiences are reflected in the language and imagery of the book of Ezekiel (Garber 2004, 2011; Smith-Christopher 2002, 2011).

It is obvious from the descriptions above that the narrative of the book depicts an exilic setting. But what about the setting of the book of Ezekiel as a composition? One of the enduring insights of the historical-critical approach to biblical texts is that the setting and concerns which give rise to a literary work may be considerably later than events depicted in it. In the case of Ezekiel, though, most commentators believe that the setting reflected by the earliest form of the book is also exilic. Such a setting is suggested by the explanations of exile as punishment for violence, idolatry, and Sabbath violation (and the numerous accompanying accusations); the critiques of King Zedekiah (Ezek 17.1–21; 21.30–32 [ET vv. 25–27]); the critique of foreign alliances (Ezek 23.14–17); the reaction to the responses of surrounding nations at the fall of Jerusalem (Ezek 25.1–7; 35.1–15); the observation that Egypt failed to provide aid (Ezek 29.6–7); the hopes for military action by Babylon against surrounding nations (e.g., Ezek 26.7; 29.18–20; 30.24–25); statements that reflect tension between the exilic community and those living in Judah (Ezek 11.1–11, 15; 33.23–29); and arguments that a return from exile lies in the future (Ezek 11.17; 20.34–38, 41–42; 37.12). The majority of commentators also acknowledge the Babylonian provenance of the earliest form of the book, evident from the presence of Akkadian loanwords (e.g., *swgr* "neck stock," Ezek 19.9; *škr* "payment," Ezek 27.15) and familiarity with Mesopotamian imagery and religious-political ideology (Bodi 1991: 35–51; Kutsko 2000: 101–49; Renz 1999: 27–38). This does not, of course, exclude the presence of redactional material in the book that reflects a later setting (see Chapter 2).

For many prophetic books, there is a considerable distance between the audience of the spoken messages of the prophet and the audience of the book composed from those speeches. For example, in the book of Amos we can reconstruct spoken oracles directed to a pre-722 BCE Israelite audience (e.g., Amos 4.1–3, which critiques social injustice in Samaria). Yet these oracles have been collected, edited, and composed into a book for a later reading audience. The paradigmatic nature of the older material for later readers is created by a complex compositional process involving the juxtaposition of generically diverse and originally separate units of material, the insertion of explicit theological reflection about divine election and the extent of judgment (e.g., Amos 9.7–10), and the insertion of material linking hope for restoration with the renewal of the "fallen booth of David" (e.g., Amos 9.11–15; note the temporal perspective of vv. 14–15).

In the case of Ezekiel, however, the situation is different. If we assume on the basis of passages such as Ezek 21.5 [ET 20.49]; 33.30–31 that the prophet Ezekiel did make oral proclamation, the settings of both the audience of prophetic speech and of the readers of the earliest form of the prophetic book are exilic. To be sure, there is inevitably some rhetorical distance even here (Renz 1999: 14–18, 41–42). The book of Ezekiel is actually a narrative about what God told the prophet to say, not a simple transcript of what the prophet actually said. The audience of the speaking prophet would have heard him proclaim disaster against the city prior to its fall; for the readers of the book, Jerusalem had already fallen. Sign acts performed by a speaking prophet are intended to persuade a listening audience; the report of a sign act is intended to make an argument for a reading audience. The reader of the rare appeals to repent (Ezek 14.6; 18.30, 32; 33.11) approaches these passages with a pessimism about their viability that is instilled at the very beginning of the narrative (Ezek 2.3–5; 3.7). The book, then, shows the reader that Ezekiel's listening audience did not respond to his appeals (cf. Ezek 33.30–32). Yet for both listener and reader, hope for restoration stands in the future. The earliest form of the book of Ezekiel shows no indication that a return from exile was an available option; it attempts to convince the reader that Yhwh would make a return possible. The rhetorical setting of the book's reading audience, then, is very similar to the rhetorical setting of the prophet's listening audience, even if we cannot get behind the book to reconstruct the exact form of his oral speeches.

The unique compositional nature of the book of Ezekiel will be discussed at greater length in Chapter 2. For now, I want to emphasize the rhetorical significance of the book of Ezekiel as a literary composition. This is not to suggest that Ezekiel the prophet never spoke. As Thomas Renz (1999: 16) notes, it is important that we read the book of Ezekiel as rhetorical literature while at the same time acknowledging that "the written book derives from an oral debate." But we must take seriously the shape and contents of the book as a literary attempt to solve the problems of an exilic audience. Renz concludes:

... one must not overlook the fact that the book invites its readers to identify with the exilic community. It does not address directly a world beyond the world of the prophet Ezekiel, but rather invites prospective readers to enter into the world of refugees in "Tel Aviv" and their prophet. The book of Ezekiel develops its argument with the reader by narrating the story of a prophet's unfolding argument with his exilic audience. In this way the book addresses its own audience by having the audience in the book addressed by the prophet. In other words, it is a communication by being a narrative about a communication.

b. Ezekiel as a prophet of Yhwh

Prevalent in some earlier studies of Israelite prophecy is a dichotomy between "pre-classical" and "classical" prophecy (sometimes framed as a contrast between "early prophets" and "writing prophets"). Pre-classical prophecy was associated with wandering ecstatics who often operated in groups and who seemed to be associated with regional sanctuaries. In contrast, classical prophecy was thought to be marked by ethical monotheism, and was distinguished both from earlier prophecy (often deprecated as "primitive") and from later "priestly" religion (often deprecated as "legalistic"). Classical prophecy was not typically associated with the cult, and it was not understood to be characterized by ecstatic behavior (or if it was, the ecstatic behavior was thought to be of a different kind than attested in earlier prophecy). We can see this dichotomy in a 1934 essay by S. Mowinckel, who contrasts "older, primitive 'nebhi'ism'" with later "pre-exilic reforming prophets." Mowinckel goes on to argue that if these later "literary prophets" had ecstatic experiences, they were "manifested not in convulsions, delirious frenzy and glossolaly, but in tranquil visions and trances" (1934: 199, 209–10).

This model of ancient Israelite prophecy has shortcomings that are clear in hindsight (see Wilson 1978, 1979), but it proved to be particularly detrimental to the study of the book of Ezekiel (McKeating 1993: 40–41). Because the book seemed to bear features of both "pre-classical" and "classical" prophecy, commentators inevitably attempted to explain away certain details in order to make it fit their model. Material that resembled priestly law was judged to be later interpolation, and descriptions of sign acts or visionary experience were taken as evidence of sickness or a disturbed mind. Commentators felt compelled to address the "bizarre" nature of Ezekiel's actions. Because the prophet was considered to be abnormal, it was perhaps inevitable that he was subjected to psychiatric assessment: Edwin Broome (1943: 291) claimed that "Ezekiel exhibits behavioristic abnormalities consistent with paranoid schizophrenia. There can be no doubt that we are dealing with a true psychotic," and David Halperin (1993) used a Freudian approach in an attempt to uncover the sexual terrors and desires behind Ezekiel's actions.

Much of this could have been avoided by the application of proper models, or at the least by a critical attitude towards inherited models. The depictions of Ezekiel's experience and behavior should not simply be dismissed as "bizarre." Rather, they can and should be cross-culturally situated and interpreted using the disciplines of cultural anthropology, psychology, trauma theory, and rhetorical criticism. Fortunately, such studies have become increasingly common, resulting in the rehabilitation of the prophet: Ezekiel is no longer as strange to readers as he was once thought to be. His experiences and behavior fall into the normal range of what can be defined as prophetic experience.

But what does it mean to say that Ezekiel is depicted as a "prophet"? What is "prophecy"? Manfred Weippert offers the following definition:

> prophecy is present when a person (a) through a cognitive experience (a vision, an auditory experience, an audio-visual appearance, a dream or the like) becomes the subject of the revelation of a deity, or several deities and, in addition, (b) is conscious of being commissioned by the deity or deities in question to convey the revelation in a verbal form (as a "prophecy" or a "prophetic speech"), or through nonverbal communicative acts ("symbolic acts"), to a third party who constitutes the actual addressee of the message.
>
> Quoted in Nissinen 2004: 20

The depiction of Ezekiel as having a revelatory experience (Ezek 1–3), then being told to "prophesy" and "speak [God's] words" (Ezek 2.7; 3.1, 4, 11; cf. 2.5; 33.33), fits this definition.

It is possible to sharpen our understanding of prophecy by contextualizing it in various ways. For example, a number of scholars (e.g., Nissinen 2004: 21–22; Stökl 2012: 8–11) have suggested that prophecy can be fit into a broader spectrum of beliefs and practices relating to what we could think of as "divine information technology": on one end of the spectrum are forms of "intuitive divination" (associated with prophets and dreamers), and on the other end are forms of "technical divination" (associated with dream interpreters, astrologers, haruspices, etc.). Other scholars—such as Robert Wilson (1980) and Thomas Overholt (1989)—have studied the social function of prophecy, which they define as intermediation between the divine and the human spheres. This idea of intermediation is particularly noticeable in Ezek 20.1 (where the elders come to "inquire of Yhwh") and in Ezek 14.4–6 (in which it is argued that Israel's prophets have not properly functioned as intermediaries). The depiction of Ezekiel as a prophetic intermediary figure explains the diverse strategies—the critique of behavior, the explanation of the exilic situation, the argument that there is hope for restoration—that are attested in the book.

How then should the reader understand the descriptions of Ezekiel's experiences? The category of "ecstasy" was already being used to describe prophetic experience and behavior by both G. Hölscher and H. Gunkel in the early 1900s. Robert Wilson's influential work (1980) on Israelite prophecy drew on comparative anthropology as well as psychological research into altered states of consciousness. Wilson's categories and definitions can easily accommodate the accounts of Ezekiel's experience: we find in the book visions of divine entities (Ezek 1–3); sensations of terror and awe (Ezek 1.28); sensations of possession and enablement (Ezek 2.2; 3.24); a feeling of compulsion (Ezek 3.14; 8.1)—specifically, the compulsion to speak a message given by God, associated with the loss of independent speech faculties (Ezek 2.4, 7; 3.26–27); and sensations of transportation within the visionary experience (Ezek 3.12,

14; 8.3; 11.1, 24; 40.2). Current research has demonstrated that ecstatic experience is in fact cross-culturally attested and may be widespread within individual cultures. Social responses to ecstatic experience vary considerably: in some cultures it is recognized as "normal" (at least in certain social settings, or for certain socially recognized roles, such as the shaman), while in other cultures it is considered to be "abnormal" or undesirable. Ecstatic experience can be religious or non-religious, and can be analyzed using sociological, physiological, and neurological categories (see Bourguignon 1973; Lewis 1989; Ludwig 1969; McNamara 2009; Price-Williams and Hughes 1994). It is worth noting just how significant this comparative research has been for the study of the book of Ezekiel: whereas many earlier discussions of Ezek 8.3; 11.1 treated these verses as fodder for debates over whether the prophet actually had a ministry in Jerusalem as opposed to Babylon, modern commentators treat these descriptions of the sensation of physical displacement as a typical feature of ecstatic experience.

Insofar as we can reconstruct the phenomenon of Israelite prophecy from biblical texts (which were not written to provide this information, and which are often radically dissimilar in genre and purpose), we can say that there are many parallels between what we see in the book of Ezekiel and what we see in other texts (Carley 1975). Like other prophets, Ezekiel believes that God has given him a message to proclaim to his contemporaries. Like other prophets, he has visionary experiences, he makes persuasive speeches, and he performs symbolic actions. His speeches contain familiar criticisms and instructions, and they employ familiar prophetic genres and formulas. The unique features of the book of Ezekiel lie less in the depiction of prophetic experience than in the message proclaimed by the prophet and in the language and setting in which this message is given.

c. Ezekiel as a priest

In Ezek 1.3, Ezekiel is identified as "the son of Buzi, the priest." In addition, most take the reference to the "thirtieth year" (Ezek 1.1) to be a reference to Ezekiel's age at his first vision, which is also the age at which Levitical service began (Num 4.1–3, 23, 30; note that the terminus of Levitical service at the age of fifty corresponds to the last date notice in Ezek 40.1, twenty years after the date in Ezek 1.1, 3). The prophet refers to his priestly upbringing in Ezek 4.14 when, after having been told to eat bread cooked over human excrement, he protests that he has never defiled himself by "eating what died naturally, what was torn by animals, or meat that is ritually unacceptable." All these are mentioned in Lev 7.18; 19.7–8; 22.8 as actions that are incompatible with priestly service. But how is the depiction of Ezekiel's priestly heritage significant for how we read the book?

Scholars have expressed opposing views as to whether Ezekiel is best described as a priestly prophet or as a prophetic priest (see Cook and Patton 2004; Mein 2001a; Sweeney 2005). On the one hand, one could argue that in some sense Ezekiel indirectly mediates the divine presence to his community by encountering Yhwh in exile (Ezek 1–3) and by affirming the presence of Yhwh for the exilic community (Ezek 11.16). On the other hand, the role that the prophet plays cannot be said to be in any sense cultic, since he is in exile and separated from the Jerusalem temple. One could also argue that Ezekiel carries out a priestly function by giving rulings and instruction, such as the discussion of behavior that results in life or death (Ezek 18) or the procedures for the restored temple (Ezek 40–48; see esp. 43.12, 18). However, the material in Ezek 18 does not actually constitute a legal ruling (compare Hag 2.11–13), but is a rhetorical appeal based on priestly instruction. Moreover, while much of the material in Ezek 40–48 is legal instruction concerning the cult, it is presented in a vision report. The forms and function of priestly Torah have therefore been subordinated to the forms and function of prophetic literature. Some have argued that Ezekiel is described as a priestly "new Moses" figure inasmuch as he is instructed to consecrate the altar in the restored temple (Ezek 43.18–27). But the matter is not quite so simple as it appears. The second person singular forms in Ezek 43.19–25 may not be directly addressed to Ezekiel at all, but may simply be a feature of the genre. After all, one could hardly argue that the second person singular forms in Exod 20.24-26 mean that ancient Israelite authors imagined only Moses was intended to build altars. Furthermore, the cosmic-mythic features of the temple described in Ezek 40-48 challenge a reading in which these chapters function as a simple building-plan and procedural guide for Ezekiel himself.

The depiction of Ezekiel as priest is significant not because the prophet actually performs priestly duties, but because the prophet diagnoses Israel's problem and offers a solution using priestly ideology and traditions. For example, the book repeatedly argues that the people and land have become unclean because of bloodshed, idolatry, and prohibited sexual relations (e.g., Ezek 14.11; 20.7, 18, 26, 30, 31, 43; 22.3, 4, 11; 23.7, 13, 30; 36.17-18; 37.23; etc.). Ezekiel's accusations are articulated as specifically priestly concerns, because these actions were believed to defile the land (cf. Lev 18.24-28; Num 35.33-34). Not only are people and land defiled, but Yhwh's very name has been profaned by the people's actions (Ezek 36.20-22; 43.7-8). One of the functions of a priest is to distinguish between pure and impure, between holy and common, but Ezekiel accuses the priests of failing to perform this function (Ezek 22.26). Both the Sabbath (Ezek 20.13, 16, 21, 24; 22.8; 23.38) and the temple (Ezek 5.11; 23.38, 39; 44.7) have been profaned. This poses a threat because the correct observance of sacred time and sacred space reflects the maintenance of cosmic order (the temple is, after all, a model of the cosmos). And because the people have profaned the temple, God will respond in kind. To be sure, the temple was destroyed by the invading Babylonians, but this destruction is interpreted as divinely authorized (Ezek 7.21-22; 25.3) and indeed as undertaken by Yhwh himself (Ezek 24.21; cf. Ezek 9.6-7). Finally, the condition of exile is described in terms of eating unclean food (Ezek 4.13). These are thoroughly priestly problems, and require a priestly solution.

Such a solution is described in the following ways: the people's idolatrous practices will be judged in kind, by the desecration of their cultic sites by their corpses (Ezek 6.4, 5, 13). God will "purge" the rebels from the people (Ezek 20.38). He will "make atonement" for the people (Ezek 16.63). He will "destroy" their uncleanness (Ezek 22.15). He will "cleanse" them and "save" them from their iniquity, their idols, and their uncleanness (Ezek 36.25, 29, 33; 37.23). The sanctity of the temple, cultic practice, and cult personnel will be restored, and Y<small>HWH</small> will again reside in his temple (Ezek 20.39-40; 37.27-28; 43.1-12; 44.6-31). The temple will regain its function as the locus of cosmic order and the source of life (Ezek 47.1-12). The land will be purified from its uncleanness (Ezek 11.18) and its purity will be safeguarded (Ezek 47-48). Y<small>HWH</small>'s name will be sanctified by what he will do (Ezek 36.23). Not only does Ezekiel accuse his audience with locutions taken from traditional priestly material (e.g., Ezek 20.13, 16, 21, 24 // Lev 18.4-5; Ezek 22.7-12 // Lev 18.7-9, 15, 19; 19.3, 8, 13, 16; 20.9-11; 25.36), the book describes the people's restoration using locutions taken (and creatively modified) from the same material (Ezek 34.25-30 // Lev 26.4-6, 12-13; see the next chapter for further discussion). Beyond this, we see in the book typical priestly concerns with matters of both moral purity or impurity (e.g., Ezek 18.5-13; 33.15) and ritual impurity (e.g., menstruation, Ezek 18.6; corpse contact, Ezek 39.12, 14-16; 43.7-9; laws specifically for priests, Ezek 44.17-31).

2. The book of Ezekiel

a. Structure

A glance at the standard commentaries and introductions to the book of Ezekiel reveals a surprising fact: while all scholars seem to agree that the book is highly structured, there is considerable disagreement about what the structure of the book actually is. For example, the majority of scholars see the book of Ezekiel arranged according to a "tripartite eschatological schema" (similar to that found in Zephaniah or LXX Jeremiah) of "judgment on Israel" (Ezek 1-24), "judgment on surrounding nations" (25-32), and "hope for Israel" (33-48). This position is held by, for example, Fohrer (1968: 414), Zimmerli (1979: 2), Pohlmann (1996: 18-20), and Darr (2001: 1089). However, others divide the book into two sections (chs. 1-33, concerning judgment; chs. 34-48, concerning hope), four sections (chs. 1–24, judgment on Israel; 25–32, judgment against the nations; 33–39, hope for Israel; 40–48, the vision of a restored temple), or even seven sections (chs. 1–3; 4–24; 25–32; 33; 34–37; 38–39; 40–48).

According to Mayfield (2010), it is not only the differences between these proposals listed above that suggest confusion about the definition of literary structure, but the very categories themselves that are employed. First, is it really the case that a three-part "judgment on Israel—judgment on foreign nations—hope for Israel" pattern represents the structure of the book if there are significant statements of hope within the first and second parts (e.g., Ezek 11.17–21; 14.11; 16.60–63; 17.22–24; 20.33–38, 39–44; 28.24, 25–26; 29.21a), and judgment against the nations in the third part (e.g., Ezek 35)? Second, the proposed "structural sections" mentioned above are based on a variety of different criteria, including outlook (doom vs. hope), addressee (Israel/Judah vs. foreign nations), genre (call narratives vs. prophetic speech vs. proto-apocalyptic), and content (a vision of a restored temple vs. other content). But while one may isolate and identify *sections* using any number of formal and content-based criteria, it seems desirable that one look for identical and recurring features to determine the *structure* of a literary work. Mayfield addresses this problem by distinguishing between genre structure and text structure on the one hand, and between conceptual structure and surface structure on the other. He argues that the literary structure of a book should be built on a hierarchy of surface-level features alone. In the case of the book of Ezekiel, this structure consists of thirteen sections created by chronological formulas (the first structural level of the book; see the discussion below), which in turn are made up of shorter oracles marked by the prophetic word formula (the second structural level). These chronological formulas are for the most part calculated from the year in which King Jehoiachin and the upper class of Jerusalem (including Ezekiel) were taken into exile by King Nebuchadnezzar of Babylon (c. 597 BCE). They are also for the most part fixed in form (typically: "and it came about in the year X, in the Y [month], on the Z of the month"), and regularly occur throughout the book. To be sure, there are some variations in form: the chronological formulas differ according to whether the word "year" precedes its identifying number (Ezek 8.1; 20.1; 29.1) or follows it (Ezek 29.17; 30.20; 31.1; 32.1); the formula in Ezek 24.1 follows the system of chronology used in 2 Kgs 25.1; Jer 39.1; the formula in Ezek 32.1 adds the word "month" to its identifying number; and the formulas in Ezek 1.2; 26.1; and MT 32.17 omit the number of the month altogether. But these variations do not pose a challenge to the structural function of the chronological formulas.

It is important to note that the literary structure of a book should not be confused with its compositional history. It is also important to note that even if we argue that chronological formulas create the literary structure of Ezekiel, this does not exclude the presence of other organizational features operating simultaneously in the book. While the chronological formulas separate or bring together surrounding text-segments, this same result can be accomplished by other means and at other levels. For example, text-segments can be clustered together on the basis of shared themes, or linked together by keywords or refrains. Readers should be aware of the variety of organizational features that are employed in the book (such as, e.g., the placement of the vision reports). In the following chapter, I will explore how these features affect the reading process.

b. The chronological formulas

The fourteen chronological formulas in Table 1.1 create the dating scheme of the book. There are three oddities in this dating scheme that are worthy of particular attention, the first of which is the reference to the unidentified "thirtieth year" in Ezek 1.1. To incorporate this date in the chronological scheme used in the rest of the book (that is, as the thirtieth year from the exile of Jehoiachin) would result in a date later than anything in the entire book and in a vision report that is inexplicably out of sequence. Several other explanations have therefore been proposed. According to the explanation given in the Targum to Ezekiel, the "thirtieth year" of Ezek 1.1 should be calculated back from the year given in Ezek 1.2. Thirty years before Ezekiel's first vision in

The Prophet Ezekiel and the Book of Ezekiel

Table 1.1 The fourteen chronological formulas

Ref.	Day/Mo/Yr (MT)	Material introduced by formula	Date
1.1	(5/4/30)	Vision at Chebar (= 30th year of ?)	593
1.2	5/__/5	Supplementary introduction (= 5th year of Jehoiachin's captivity, c. 597 BCE)	593
8.1	5/6/6	Vision of Jerusalem temple	592
20.1	10/5/7	Inquiry of elders	591
24.1	10/10/9 [10]	Beginning of siege of Jerusalem (*uses dating format of 2 Kgs 25.1, corresponds to 10/10/10 in Ezekiel's system*)	587
26.1	1/__/11	Oracle against Tyre	586
29.1	12/10/10	Oracle against Egypt	587
29.17	1/1/27	Oracle against Egypt (response to oracle in 26.7–14)	571
30.20	7/1/11	Oracle against Egypt	586
31.1	1/3/11	Oracle against Egypt	586
32.1	1/12/12	Lament over Egypt	585
32.17	15/__/12	Lament over Egypt (*some reconstruct as 15/1/12 using the LXX; others reconstruct as 15/12/12*)	585
33.21	5/10/12	News of Jerusalem's fall	585
40.1	10/1/25	Vision of Restored Temple	573

593 (the fifth year of King Jehoiachin's captivity) would correspond to the eighteenth year of King Josiah (2 Kgs 22.3). According to 2 Kgs 22.11–17, it was in this year that the Book of the Law (which contained curses for covenant unfaithfulness) was found in the temple. This explanation is taken up by Renz (1999: 134–35), who argues that Ezekiel's "thirtieth year" constitutes a deliberate allusion meant to create a connection between the earlier promise of judgment and the depiction of its fulfillment in the book of Ezekiel. But most commentators maintain that the "thirtieth year" refers to the age of the prophet, and that it may also refer to the age at which Ezekiel was eligible to begin priestly service (cf. Num 4).

The second oddity is closely related: why are there *two* date formulas in the introduction to the book? Most commentators argue that the additional date formula in Ezek 1.2-3 was supplied by a later editor to correlate the date in 1.1 with the dating scheme in the rest of the book and with the format of the introductory formulas in other prophetic books (cf. Hag 1.1; Zech 1.1).

The third feature worthy of note is the presence of date formulas (and their accompanying oracles) that are out of chronological sequence. For example, the formula and the following oracle in Ezek 29.17-20 are dated later than any of the other dated oracles in the book. This oracle concerns Egypt, and is a response to the oracle in 26.1-14; it has been placed in its current position for thematic reasons, along with the rest of the Egypt oracles. Similarly, the date formula in Ezek 26.1 (= 586 BCE) is out of sequence with respect to the next date formula in Ezek 29.1 (= 587 BCE); it has been moved earlier so that all the Tyre oracles (chs. 26-28) precede all the Egypt oracles. The date formula in Ezek 33.21 (= the tenth month of 585 BCE) is out of sequence with respect to the earlier date formula in Ezek 32.1 (= the twelfth month of 585 BCE); it has been moved later so that all the Egypt oracles in chs. 29-32 form an uninterrupted unit. So while most of the book is arranged according to a chronological sequence, occasionally a thematic organization is given priority.

c. General literary characteristics

One of the most prominent literary features of the book of Ezekiel is that the contents of the entire book have been presented in a first-person narrative frame. In this respect, Ezekiel is unique in the prophetic corpus. While there are sections where the narrative describes what the prophet sees (e.g., Ezek 1, 10-11, 40-48), the bulk of the book is a story of what God tells the prophet to say. Of course, the book of Ezekiel is known for its poetry as well: representative examples may be found in the laments for the lioness and the vine (Ezek 19.1-9, 10-14) and the laments over Tyre (Ezek 26-28), as well as in shorter poetic speeches (e.g., Ezek 23.32–34). Commentators have also noted that the prose of Ezekiel is marked by the presence of rhythm and the extensive use of imagery, features which are usually associated with poetry.

If the book of Ezekiel is actually a narrative, what would we gain by consciously reading it in light of the categories of plot, setting, and characterization? We would see little plot development, but the plot line that is present is essential to the argument in that it highlights the fall of Jerusalem and creates a causal connection between Israel's rebellion against God and the deportation to Babylon. The narrative ends without a resolution of the problems of rebellion and exile, though the solution is presented as something that will be realized in the future. The setting is likewise important: with the exception of the two large vision reports (Ezek 8–11, 40–48, focusing on temple and city), the action takes place among the exilic community in Babylon and emphasizes the plight of the exiles as a problem to be solved. Within the vision reports, rapid local scene changes are used to focus on the "abominations" that defile the temple and warrant its destruction (Ezek 8–11) and the architectural features that are necessary to ensure a new and purified temple (Ezek 40–48).

It is the characterization in the book that has perhaps received the most attention. The *dramatis personae* include Israel's God YHWH, the prophet Ezekiel, the prophet's fellow Israelites (both those in Jerusalem and the community in exile), surrounding nations and their leaders, and—though only mentioned briefly—the mysterious enemy named "Gog" of Ezek 38–39 and the angelic messenger/guide figure of Ezek 40–48. It is noteworthy that the characters display little if any development—which, in the case of the prophet's fellow Israelites, is highlighted as a problem. The prophet's contemporaries are described as "rebellious" (Ezek 2.3–8), and the prophet is warned that no one will listen to him (Ezek 3.7). The possibility that a wicked person will change after being warned is not envisioned as a possibility (Ezek 3.17–21), and the presentation of Israelite history in Ezek 20 argues that the people are fixed in a pattern of rebellious behavior. Change, then, is something that will happen in the future—which is in keeping with Ezekiel's pessimism about the present. And yet the prophet's fellow Israelites are not depicted in a completely monolithic fashion: there are important differences between the characterization of the citizens of Jerusalem and the exilic community.

A second notable feature is that while the character Ezekiel is narrating what he sees and hears, it is the perspective attributed to Yhwh that is given highest priority. For example, the only report of Ezekiel's inner thoughts is in Ezek 3.14, and verbalization of the prophet's thoughts is found only in Ezek 4.14; 9.8; 11.13; 21.5 [ET 20.49]; 37.3. Occasionally the thoughts or speeches of other characters are reported as quoted speech (e.g., the nations, Ezek 26.16–18; 27.32; Edom, Ezek 35.10; Gog, Ezek 38.11). When we hear the voices of Ezekiel's contemporaries quoted by God or the prophet, it is either to show the people's bewilderment at what the prophet has said or acted out (e.g., Ezek 12.9; 24.19; 37.18) or to present the people's speech as negative, incorrect, or in need of response (e.g., Ezek 8.12; 9.9; 11.3, 15; 12.22, 27; 13.6, 10; 18.2, 19, 25, 29; 20.32; 21.5 [ET 20.49]; 33.10, 17, 20, 24, 30; 37.11). It is clear that the depiction of the thoughts, emotions, and speech of the prophet (and of all other characters) has been under-represented in favor of reporting Yhwh's speech and representing his point of view (that is to say, the author's point of view). Moreover, the depiction of Yhwh himself is unique in several ways when compared to other prophetic books (see the discussion of language and imagery below).

d. Use of traditional genres

The appearance of a recognizable genre elicits certain expectations in a reader. An author can exploit these expectations either by building on them (in this case, new arguments are based on shared knowledge), or by shattering them (in this case, the author modifies elements in the genre and/or employs the genre in new ways for surprising effect). Many of the genres found in the book of Ezekiel are familiar to readers from other prophetic books, such as accusation and announcement of judgment (e.g., Ezek 7.20–21; 22.1–16; 22.17–22). Of course, in the book of Ezekiel these are framed not as reports of speech, but as what Ezekiel was told to say. We also see the parodic use of dirges, as in Ezek 19; 26.17–18; 27.32; 28.12–19 (though these are substantially longer than what we see in other prophetic books; cf. Jer 9.19–20 [ET vv. 20–21]; 48.17; Amos 5.1–2). Of particular interest is the way that call narratives, vision reports, sign acts, and oracles against foreign nations (OAN) are employed in the book.

The book of Ezekiel begins with a call narrative (*Berufungsbericht*) embedded in a vision report. The function of a call narrative is to legitimate the prophet as a representative of Yhwh. Habel (1965) isolates the following six elements typical of a call narrative: (a) divine confrontation (e.g., Judg 6.11b–12a; Isa 6.1–7; Jer 1.4); (b) introductory word (e.g., Exod 3.4–9; Judg 6.12b–13; Isa 6.8; Jer 1.5); (c) commission (e.g., Exod 3.10; Judg 6.14; Isa 6.9–10; Jer 1.7); (d) objection by the prophet (e.g., Exod 3.11; 4.1, 10, 13; Judg 6.15; Isa 6.5; Jer 1.6); (e) reassurance (e.g., Exod 3.12; 4.2–9, 11–12, 14–16; Judg 6.16; Isa 6.7b; Jer 1.8, 17–19); and (f) the giving of a sign (e.g., Exod 3.12; 4.2–9; Judg 6.17; Isa 6.6–7a; Jer 1.9–10, 11–16). These six elements are also present in Ezekiel, though with significant modifications. The divine confrontation occurs in Ezek 1.1–28, embedded in a lengthy report of Ezekiel's vision of the divine throne-chariot. The introductory word occurs in Ezek 2.1–2. According to Habel, this element usually contains the grounds for the commission. Here, however, the emphasis is on the controlling power of Yhwh's spirit—an important theme in the book of Ezekiel. The commission is found in Ezek 2.3–4, where God tells Ezekiel "I am sending you ... you shall say to them." The expected objection by the prophet is lacking, at least in an overt external form. Instead, the book provides a description of the prophet's internal emotions ("bitter in the rage of my spirit," Ezek 3.14). Any objection that might have been forthcoming is forestalled by a warning not to be rebellious like his audience (Ezek 2.8), and the report of Ezekiel's emotional response is followed by a warning that he will be held accountable if he does not warn his audience (Ezek 3.16–21). The element of objection, then, has been suppressed to highlight Yhwh's superior power. The prophet receives reassurance in Ezek 2.6; 3.8–9. It is noteworthy that this element is repeated multiple times. The stubbornness of Ezekiel's audience is given prominence, and in response the prophet is told that God will make him even more stubborn than his audience. Finally, the sign occurs in Ezek 2.8–3.3. But this is not a sign whereby the prophet is reassured of Yhwh's presence and empowerment, as in other call narratives; rather, it is an indication of what his message will be: "lamentations, mourning, and woe."

The book of Ezekiel is also notable for its vision reports, which can be found in Ezek 1.1–3.14; 3.22–27; 8.1–11.25; 37.1–14; 40.1–48.35. Vision reports have a distinctive rhetorical function in that they present information to the reader through a description of the prophet's visual experience. This use of this genre represents an attempt to bring about a shared perspective between the narrator (or prophetic character) and the reader. Features of the vision report (see Long 1976; Niditch 1983) include: (a) the use of the word "vision" (*mr'h*) to introduce the material (Ezek 1.1; 8.3, 4; 11.24; 40.2; cf. 43.3); (b) the use of "sight" terminology, such as "I saw" (Ezek 1.4, 28; 8.2, 4, 6, etc.; 11.24; 37.8; 41.8; 43.3; 44.3), "show/be shown" (Ezek 11.25; 40.4), and "see with your eyes" (Ezek 40.4; 44.5); (c) a first-person report of what the prophet saw and heard. The vision reports in Ezekiel also make reference to the Spirit of Yhwh entering, raising up, or transporting the prophet (Ezek 2.2; 3.12, 14, 24; 8.3; 11.1, 24; 37.1; 43.5), or to the "hand of Yhwh" being upon the prophet (Ezek 3.14; 8.1; 37.1; 40.1). Other occurrences of the genre can be found in Isa 6; Jer 1; 24; Amos 7–9; Zech 1–6; Dan 7–8. The vision report in Ezek 40–48 is particularly notable, not only for its length, but also because it contains four content-related features that are found only here and in later vision reports (Lyons 2014). These innovations include the use of an angelic interpreter/guide figure in the vision, the presence of cosmic-mythic imagery, an extensive description of sacred space, and the embedding of legal material. All of these innovations contribute to an argument about restoration—that Yhwh will return to live among his people, that Yhwh's restored temple will be a locus of sanctity and healing, and that past abuses to the cult will be remedied.

Another traditional genre used in the book of Ezekiel is the report of a command to perform a sign act. The prophetic sign acts in Jeremiah and Ezekiel were the subject of a comprehensive study by Kelvin Friebel (1999), who examined instances of what he classified as "non-verbal communication." These included both longer performances (e.g., Ezek 4–5; 12.1–12, 17–20; 21.24–27 [ET 21.19–22]; 24.15–24; 37.15–22) and shorter expressive actions (e.g., Ezek 6.11; 21.11–12, 17, 19 [ET vv. 6–7, 12, 14]). Typical features of this genre include: (a) a command to the prophet to perform an action that is unusual (e.g., Ezek 4.12, cooking food over human excrement; Ezek 5.1–2, shaving one's head and burning or scattering the hair; Ezek 37.16–17, holding two sticks together); (b) the use of the term "sign" (*'wt, mwpt*; Ezek 4.3; 12.6, 11; 24.24, 27); (c) a question by the audience (either quoted or anticipated: Ezek 12.9; 24.19; 37.18); and (d) an interpretation of the sign act (e.g., Ezek 4.13 "In this way the sons of Israel will eat . . ."; Ezek 5.5 "This is Jerusalem"). The rhetorical function of prophetic sign acts is clear: the unusual and obscure nature of these actions is meant to gather an audience and provoke curiosity, at which point the prophet interprets the sign act and verbalizes the argument to the audience. The rhetorical function of the *report* of a sign act, however, is different: it forces the reader of the book to determine whether the prophet's contemporaries did or did not respond to his message and to evaluate them accordingly. Noteworthy features of the genre as employed in Ezekiel include the juxtaposition of diverse sign acts in chs. 4–5, the frequent presence of ambiguity or absence of interpretation (what is the significance of the "iron plate" in Ezek 4.3? What is the referent of the "390 days" in Ezek 4.4–5? Why is the action described in Ezek 5.3 uninterpreted? Why won't the people weep in Ezek 24.23?), and the remarkable range of events (siege, effects of siege, exile, restoration) described by the sign acts.

Like several other prophetic books, the book of Ezekiel contains oracles concerning foreign nations (cf. Isa 14–21, 23; Jer 46–51; Amos 1; Zeph 2). It is generally accepted that these oracles grew out of an older "war oracle" genre (Christensen 1975; cf. 1 Kgs 22.10–12). When considering the function of these oracles, it is essential to make a distinction between their *addressees* and their *audience*. While these oracles are addressed to various foreign nations (e.g., Moab, Edom, Tyre), they are directed to an exilic Israelite audience and are designed to have an effect on this audience.

With one exception (the oracle against Edom in Ezek 35), the oracles concerning foreign nations are clustered together in Ezek 25–32. These oracles display many shared words, phrases, and images, and display clear signs of editorial placement and linking (for examples, see the following chapter). They are addressed to seven named countries: Moab, Edom, Ammon, and Philistia (in Ezek 25), Tyre and Sidon (in Ezek 26–28), and Egypt (in Ezek 29–32). The number of addressees is probably deliberate; the oracle concerning Sidon lacks an accusation and is very short (only four verses long), and seems to have been placed here to create a seven-addressee oracle collection. It is important to note that the selection of foreign nations is also deliberate; the oracles are specifically related to the fall of Jerusalem and to Nebuchadnezzar's western campaigns. One nation that is not listed in Ezek 25–32 is Babylon. This might strike the reader as a curious omission, since other prophetic books contain oracles addressing the dominant empires under which the prophetic traditions originated and were collected. In fact, there *is* an oracle concerning Babylon in the book of Ezekiel, one which can be found in Ezek 21.33–37 [ET vv. 28–32]. This oracle is actually addressed to Ammon, and never even mentions the name "Babylon." Nevertheless, the identity of the "sword" that will be "drawn against Ammon" and then subsequently destroyed is obvious in light of the preceding verses. The oblique nature of this oracle might be explained with reference to how one living under empire might cleverly criticize it.

The oracles concerning foreign nations in Ezekiel contain accusations listing offences that are familiar from other occurrences of the genre. We see accusations of hostile speech—in particular, expressions of joy and scorn at the downfall of Jerusalem in Ezek 25.3, 6, 8; 26.2; 35.15; 36.6 (cf. Obad 1.12). We see accusations of hostile activity ("revenge") by Edom and Philistia against Jerusalem in Ezek 25.12, 15 (cf. Obad

1.10-14), and of designs on the land of Israel (by Edom and "the rest of the nations") in Ezek 35.10; 36.5. We find references to the pride of Tyre in Ezek 27.3; 28.2-6, 17, and to the pride of Egypt in Ezek 29.3; 31.10; 32.2 (cf. Isa 10.12-14; 16.6). Less common are the references to the "violence" done by Tyre in Ezek 28.16 (per Ezek 28.18, this is apparently economic in nature), and to Egypt's failure to come to the aid of Judah when requested (Ezek 29.6-7). According to the logic of the oracles, these nations will be punished by Yhwh, typically through invasion and military destruction. The punishment is usually "in kind"—that is, the punishment described corresponds to the offence in some way: because Edom "took vengeance" (*nqm*, Ezek 25.12) against Judah, God will respond by "laying vengeance" (*nqmh*, Ezek 25.14) on Edom. Likewise, because Egypt is proud, like a tall tree (Ezek 31.10; cf. vv. 2-9), God will hand Egypt over to attackers who will humble it in the same way that a tree is cut down (Ezek 31.11-14). In some instances, however, we see the same judgment language used for these foreign nations that is elsewhere used for Jerusalem: the expression "cut off man and cattle" (Ezek 25.13; 29.8) can be found in Ezek 14.13, 17, 19, 21; the expression "bring a sword against you" (Ezek 29.8) can be found in Ezek 5.17; 6.3; 11.8; the expression "scatter among the nations, disperse among the lands" (Ezek 29.12; 30.23, 26) can be found in Ezek 12.15; 20.23; 22.15; 36.19; the expression "strong pride" (Ezek 30.6, 18) can be found in Ezek 24.21; 33.28. It is noteworthy that each of these locutions can also be found in the Holiness Code (Lev 26.19, 22 [here, only "cut off cattle"], 25, 33).

What is the function of these oracles in the book of Ezekiel? According to Paul Raabe (2010: 201-6), they "serve a theocentric purpose" by "direct[ing] attention away from the nations and toward Yahweh." This purpose is underscored by the repetition of the Recognition Formula in these oracles (Ezek 25.5, 7, 11, 14, 17; 26.6, 9, 16; etc.). The divine actions depicted in these oracles are expressions of Yhwh's holiness (Ezek 28.22, 25). Another function of these oracles is to depict Yhwh as a deity who vindicates Israel from enemies and to create hope for future security for Israel (particularly noticeable in

Ezek 28.24–26). Finally, these oracles serve as a warning. As Thomas Renz (1999: 230–31) notes,

> in the oracles against the nations the readers were invited to see the same pattern of rebellion against Yahweh at work which had brought Jerusalem to its end. The readers are encouraged to see that rebellion against Yahweh reduces Israel to the level of other nations and does not have a future, since Yahweh will destroy pride against him everywhere. Thus they will realise that assimilation into other nations will only continue the rebellious history of the past and consequently will not open up a future for their community.

e. Distinctive language

Any reader of the book of Ezekiel will quickly discover that it contains highly repetitive (and often distinctive) language. Some of the most frequently repeated phrases are formulas typical of prophetic books: "the word of Yhwh came to me" (the Prophetic Word Formula), "Thus says Yhwh" (the Messenger Formula), and "utterance of Lord Yhwh" (the Prophetic Utterance Formula). These are typically found at the introductions or conclusions of speech units. But the book also contains additional formulas that are absent from other books, or at least appear with a much higher frequency in Ezekiel than they do in other books, such as "I am Yhwh" (the Self-Introduction Formula) and the related "then X will know that I am Yhwh" (the Recognition Formula). The Self-Introduction Formula is often coupled with a verb to denote the inevitability of an event; Block (1997: 38) relates this to other passages that emphasize the irrepressible action of God, such as Ezek 21.4, 10 [ET 20.48; 21.5]. According to Zimmerli (1979: 38), the Recognition Formula appears roughly seventy times in the book of Ezekiel, and points to the centrality of the theme of the knowledge of God—in particular, the argument that certain events will bring about a new knowledge of the God of Israel in the observer. This formula may be familiar to readers of the story of the exodus from Egypt, where God's actions in liberating Israel from slavery are said to result in a knowledge among both Israelites and Egyptians that he is Yhwh (e.g., Exod 6.7; 7.5, 17; 8.18; 10.2; 14.4).

The book also contains a number of expressions that are used to make arguments about God's reputation or appearance in the eyes of observers. For example, God is said to act "for the sake of his name" (i.e., his reputation) in Ezek 20.9, 14, 22, 44; 36.22. He will act in response to the "profanation" (Ezek 36.20–23) and "defilement" (Ezek 43.8) of his name by ensuring that it is no longer "profaned" (Ezek 20.39; 39.7) or "defiled" (Ezek 43.7). He "has concern for his name" in Ezek 36.21; he "vindicates the holiness of his name" in Ezek 36.23; he will "make his holy name known" and will "be jealous for his holy name" in Ezek 39.7, 25. Similarly, God is described as acting in order to "display his holiness" (Ezek 20.41; 28.22, 25; 36.23; 38.16; 39.27). He is also depicted as being extraordinarily concerned about how his actions towards Israel appear to others, as we see in the use of the phrase "in the eyes of the nations" (Ezek 5.8; 20.9, 14, 22, 41; 22.16 [?]; 28.25; 38.23; 39.27; cf. also 36.20, where God is concerned about what the nations are saying). These locutions are used to depict the motivations for God's actions, a theme to which we will return below in Chapter 3.

We also see a high frequency of prophetic speech formulas denoting hostility: "set your/my face against" (fourteen times, e.g., Ezek 6.1), "Behold, I am against you" (thirteen times, e.g., Ezek 5.8), and "my eye will not spare and I will not have pity" (six times, e.g., Ezek 7.4). These are congruent with the similarly high frequency of words for hostile emotions, such as "anger" ('*p*, fifteen times) and "wrath" (*ḥmh*, thirty-three times). In a similar vein, we find closely-related locutions for the expression of these hostile emotions: "my anger will spend itself" (Ezek 5.13a); "I will finish off my anger on X" (Ezek 5.13b; 6.12; 7.8; 13.15; 20.8, 21); "I will finish X off [in my anger]" (Ezek 20.13; 22.31; 43.8); "I will vent my fury" (Ezek 5.13; 16.42; 21.22 [ET 21.17]; 24.13); "I will pour out my anger/indignation" (Ezek 7.8; 9.8; 14.19; 20.8, 13, 21, 33, 34; 21.36 [ET 21.31]; 22.22, 31; 30.15; 36.18). It is not surprising that the biblical authors universally depict Yhwh as opposed to certain kinds of behavior; but Ezekiel seems to go far beyond other authors in his depiction of Yhwh's extremely negative emotional response and reaction to such behavior. It is for this reason that Raitt (1977: 35–58) speaks of a "radicalization of the judgment message" in the book of Ezekiel, and argues that it arises out of the failure of the people to respond to earlier offers of repentance.

The book of Ezekiel is argumentative literature: both the book as a whole and the speeches within the book represent attempts to persuade an audience of something. Nearly all of the literary and lexical features of the book that I am discussing in this section can be described in terms of their rhetorical function. For example, we find in the book of Ezekiel almost half (forty out of ninety-nine times in the Hebrew Bible) of the occurrences of the word "because" (*y'n*). This reflects the book's emphasis on causality and the connection between actions and consequences (e.g., Ezek 5.9 "... *because of* all your abominations"; 5.11 "*because* you defiled my sanctuary ..."; 13.8 "*because* you spoke falsehood .."). It represents a positive form of persuasion insofar as it offers evidence to convince someone of a new idea. We can also find examples of negative forms of persuasion, where the book provides evidence in the process of countering or preventing an idea or action. For example, we see a very frequent use of quoted speech to express a sentiment which is in turn opposed in some way in the following verses (Ezek 8.12; 11.3; 12.22, 27; 13.6, 7, 10; 18.2, 19, 25, 29; 20.32; 22.28; 25.3, 8; 26.2; 27.2; 28.2, 9; 29.3, 9; 33.17, 20, 24; 35.10, 12; 36.2, 13, 20; 37.11; 38.11). Persuasive attempts can be more subtle, as in the case of rhetorical questions. Here a question is posed, even though the answer is obvious; the point is to evoke an involuntary agreement with the person who is asking the question. Rhetorical questions are very widely used in the book of Ezekiel (Ezek 13.7, 18; 16.20, 56; 17.9, 10, 12, 15; 18.13, 23, 24, 25, 29; 26.15; 27.32; 28.9; 31.2, 18; 32.19; 33.25, 26; 34.2, 18; 38.13, 14, 17), mostly in contexts of divine accusation and judgment. In addition to these are instances in which God addresses the prophet with a rhetorical question (Ezek 8.6, 12, 15, 17; 12.9; 15.2–4; 20.3, 4, 30, 31; 22.2, 14; 23.36; 24.25–26). We even see the repetition of a particular question, such as "Do you see, son of man?" (Ezek 8.6, 12, 15, 17), or "Will you judge, son of man?" (Ezek 20.4; 22.2; 23.36). Inside the story, these questions invite Ezekiel to share God's perspective; outside the story, they invite the reader to share the same perspective, since the author is promoting a value system expressed through his depiction of God.

Other distinctive language includes a preference for a longer form of divine address ("Lord Yhwh"), and for the use of the term "Son of Man" (often translated "Mortal") when God addresses Ezekiel. These are in keeping with the book's emphasis on divine transcendence and on the subordinate place of humanity in relation to God. Other distinctive terms of address are the terms "House of Israel" and "Mountains of Israel," and the term "prince" (*nśy'*) rather than the term "king" (*mlk*) when referring to the Israelite political leader. Because the term "prince" is typically used in biblical literature for pre-monarchic Israelite leaders, Ezekiel's preference for the term is sometimes thought to be an expression of the low view he has of the Israelite monarchy, or of the subordinated status that the Israelite leader will have in the future according to Ezek 40–48. Still, we do see exceptions to this preference in Ezek 17.12, 16; 37.22, 24; 43.7.

Distinctive descriptive words used in the book include the negative terms "rebellious house" (*byt mry*, thirteen times, only in Ezekiel) and "abomination" (*twʻbh*, forty-three times; this constitutes almost half of the total occurrences of this word in the Hebrew Bible). Another negative descriptive word is *glwlym* (occurring in Ezekiel thirty-nine out of a total forty-eight times in the Bible). This word is often translated as "idols," but it has a particularly pejorative connotation: it is derived from the root *gll* "to be round," from which the word *gl* "turds, dung" (Ezek 4.12, 15; Job 20.7) is also derived. Moreover, it is vocalized with the same vowels as the Hebrew word for "detestable thing" (*šqwṣ*)—a kind of dysphemism which often occurs in Israelite scribal practice when referring to other gods. The animosity with which Ezekiel regards these representations of other deities—"detestable turds"—can be seen in e.g. Ezek 6.4–6; 16.36.

Since the prophet Ezekiel is also depicted as a priest, the frequent use of priestly language is not surprising. For example, the verb "to profane" or "be profaned" (*ḥll*) is used twenty-four times, and the verb "to be unclean" or "defile" (*ṭm'*) is used thirty times. The things that are described as "profaned" include the temple (Ezek 7.21, 22; 23.39; 24.21; 25.3; 44.7), the Sabbath (20.13, 16, 21, 24; 22.8; 23.38), sacred contributions (22.26), God (13.19; 22.26) or God's name (20.9, 14, 22, 39; 36.20, 21, 22, 23; 39.7), the people of Israel (22.16), and the King of Tyre (28.7, 16). Similarly, things described as "unclean" or "defiled" include the Israelites themselves (through idolatry or prohibited sexual relations, e.g., Ezek 14.11; 18.6, 11, 15; 22.11; 20.7, 18, 26, 30, 31; 22.3, 4; 23.7, 13, 30; 37.23; etc.), priests (by corpse contact, Ezek 44.25), God's name (by idolatry and by the proximity of what may be funerary steles next to the temple, Ezek 43.7, 8), the temple (Ezek 5.11; 9.7; 23.38), and the land (by idolatry, Ezek 36.18). We find language for offerings (Ezek 20.28, 31, 40; etc.) and the use of the priestly term "soothing aroma" for describing sacrifices (Ezek 6.13; 16.19; 20.28, 41). We see reference to the act of priestly instruction (or the lack thereof) in Ezek 22.26, and accusations based on priestly instruction in Ezek 22.6–12. The most obvious use of priestly language lies in the description of the temple and regulations for temple service embedded in the vision report of Ezek 40–48.

Given the amount of priestly language and imagery, the lack of any reference in the book of Ezekiel to Moses or to Sinai is puzzling. Also, the word "commandment" (*mṣwh*) is never used, and the word "law, instruction" (*twrh*) occurs only nine times, mostly in Ezek 43–44. Ezekiel prefers to use the terms "statute" (*ḥqh, ḥq*) and "ordinance" (*mšpṭ*) for divine regulations. These words typically occur in the two-clause expression "to [not] walk in my statutes and keep/do my ordinances" (e.g., Ezek 5.7; 11.12, 20; 18.9, 17; 20.11, 13, 16, 19; 36.27; 37.24; etc.). This widely-used locution seems to have been taken from Lev 18.4–5. In fact, there are a startling number of locutions that are shared by both Ezekiel and Lev 17–26 (the "Holiness Code"), a relationship which scholars now explain in terms of literary dependence. I will discuss this relationship in more detail in the following chapter.

Almost as significant as words that are distinctive or unusually frequent in Ezekiel are words that are *not* used—particularly words that express a positive orientation of God towards others. For example, we never see the nouns "love" (*'hbh*) or "kindness" (*ḥsd*), and the verb "love" is only used metaphorically in Ezek 16 and 23 to speak of Israel's "lovers"—i.e., those with whom Israel made political alliances. We never see in Ezekiel the words for redemption (*pdh, g'l*) that are used in Isaiah and Jeremiah. The verb "to comfort" (*nḥm*) is used in very atypical ways in the book of Ezekiel: to refer to God's satisfaction at punishing Israel (Ezek 5.13); to the exiles' realization that there was a reason for the fall of Jerusalem (Ezek 14.22, 23); to what is felt by Sodom and Samaria at seeing the restoration of Judah (Ezek 16.54); to what is felt by other nations in the Underworld at seeing Egypt join them (Ezek 31.16); to what Pharaoh feels when he sees the other nations he is joining in the Underworld (Ezek 32.31). This is a very odd sort of comfort indeed—certainly not the kind of comfort we see spoken of in e.g. Isa 12.1; 40.1; 49.13; Jer 31.13! The absence of these words (or of the usual use of these words) as predications of God in the book of Ezekiel is likely a deliberate rhetorical ploy to prevent the prophet's audience from presuming that God will overlook their offences. We see a similar rhetorical ploy at work in Ezek 20, where Ezekiel omits any mention of a time of obedience in Israel's history—probably to deny his audience an opportunity to claim that they deserve divine favor for past faithfulness.

The word "Zion" is never used (though see the references to "my holy mountain," Ezek 20.40; "my hill," Ezek 34.26; and the "very high mountain" in Ezek 40.2)—again, probably to avoid reminding Ezekiel's audience of a past relationship that they could attempt to claim to their advantage. The use of the word "repent, turn" (*šwb*) for an offer made by God to Israel occurs only four times in the entire book (Ezek 14.6; 18.30, 32; 33.11), even though God's openness to repentance is discussed at length in chs. 18 and 33. The infrequent use of this word is likely due to Ezekiel's pessimism about the spiritual condition of his audience—a theme that will be discussed below in Chapter 3.

f. Distinctive imagery

Much of Ezekiel's language is highly visual, evoking images in the mind of the reader. For example, the book begins with a vision report describing what Ezekiel sees: in the distance, a glowing storm cloud with lightning flashing about it. As the vision report proceeds, the description follows both a horizontal axis (describing the movement of the glowing storm cloud toward the viewer, at which point greater detail can be seen) and a vertical axis (describing the appearance of the supernatural winged creatures, then moving up to describe the platform that they support, the throne on the platform, and finally the deity seated on the throne). As Greenberg (1983: 52–53) notes, this manner of deliberate description and the constant comparisons to known things (e.g., v. 5 "*something like* four living creatures"; v. 7 "*like* a calf's foot ... *like* burnished bronze"; v. 27 "*like the appearance* of fire") point to the precision and attention to detail with which the report was composed. This speaks against the tendency of some commentators (e.g., Wilson 1984: 124) to describe the vision report as "vague."

Ezekiel's report of Yhwh enthroned and embodied resembles imagery found elsewhere in the Bible. For example, the prophet's description of Yhwh as a humanoid figure seated on a throne resting on a platform (Ezek 1.26; 10.1) has similarities to the description of what Moses and the elders see in Exod 24.9–10, and to Isaiah's vision of the enthroned deity with surrounding winged beings in Isa 6. While the logical and textual problems in Ezek 1, 10 are formidable (see Wood 2008: 105–38, esp. 134–35), we can say that Ezek 10.15, 20 attempts to identify the "living creatures" of Ezek 1 as "cherubs"—not the *putti* of Renaissance art, but winged supernatural creatures upon which Yhwh is enthroned. We see winged supernatural beings with hybrid human-animal characteristics (lion, bull, eagle, human) depicted in ancient Near Eastern carvings and statues; some of these are bearers of a deity's throne platform (Keel-Leu 1977: 125–273), others are carved on a throne itself (as we see in some of the Megiddo ivories, on the sarcophagus of King Ahiram of Byblos, and on the throne of Ashtarte in the Phoenician temple of Eshmun), and still others are guardians at gates of temples and palaces (as we see on the palace of Ashurbanipal II at Nimrud). The image of Yhwh enthroned on cherubs can be seen in Exod 25.18–19, 22; 1 Sam 4.4; Ps 99.1 (the description of Yhwh "riding on a cherub" in Ps 18.11–13 [ET vv. 10–12] is somewhat different, though the images of storm, "radiance," and "coals of fire" in these verses also appear in Ezekiel). But the description of the enthroned deity in Ezekiel goes far beyond what we see in these other texts in terms of length and detail.

There is also a distinctive use of cosmic and mythic imagery in Ezekiel, particularly in the oracles against the nations (OAN; see Boadt 1980: 173; Crouch 2011; Strine and Crouch 2013). For example, we can find Underworld imagery scattered throughout the Hebrew Bible, particularly in poetry (e.g., Isa 5.14; 14.9–11, 15; Ps 49.13–15 [ET vv. 12–14]; 88.4–7, 11–13 [ET vv. 3–6, 10–12]; Job 17.13–16). But Ezekiel's use of this imagery is more concentrated than in other biblical compositions (cf. Ezek 26.20; 28.8; 31.14–18; 32.18–32, where the Underworld is referred to by its proper name "Sheol" as well as the terms "The Pit" and "The World Beneath"). In the taunt-song of Isa 14, the dead in Sheol wake up at the arrival of the King of Babylon to observe that he is in fact just as mortal as anyone else, despite his godlike pretensions. In Ezekiel, we see these motifs separately applied to two different nations: the King of Tyre is described as descending to Sheol despite his godlike pretensions (Ezek 28.2, 6–10), and the dead in Sheol are described as commenting on the arrival of Pharaoh and the army of Egypt (Ezek 32.21). We also find references to the dragon in the sea (Ezek 29.3; 32.2), to the world tree (Ezek 31), and to cosmic distress at the actions of the divine warrior Yhwh (Ezek 32.7–8). As Crouch (2011: 478) argues,

> the defeat of Yahweh's human king in Jerusalem and Judah's fall to the Babylonians posed a major theological and ideological challenge to the adherents of the royal military ideology—in other words, the elites who were subsequently deported to Babylon. Ezekiel's use of these cosmological mythological motifs in his

OANs is directly related to the theological threat posed by this disaster, namely, the possibility that Yahweh had lost his status as divine king and creator. By using these traditions Ezekiel is reasserting Yahweh's claims to these titles.

Strine and Crouch (2013) also demonstrate how Ezekiel creatively reworks traditional *Chaoskampf* imagery to critique Judah's reliance on Egypt.

Other cosmic-mythic images can be found in Ezekiel's descriptions of the "very high mountain" (Ezek 40.2), the life-giving river (Ezek 47.1–12), and the trees of life (Ezek 47.12), all employed in the final vision report of the book. These images are familiar from Ugaritic texts, where the gods are described as dwelling on the tops of mountains or at the source of cosmic rivers. They also appear in biblical texts, where Sinai and Zion are described as the dwelling of Yhwh (Deut 33.2; Ps 48.2–3 [ET vv. 1–2]; 68.17–19 [ET vv. 16–18]), and where the Garden of God is described as containing the tree of life and as watered by a cosmic river (Gen 2.9–14; see also Zion in Ps 46.5 [ET v. 4]). Ezekiel uses these symbols of cosmic order, life, and healing to depict future restoration. Levenson (1976: 7–8, 18, 33) has argued that Ezek 40.2 picks up the promise of hope on the "high and lofty mountain" from Ezek 17.22–24. The reconstitution of the temple is thus depicted as the end result of the return from exile. But by employing these cosmic-mythic images, Ezekiel points to a reality beyond the catastrophe of exile: "What [Ezekiel] sees is the security of Zion, whose historical end he saw and narrated in chs. 8–11, but whose supra-historical foundation can never be razed." According to Levenson, Ezekiel also engages in political critique by combining Zion imagery with "pre-political" Eden imagery (e.g., the trees and river of life).

Some of the most extensively used images in the book of Ezekiel are those associated with the various stages of siege warfare and its consequences. Ezekiel visualizes the approach of the Babylonian army, and describes it as performing divination to decide which city to attack first (Ezek 21.23–27 [ET vv. 18–22]). He uses the metaphor of a city watchman who warns of an approaching attack (Ezek 33.1–6). He describes the details of the siege proper, including the strategic location of enemy camps around a city and the use of walls, ramps, and battering rams (Ezek 4.1–3; 17.17; 21.27 [ET v. 22]; 26.7–9), and makes special reference to the difficulty experienced by the attackers (Ezek 29.17–20). Ezekiel also describes the conditions inside a city during the siege: first, the rationing of food and water (Ezek 4.9–11, 16–17), then the absence of any food (Ezek 5.12, 16; 7.15), culminating in cannibalism (Ezek 5.10). Eventually, the city walls are breached by the enemy, who plunders the city and kills its citizens (Ezek 23.22–26; 26.9–12). Some of the city's inhabitants escape (Ezek 7.16; 17.21), but most are taken captive and led off into exile (Ezek 12.1–6; 17.20). The city is now the object of scorn from surrounding nations and passers-by (Ezek 5.14–15; 25.3). Because the land is devastated and laid waste (Ezek 12.20), wild animals are a threat to any who remain (Ezek 5.17; 34.25). Hence we see Ezekiel refer to the consequences of siege warfare using a three-element merism structure reflecting the fates of death by sword, death by famine or plague, and scattering (Ezek 5.2, 12; 6.11–12; 7.15; 12.16), or the four fates of sword, famine, plague, and wild animals (Ezek 14.12–21). To be sure, this is stereotypical language (cf. Lev 26.21–38; Jer 14.12, 18; 15.2–3; 18.21; 21.7, 9), but it is based on all-too-common realities in the ancient Near East.

Some of Ezekiel's most well-known images are taken from nature: mountains (note the contrast between the two mountains in Ezek 35.1–36.15), the sea (Ezek 27), the Nile River (Ezek 29.3), trees (Ezek 17.22–24; 21.3 [ET 20.47]; 31.1–18; 47.12), vines (Ezek 15.1–6; 17.1–10; 19.10–14), a lioness and her cubs (19.1–9), eagles (Ezek 17.1–7), and sheep (Ezek 34.1–23, 31; 36.37–38). We also see an intense interest in land in the book of Ezekiel—land as profaned, devastated, and laid waste (Ezek 6.14; 12.20; 33.29; 36.18), land that "devours its inhabitants" (Ezek 36.12–14), land as cleansed, occupied, and fertile (Ezek 11.17–18; 34.25–29; 36.8–12, 33–38), and land as arranged by boundaries and tribal territories (Ezek 47–48).

Among the images we do not see in the book of Ezekiel are depictions of global or cosmic restoration, as we find in, for example, Isa 11.6–9;

25.6–8. Depictions of restoration in the book of Ezekiel (e.g., Ezek 34, 36, 47) are limited to the land of Israel alone. Nor do we see in Ezekiel any reference to transformation of foreign nations, or of the nations as involved in the restoration of Israel (as we find in e.g. Isa 2.2–4; 19.19–25; 49.6; 56.6–8; 60.3–9; Jer 3.17; Zech 8.20–23). This absence is highlighted by the way in which Ezekiel is used in John's Apocalypse; here Ezek 47.12 is repeated in Rev 22.2, but the author universalizes Ezekiel's strictly local vision of restoration by specifying that the leaves of the tree are for healing "the nations." We do however see a reversal of judgment and a very limited restoration for Egypt in Ezek 29.13–16, which could be compared to Jer 48.47; 49.6, 39. Another image that we do not see in the book of Ezekiel is that of a future Davidic ruler with a global rule or role, as in Isa 11.1–5, 10; Zech 9.9–10. Again, the conception of restoration in Ezekiel is restrained; the future Davidic ruler is depicted as a shepherd of Israel alone (Ezek 34.23–24; 37.22, 24). Finally, when we think of biblical depictions of God as being tender or compassionate, it is highly unlikely that the book of Ezekiel would come to mind. As I noted above, Ezekiel is known for his extensive depictions of an enraged deity. There are, however, a few exceptions to the harsh language that I will discuss in Chapter 3.

g. Figurative and symbolic language

Like other prophetic books, Ezekiel contains a great deal of figurative and symbolic language (we could also include the book's numerous descriptions of sign acts in this category). Karin Schöpflin (2005: 101) argues that the metaphors in Ezekiel "seem to be employed in an almost systematic fashion, and the arrangement of the metaphorical passages within the book appears to be a deliberate composition." She points to the clustering of fire/heat images as metaphors for judgment on Jerusalem: Jerusalem will be burned like a useless vine (Ezek 15); God will kindle an unquenchable fire which will consume the trees of the southland (Ezek 20.1–4); God will smelt the people of Jerusalem like metal in a furnace (Ezek 22.20–22); the judgment on Jerusalem is compared to a pot heated to cook meat, then heated to burn the filth cooked onto it (Ezek 24.3–13). To these we could add the use of fire for describing judgment in Ezek 16.41; 23.25, 47, and the description of the burned vine in Ezek 19.12, 14. The use of this fire imagery conveys the finality and irreversibility of judgment.

The book of Ezekiel is also particularly notable for the number of extended metaphors (sometimes classified as allegories) that are employed. For example, in ch. 16 the story of Israel's relationship with God is told as a story of a foundling child who grows up, is married, turns to prostitution, and is turned over to her lovers to be brutally killed. In ch. 17, the recent history of Israel's monarchy is described in a story of two eagles and a vine. In ch. 19, the downfall of Israel's monarchy is described using two extended metaphors: the story of a lioness and her captured cubs, and the story of a fruitful vine that is plucked up. In ch. 23, the cities of Samaria and Jerusalem are described as a story of two sisters.

Not only does the book of Ezekiel make use of extended metaphors, but it also contains instances where a single symbolic image is used in multiple ways. For example, in ch. 11 the elders of Jerusalem are depicted as saying, "The time to build houses is not near; this [city] is the pot, and we are the meat" (v. 3). Presumably, this is a proverb quoted by the elders as the *nouveaux riches*, the ones who are taking over the housing of the recently exiled upper class and boasting about their own newly acquired status. The metaphor of meat in a pot seems to be used to suggest the appropriateness or proper fit of these elders in the city (compare our idiom "hand in glove" to signify an appropriate fit). But in the following verses the prophet counters their use of this proverb by subverting the meaning of the image in two different ways. In the first, he affirms that the city is the pot, but denies that the elders are the meat; rather, the meat represents those who have been killed by the elders of the city (vv. 6–7a). In the second, he affirms that the city is the pot and the elders are the meat, but changes the signification of the image from that of proper fit to that of security. He then proceeds to deny the elders security by claiming that they will be like meat that is taken *out* of a pot

(vv. 7b-11). The next time we see the "meat in pot" image is in ch. 24, where it is again used in two different metaphors—one depicting judgment as the cooking of indiscriminately chosen cuts of meat, and the other depicting judgment as the burning away of baked-on filth. Other examples of a single image used in multiple ways include the vine image employed in Ezek 15 and 17, and the cedar tree image employed in Ezek 17 and 31.

When employing symbolic language, Ezekiel has a notable tendency to move back and forth between symbol and interpretation, or between symbol and reality. For example, in the sign act described in Ezek 5.2, God tells the prophet to divide his hair into thirds, then burn it, chase it with a sword, and scatter it to the wind. At the end of the verse, however, we find the comment "and I will unsheathe a sword behind them." Here reality begins to intrude into the symbol, as can be seen by the sudden shift from "you" to "I." The image of God scattering the people, then unsheathing a sword behind them, comes from Lev 26.33 and is picked up in Ezek 5.12, where the interpretation of the sign act is given. But in v. 2 the interpretation is already beginning to creep in. Likewise, in Ezek 16.24–25 the actual details of siege warfare intrude into the metaphorical judgment of the unfaithful wife. A similar flexibility can be seen in the way Ezekiel moves between metaphors, as in Ezek 16 where Jerusalem is depicted in succession as adopted daughter, then wife, then sister; or in Ezek 23, where Yhwh is depicted as having two wives (Samaria and Jerusalem)—even though Ezek 16 depicted Jerusalem as Yhwh's sole wife.

Ezekiel's protest "They are saying of me, 'Isn't he just a maker of metaphors?'" (Ezek 21.5 [ET 20.49]) is a testimony to his effectiveness in metaphor-making. Carol Newsom (1984) notes that a well-constructed metaphor exploits existing relationships of similarity and dissimilarity in the real world and forces readers to process the nature of these relationships when construing the metaphor. As she points out, Ezekiel's choice of images (a rock and a ship) in constructing metaphors for Tyre in Ezek 26–27 is particularly fitting. To compare Tyre to a rock exploits the fact that the city of Tyre was built on a rocky island just off the coast (the name "Tyre" actually means "rock"). This location provided defense from invading armies (as King Nebuchadnezzar discovered, Ezek 29.18) as well as an excellent base for the highly profitable Phoenician shipping industry in the Mediterranean. In Ezek 26, the prophet uses the metaphor "Tyre is a rock," but reverses the image of rock-as-security to the image of a bare rock, swept completely free of walls, houses, and inhabitants, and suitable only for drying fishing nets (Ezek 26.4–5, 12, 14). Likewise, in Ezek 27 the prophet takes into account Tyre's success at nautical trade by comparing the city to a ship and its inhabitants to sailors on the ship (Ezek 27.4–9). Tyre's trading partners and the goods it transported are enumerated in great detail (vv. 10–25). But ships and their contents are vulnerable to the sea, the very thing that makes nautical trading possible and profitable; and so in the metaphor, Ezekiel sinks Tyre-as-ship and plunges its inhabitants and trade goods into the sea (Ezek 27.26–27). Tyre, which has derived all of its benefits from being "in the heart of the seas" (Ezek 27.4), has in the metaphor been destroyed "in the heart of the seas" (Ezek 27.26, 34).

Cognitive linguists who study metaphor have noted that many metaphors are built from embodied human existence in the world, and can serve as the basis for further metaphors. One such metaphor, used widely in prophetic literature, is A CITY IS A WOMAN (for recent research, see the discussion and literature cited in Day 1995 and Kelle 2008). In fact, Galambush (1992) has argued that this metaphor is central to the entire book of Ezekiel. We also see it used to generate other metaphors, as the following examples demonstrate:

- JERUSALEM IS A BRIDE/WIFE: in Ezek 16.2, 8–14, a marriage covenant is metaphorically mapped onto a religious covenant, the latter already being a metaphor derived originally from the sphere of international politics; in Ezek 24.15–24, the sign act relating to the death of Ezekiel's wife presumes the metaphor of Jerusalem as wife. For other examples, see Isa 49.18; 62.5; Jer 2.2.
- JERUSALEM IS A MOTHER: Ezek 16.20, 55; 23.4 (in this last verse, used of Samaria as well). What is curious in the use of this

metaphor is the way the mother/child relationship is expressed: in Ezek 16.20 the reference is to literal children offered to other gods, whereas in Ezek 16.55 "daughters" is a metaphor for surrounding villages. For other examples, see Isa 60.4; 66.10–11.

- JERUSALEM IS A WOMAN BEREAVED: Ezek 23.25. For other examples, see Isa 3.25–26; Mic 1.16; Lam 2.21–22; note a reversal of this metaphor in Isa 49.19–22.
- JERUSALEM IS A PROSTITUTE/ADULTEROUS WIFE: Ezek 16.15–34; 23.1–21, 40–44 (note that Samaria is included as sister/wife in ch. 23). Here adultery and prostitution—images of sexual unfaithfulness and promiscuity—are metaphorically mapped onto devotion to non-Israelite deities and onto political alliances with other countries (of course, this metaphor presumes the mapping of the marriage covenant metaphor onto the religious covenant metaphor as mentioned above). For other examples, see Isa 1.21; Jer 2.20, 33; 3.1–10, 20; 5.7–8; Hos 1.2; 4.12–13. However, while this metaphor is used in other prophetic books, Moughtin-Mumby (2008: 22–30) rightly cautions against assuming that a single conceptual story lies behind every use of the metaphor. Note that the language of divorce and remarriage is not explicitly employed in Ezekiel (as it is in Isa 50.1; Jer 3.8; Hos 2.4, 21–22 [ET vv. 2, 19–20]), though one could argue that the concepts of divorce and remarriage are assumed in Ezek 16.38–39, 59–63.

The metaphorical use of gendered imagery in Ezek 16 and 23, two chapters in which Jerusalem and Samaria are compared to married women who endlessly pursue other sexual partners, presents a number of problems for readers (see Moughtin-Mumby 2008: 156–205 for a discussion of the imagery and a survey of past research). First, Ezekiel makes extensive use of crude, explicit, and highly graphic sexual imagery (e.g., Ezek 16.25, 26, 28, 29, 36; 23.3, 20–21). Some commentators even suggest that the imagery is pornographic, meant to arouse male desire. Others, however, point out that Ezekiel's sexual language is intended to shame, not titillate: he applies the female imagery to a primarily *male* Israelite audience in order to accuse them of religious and political unfaithfulness.

Second, Ezekiel depicts Yhwh's response to Jerusalem (the metaphorical wife) in extremely violent terms: Yhwh is described as handing her over to her lovers to be stripped naked, stoned, dismembered, and burned (e.g., Ezek 16.37–42; 23.25–26, 28–29, 46–47). For some, this is reminiscent of the experiences of battered women whose husbands are controlling and abusive. In the interest of precision, we should note that the imagery in these chapters does not resemble an abusive relational cycle alternating between violence and attempts at reconciliation. Nor does it depict Jerusalem as one who tragically remains attracted to a violent spouse. Ezekiel's argument is nothing less than this: the relationship is over, no reconciliation is possible, and Jerusalem must be utterly destroyed. This depiction of divine participation in violence understandably constitutes a theological problem for some readers. While this violent imagery should not be ignored or explained away, we must note that many commentators now argue that it reflects historical realities rather than misogynistic fantasies: Ezekiel is describing (and attempting to make sense of) the actual violence suffered by citizens of Jerusalem when the city was conquered.

Third, the language of possession ("you became mine," Ezek 16.8; 23.4) and the absence of any female perspective are offensive to many modern readers, because they depict male-female relationships solely in terms of male control. Finally, it has been noted that this metaphorical language makes it possible for male readers to legitimate relational control and violence insofar as this behavior can be ascribed to God (depicted as the metaphorical husband in these chapters). History offers many examples of religious communities that have justified unethical behavior—slavery, apartheid, anti-Semitism, marginalization of women—by appealing to their sacred texts. And while a careful reader may be able to see why Ezekiel combines the metaphors of a marriage covenant and a political covenant, there is no denying that this combination presents dangerous possibilities for those who read these chapters uncritically. Fortunately, a number of modern commentators are aware of the danger and offer sensitive and creative suggestions for preventing unethical readings (Darr 1992; Kelle 2013: 179–83, 202–4; Patton 2000).

Further reading

For a discussion of sixth-century BCE Israelite literature, see Albertz (2003); on the events leading up to the fall of Jerusalem, and the ensuing seige and deportation, see Grayson (2000: 93–102); Albertz (2003: 70–90); Lipschits (2005). For a detailed discussion of the literary depiction of Ezekiel the prophet, see Schöpflin (2002). For a survey of the study of the phenomenon of Israelite prophecy in recent scholarship, see Kelle (2014).

2

From Prophetic Speech to Prophetic Book

In this chapter I will discuss models that attempt to explain how the book of Ezekiel came into being and how it was subsequently modified and copied. I will also give examples of compositional and redactional strategies—that is, the editorial choices about form and content that resulted in the shape and argument structure of the book. It should be noted that the book itself does not directly refer to its own formation. The models that I discuss below are inferred from features in the book, and they remain *models*—our best attempts to account for the data that we see, and not definitive or universally agreed-on statements of how the book grew into the form(s) in which we now have it. That there are considerable differences between these compositional models is to be expected; these point to the complexity of the data, and reflect the various ways in which readers construe the contents and shape of the book of Ezekiel.

1. The formation of prophetic literature

In the popular imagination, a prophet is the disturbing person on the sidewalk ranting about coming judgment to passersby. And for good reason: this is both how some prophets are depicted in biblical literature (e.g., Jer 7.1–15; Amos 7.10–13; Jon 3.4) and how some people who self-identify as prophets today appear. But if the popular view of Israel's prophets as "manic street preachers" is in some limited sense correct, how do we explain the fact that the words attributed to them survive in books—books that are complex, and display literary and theological sophistication?

With a few exceptions, pre-critical readers simply assumed that prophets wrote the books that mention their names. However, when Hermann Gunkel set about reconstructing a history of literary types in ancient Israel, he noted that the prophetic literature which we now have is made up of short, originally oral units of speech. In 1923, he argued that ancient Israelite prophets were primarily and originally speakers, not writers (Gunkel 1987: 24). This assessment fits the depiction of prophecy in the biblical text, in which prophets spoke (and sometimes acted out) messages to their audience, who could be kings (Jer 21.11–12), passers-by (Jer 7.1–12), or people who came to request an oracle (Jer 21.1–7). The constraints of effective oral communication in such contexts would mean that individual units of speech had to be short, simple, and vivid. It is not difficult for a modern reader to see these short units, distinguishable by form and content, that have been juxtaposed in the prophetic books of the Bible. As the form-critical study of prophetic literature has shown, these units of prophetic speech tend to have stereotypical features, and can be grouped into categories and labeled as pronouncements of accusation, judgment, deliverance, and so on. The short, self-contained nature of prophetic utterances and their stereotypical forms are also attested outside Israel in ancient documents from Mari and Assyria (Nissinen 2003).

But who committed prophetic speeches to writing, and why? Recent research on literacy, book production, and scribal practice in antiquity (Carr 2005; Rollston 2010: 85–135; van der Toorn 2007: 173–204) shows that individual speeches of prophets would have been written down by scribes, and later turned into prophetic books by scribes. The initial impetus for committing prophetic speech to writing would have been the socio-religious and political implications of the prophets' messages, and the desire to preserve them for authentication. Comparative evidence from the royal archives of Mari and Assyria consists of letters addressed to the king reporting the contents of prophetic speeches, as well as tablets containing scribal summaries of prophetic speeches (Nissinen 2000; van der Toorn 2000). These show us how the initial scribal recording of prophetic speech could have taken place in Israel. Israelite scribes would presumably have been connected with the palace or temple, and in some cases may have been among the supporters of a prophet.

At some point, however, earlier prophetic traditions were composed into what we now have, that is, into prophetic books (Floyd 2006; Nissinen 2005). The form in which these prophetic traditions were preserved before incorporation into a book is something we can only guess at. What we can say with certainty is that unlike prophetic speeches or even reports of speeches, prophetic books are fundamentally literature: they are lengthy and composite texts that juxtapose originally separate units of prophetic speech, they contain large-scale patterning and structuring devices, they reflect on and extend the earlier arguments on which they were based, and they are aimed at a later and wider audience than (for example) the contemporaries of the prophet standing at the temple gate. For example: the *prophet* Amos is depicted as a critic of social injustice in the northern Israelite capital city Samaria and a proclaimer of complete destruction from God (Amos 4.1-3; 6.4-7). The *book* of Amos, however, sees hope despite punishment (Amos 9.8-10). It presumes the destruction and exile of the southern capital Jerusalem, and looks forward to a restoration that is focused on the tragically fallen royal house of David (Amos 9.11-15). In the book, the connection between sin and judgment for Samaria in the north is read paradigmatically to explain what happened to Jerusalem in the south. Hymnic fragments (Amos 4.13; 5.8-9; 9.5-6) have been inserted into collections of originally separate prophetic accusations and pronouncements of judgment—a literary technique that forces a reading audience to reflect on the nature of God in relation to the surrounding judgment oracles.

It is likely that the initial impetus for the formation of prophetic books was the crisis of exile. The exilic and post-exilic Israelite communities would have attempted to explain their circumstances and ponder the possibility of hope for the future. It is natural that they would have turned to records of how they believed God had spoken in the past to explain what was happening in the present. As Michael Floyd (2006: 289) explains, "In order to discern Yahweh's involvement in the events of their own time, post-exilic prophets studied written records of the historically authenticated prophecies from pre-exilic times, and asked which patterns of divine-human interaction perceived by pre-exilic prophets were being replicated in their own day." Exilic and post-exilic scribes addressed the needs of their communities by reflecting on older prophetic messages and creating new literary compositions out of them. The end result is a book that is a prophetic message in its own right: it reflects a belief that God communicated through the spoken words of the prophets of old, but also a belief that these words could be relevant for a new generation and a wider audience (Clements 1990; Zimmerli 1995).

2. Models for explaining the formation of the book

a. The unique features of Ezekiel

When we turn to the book of Ezekiel, we see three peculiar features that add complications to the model of prophetic book formation described above. First, it is difficult (in most cases, impossible) to reconstruct the original oral form of the prophet's speeches lying behind the present book of Ezekiel (Zimmerli 1979: 25). Other prophetic books contain what can be identified as reports of prophetic speech (e.g., Isa 1.10–17; Amos 4.1–3), but what we have in Ezekiel is a presentation of what the prophet was told to say, consistently related in a first-person narrative frame. Second, many of the self-contained units in the book of Ezekiel are quite large (e.g., chs. 16, 18, 20) compared to those in other prophetic books (Gunkel 1987: 70; Zimmerli 1965: 521). This makes it unlikely that these units represent a simple record of prophetic speech. Third, the book of Ezekiel displays a widespread literary and conceptual cohesion of a kind that is different from what we see in other prophetic books. This led S. R. Driver (1891: 261) to remark that "the whole from beginning to end bear[s] unmistakably the stamp of a single mind." While this assessment has been challenged in a variety of ways over the years, modern critics still see what Driver saw, though they speak about it more cautiously. For example, Rainer Albertz (2003: 346) is able to say that in comparison to Jeremiah, Ezekiel "gives the distinct impression of being a much more unified composition." How then can we account for these features when we attempt to create a model of the book's composition?

b. A pre-literary stage for the prophetic material?

The book of Ezekiel as we have it is clearly a literary product and not a transcription of oral proclamation and performance. As I noted above, what we have is not presented as a report of what Ezekiel said and did, but as a story of what God told Ezekiel to say and do. Already in 1876, Edouard Reuss had argued that Ezekiel was a writer, not a speaker, and that the book was the result of literary reflection (Reuss 1876: 10). Modern scholars (Albertz 2003: 347) offer a similar assessment: "the evidence suggests written composition from the outset." Is there reason, then, to believe that oral proclamation lies behind what we have as literature? Was there any oral proclamation at all? Or is the presentation of Ezekiel the prophet as a speaker just a literary fiction?

It is certainly the case that the material in the book is not a transcript of speech. Moreover, we are confronted throughout the book with material that could only have originated in writing. The chronological formulas that create the book's structure, for example, would hardly have been part of oral proclamation. The narrative descriptions of the prophet's experience (cf. Ezek 3.15) are similarly literary in origin, as are the intricate legal and architectural details in Ezek 40–48. Ezekiel is said to have told the exiles what he saw in his vision (Ezek 11.25), but the vision report related before this notice (Ezek 8–11) is both enormous and complex, with reflective material inserted into it. Whatever he told his contemporaries, it is unlikely to have been the vision report as we currently have it. The placement of announcements of hope immediately after accusation and proclamation of judgment (e.g., Ezek 16.60-63; 17.22-24) is a literary strategy, not an oral strategy. Such a juxtaposition would have been rhetorically counterproductive—not to mention confusing—to a listening audience. Later redactional additions to the book, such as Ezek 38-39, are of course also purely literary (see the discussion of redaction below).

Yet the prophet Ezekiel is consistently depicted as one who is commanded to speak to his contemporaries (Ezek 2.4, 7; 3.1, 4, 17; etc.) and as one who in fact did so (Ezek 11.25; 24.18, 20; 33.30-32). He is told to speak "whether they listen or not" (Ezek 2.5, 7). It is reported that he actually performed sign acts (Ezek 12.7) and was asked for an explanation by his audience (Ezek 12.9; 24.19). Occasionally he is approached by some elders who wish to inquire of Yhwh (Ezek 14.1; 20.1). He is presented as complaining about the people's negative response to his words (Ezek 21.5 [ET 20.49]), and some passages suggest an ongoing dispute between the prophet and people about a particular issue (e.g., Ezek 18.19, 25; 33.17). This depiction fits the profile of the orality of prophecy attested in Israelite and ancient Near Eastern evidence.

The idea that there was a prophet Ezekiel who spoke publically and performed symbolic acts seems plausible for the following reasons. First, we can in a few instances reconstruct short, self-contained units that fit into well-known forms of prophetic speech, such as the fable and rhetorical questions in Ezek 17.3-10, or the woe-oracle containing an accusation and pronouncement of judgment in Ezek 13.18-23. It seems plausible that these reflect actual speeches.

Second, there are numerous descriptions of commands to carry out expressive acts in the book: "clap with your hand and stamp with your foot" (Ezek 6.11); "moan with collapse of loins and with bitterness before their eyes" (Ezek 21.11 [ET v. 6]); "strike the thigh" (Ezek 21.17 [ET v. 12]); "strike hand to hand" (Ezek 21.19 [ET v. 14]; cf. v. 22 [ET v. 17]); "I strike my hands" (Ezek 22.13). These strongly suggest that actual performance lies behind the literature that we now have.

Third, the oracle in Ezek 29.17-20 (dated to 571 BCE), which is a response to the oracle in Ezek 26.1-14 (dated to 586 BCE), is highly significant for how we understand the formation of the book. Ezek 26.1-14 envisioned the defeat of Tyre by Babylon; but as the later oracle points out, Nebuchadnezzar failed to capture the city. The fact that the later oracle acknowledges and responds to this failure suggests that the prophecy in Ezek 26.1-14 had become widely known and had achieved a fixed form. If it was not widely known, it would have been easier to simply omit it from the book during the composition process, due to embarrassment at the failure of the oracle's prediction (note the concern about the status of prophecy in Ezek 12.21-28; 13.1-16). But the deliberate acknowledgment of the issue suggests public knowledge; and how else would the first oracle have become widely known but through oral proclamation?

Fourth, the book contains material that could only have been relevant in an exilic setting, and most likely in an oral form. For example, the enormous quantity of accusations and pronouncements of judgment in the book reflects an attempt to explain the exile for those who were going through it. These look quite different from later reflections on the exilic experience (e.g., Neh 9.26-31; Dan 9.1-19). It is important to note that I am not suggesting it is possible to precisely reconstruct from these accounts what the prophet Ezekiel actually said to his contemporaries. I am simply suggesting that the book contains material with uniquely exilic concerns, and it would be highly unlikely that an exilic prophet would not have addressed these concerns in speech.

The same holds true for the sign acts described in the book of Ezekiel. For example, the reports of sign acts in Ezek 4-5 exist in a form that seems to be the result of a process of transformation from oral to literary material, a combining together and editing of what were originally short, separate units. It is difficult to account for Ezek 4-5 as a literary fiction given its composite nature; conversely, the literary unity it does possess seems more likely to be the result of an editorial process rather than *de novo* authorship. But again, while I think it likely that these sign acts were connected in some way with actual performances (see Friebel 1999: 20–34), I do not think we can read Ezek 4–5 as a simple transcript of what Ezekiel said and did.

To sum up: given the *content* of the material in the book, I think it most likely that Ezekiel the prophet addressed his contemporaries about the situation in which they found themselves. But given the *form* of the material in the book, I think it largely impossible to reconstruct the shape of what was proclaimed. Furthermore, the book of Ezekiel itself is silent about the relationship between proclamation and writing.

c. The composition of the book

If a simple "copied speech" model does not adequately reflect the pervasively literary nature of the book, how else could the formation of the book be explained? One way to classify the models that have been put forth is by examining the extent to which scholars have attributed content and/or literary activity to Ezekiel the prophet. On one end of the spectrum, there are models that attribute nothing whatsoever, or very little, to a historical exilic prophet. For example, a few scholars (e.g., Becker 1982; Torrey 1930) have understood the book as a pseudepigraphical composition produced after the exile. While this model can account for the cohesive literary nature of the book, it is difficult to explain why a pseudepigraph would be associated with an otherwise unknown priestly prophet figure rather than one of the patriarchs, or an antediluvian hero such as Enoch (both attested as central figures in pseudepigraphical apocalyptic and testamentary literature). Furthermore, the later the composition of the book of Ezekiel is dated (for Becker, in the fifth century; for Torrey, in the late Hellenistic period), the more difficult it is to explain its relevance for its putative audience given its exilic focus and the nature and quantity of its accusations. Why compose a book in the post-exilic period that castigates the exilic generation for rebellion? What problem, and whose problem, would this be attempting to solve? To be sure, we do have examples of pseudepigraphs that attempt to explain the events of their day by depicting the linkage of sin and punishment in an earlier setting (e.g., Baruch; 4 Ezra). But the literary form of these books is very different from that of Ezekiel.

Other commentators whose models could be located at this end of the spectrum include Gustav Hölscher (1924), who reconstructed a small (mostly poetic) core of doom-oracles which he attributed to the exilic prophet; this was overlaid with a large prose expansion by a fifth-century Zadokite redactor. The resulting book then underwent subsequent redaction. For Hölscher, the non-Ezekielian material could be identified not just by the presence of prose, but also by the presence of priestly language and thought and by references to hope. Today, however, most commentators do not view his use of these criteria as reliable guides for stratifying the book.

Karl-Friedrich Pohlmann (1996, 2001) reconstructs multiple layers of redactional activity behind the book as we now have it. In his model, a few poetic laments over the deportation were composed in Jerusalem, then incorporated into a short prophetic book in the late exilic period. This was enlarged by subsequent post-exilic layers of redaction, the two main layers being one which represented the interests of the Israelite communities in Babylon, and another which represented the hopes of the wider diaspora. Because the book is a product of redactional activity, Pohlmann is skeptical of our ability to recover anything about a historical exilic prophet. For him, the various stances attributed by the book to the prophet Ezekiel (visionary, watchman, pronouncer of doom oracles, etc.) are mutually exclusive.

Rainer Albertz (2003: 350) has criticized Pohlmann's model on both methodological and historical grounds, questioning the rationale behind his stratifications and wondering "why in the fifth or fourth century—150 to 200 years after the end of the exile—it should be necessary to defend the claims of the golah against the claims of those left behind in Judah." In my view, there does seem to be evidence for redactional activity that broadens the book's outlook and results in a wider hope. This wider hope can be clearly seen in the plus in MT Ezek

39.28 and in the later addition of Ezek 38–39 to the book (cf. Ezek 39.25). I therefore think it likely that subtle adjustments or expansions were made to earlier oracles, detectable by the use of the phrase "the entire house of Israel, all of it" (Ezek 20.40; 36.10; 37.11), or in the description of restoration as being "from all the places where they have been scattered" (Ezek 34.12). However, I would follow Albertz in dating the bulk of the book to a much earlier period than Pohlmann does, because I see the concerns of the book as largely exilic. The book of Ezekiel attempts to *explain why* the disaster occurred, and *convince* its audience that hope is possible, against all appearances to the contrary. In contrast, early post-exilic literature attempts to *motivate* and *assess* attempts at national and spiritual reconstitution once these had become possible.

At the other end of the spectrum, there is a model that attributes both the content and the composition of the book almost entirely to the prophet Ezekiel (though it allows for minor redactional additions). The work of Moshe Greenberg (1983, 1997) is representative of this position (see also Block 1997: 17–23; Darr 2001: 1087–88; Davis 1989; Haran 2005). To suggest that Ezekiel the prophet had a hand in the book's literary formation is not necessarily a return to a precritical stance. Even Gunkel himself—who, as I mentioned above, stressed the fundamentally oral nature of prophecy—argued that Ezekiel "composed the first prophetic book" (2003: 61). Those who hold this model argue that it is not unreasonable to suppose that the prophet would have had scribal training. After all, he is depicted as one of the priestly elites who participated in a social institution (the temple) that sponsored scribal education and book production. Furthermore, as a Jerusalem priest, he would have been trained in the use of textualized legal traditions (Davis 1989: 40). Indeed, the prophet is depicted as being commanded to write in Ezek 24.2; 37.16, 20; 43.11.

A drawback to this model is that it runs the risk of downplaying the presence of diversity, or of attributing all diversity to a single author even when other explanations are possible. For example, Greenberg believed that most attempts to account for diversity by distinguishing between material from Ezekiel and later additions are due to purely modern and artificial presuppositions (1983: 20). He claimed to "find nothing on the book of Ezekiel that necessitates supposing another hand than that of a prophet of the sixth century" (1986: 134). But his assessment of what is going on in Ezek 34.23-24—"later retouching,""secondary reflection" (1997: 702, 707)—is not substantially different from the assessments of the critics whose models he disagrees with.

In the middle of the spectrum there are models that date the bulk of the material in the book to the exilic period and give the prophet a role in the writing and editing of his own oracles, yet attribute the formation of the book itself to the "school" or "disciples" of the prophet, and find evidence for subsequent redactional additions. These models have the advantage of accounting for both cohesion (including the first-person narration and the lengthy size of the units) and coherence, for the updating (rather than omission) of Ezek 26.1–14 by Ezek 29.17–20, for the composite nature of certain sections, for material reflecting different perspectives, and for the presence of units that build on or extend the surrounding material in a reflective way. Of course, there is also a spectrum of opinions regarding the degree to which Ezekiel was involved in editing his own oracles. According to Georg Fohrer (1968: 412–14) and Rainer Albertz (2003: 351–54), Ezekiel wrote down his speeches (whether before or after he delivered them is unclear), and even supplemented and updated them; the book was then composed from these materials by his disciples shortly after his death in the sixth century BCE. G. A. Cooke (1936: xix–xxvii) and Walther Zimmerli (1979: 68–74) held a similar position, but were willing to give Ezekiel a more prominent role in the formation of the book. Zimmerli, for example, regarded Ezekiel not just as the source but also as the editor of composite texts such as Ezek 19.2–9, 10–14 and Ezek 34.1–24. The difficulties for this model lie in the absence of external sociological evidence for the existence of "prophetic schools" and in the problem of distinguishing between the prophetic and the "school" material (see further below).

d. The "school"/"disciples" of Ezekiel

Hermann Gunkel (2003: 61) seems to have been one of the earliest scholars to entertain the idea of a "school" or "disciples" of a prophet, and this idea was quickly taken up by others (Sigmund Mowinckel in particular). As we see in, for example, Jer 11.6; 18.1-2, the places where prophetic utterances were delivered were not restricted to the royal court or temple, the two obvious centers of scribal activity where such messages could have been copied down and archived. It is therefore necessary to explain how oral prophecy could have been preserved and eventually textualized. Since the book of Isaiah refers to "faithful witnesses" (Isa 8.2) and to "disciples" who received testimony and instruction from the prophet (Isa 8.16), many have postulated the existence of a circle of followers who identified with a prophet's values and teachings. These disciples would have been the ones to preserve and write down the prophet's sayings. After all, it is quite common even today for charismatic figures to attract followers who appreciate and pass on their ideas.

If many scholars believe that Ezekiel the prophet committed his own oracles to writing, why do they attribute the shape of the book as a whole to a group of the prophet's disciples? For Albertz (2003: 352-53), the literary work of disciples is necessary because the book's own chronology suggests that Ezekiel the prophet would have died too soon to compose his material into the book we now have. For Zimmerli (1979: 69-71), the literary work of disciples is necessary to explain both unity and diversity in the form, content, and outlook of material in the book. Ezekiel may have begun the process of editing his own oracles, but this process was continued and completed by his disciples. A good example can be found in the collection of sign acts in Ezek 4-5. Zimmerli believes that Ezekiel the prophet performed various sign acts before an audience of his contemporaries some time before the fall of Jerusalem. From these performances, a report was composed that described three of them: God's command to Ezekiel to besiege a model city (Ezek 4.1-2); the command to consume multigrain bread and rationed water (4.9-11); and the command to shave his head and perform various actions with his hair (5.1–2). All three sign acts begin in the same way ("And you—take for yourself …"), and these three depict the logical sequence of "siege—famine due to siege—consequences of a successful siege." But this original report was expanded: additional sign acts have been inserted without regard to logical sequence (e.g., 4.4–5, 6, 12–15); interpretations of the sign acts have been supplied (e.g., 4.16–17; 5.5), and some of the sign acts have been coordinated with each other (e.g., vv. 4.6a, 9b). Zimmerli attributes this editorial activity to Ezekiel's disciples, who are responsible for the shape of the text as we now have it.

Another example can be seen in Ezek 5.1–4. In vv. 1–2, we have what Zimmerli isolates as the third sign act in the earliest three-part collection: Ezekiel is to shave his head, then divide his hair into three parts. One third of the hair he is to burn, another third he is to strike with a sword, and the final third he is to scatter to the wind—the argument obviously being that the inhabitants of Jerusalem are completely doomed, fated to die inside or outside the city, or to be thoroughly dispersed and die after this (cf. Ezek 5.12). This would account for all the hair, so the reader is surprised to see in vv. 3–4 a command to the prophet to take some hairs, bind them in his robe, then burn them in fire. These two verses represent the addition of a new idea—an argument that even if some survivors did happen to escape the destruction of the city, one should not imagine that hope lies with them; a subsequent judgment would be meted out even upon these. Zimmerli suggests that while the argument represents the thought of Ezekiel the prophet, the expression of the argument in these verses may be the work of the prophet's disciples.

A final example can be found in Ezek 36.1–15. Zimmerli notes some peculiar literary features in this unit: an unusually high density of repeated introductory formulas, speech formulas, and statements beginning with "therefore" (*lkn*); differences in how the foe is described (v. 2, "the enemy"; vv. 3–5, "the rest of the nations"; v. 5, "all Edom"); differences in addressee (v. 1, "mountains of Israel"; v. 6, "land of

Israel"; v. 10, "all the house of Israel, all of it"); vocabulary not appearing elsewhere in the book (v. 3, *dbh* "whispering; mocking talk"); a shift from second person plural to singular in v. 12. He attributes these features to the presence of "secondary additions" and "expansions." And yet these expansions build on the surrounding material, repeating its language but extending its argument in new ways. For Zimmerli, it is this "editorial extension" (*Fortschreibung*) in which the contribution of Ezekiel's disciples is particularly noticeable.

While the attribution of the composition of the book of Ezekiel to a "prophetic school" has become widely accepted, the way the model is sometimes employed raises many questions. Is the idea of a prophetic school necessary to explain how prophetic tradition was preserved, or to explain how literary innovation was introduced into the tradition? In other words, to what extent are these disciples simply tradents who put prophetic material in written form, and to what extent are they creative figures in their own right? And what are we to make of the frequent cautions about the difficulty of distinguishing between original material from the prophet and later material from his disciples (e.g., Zimmerli 1979: 71, 177, 348, 364, 467)? If it is so difficult to distinguish between the two, how necessary is it to posit the existence of the latter? What are we to make of the fact that according to Zimmerli the prophet himself edited and commented on his own material in the same way that his disciples did? Is the idea of a prophetic school simply an heuristic device that we have created in our attempt to account for both unity and diversity of material in prophetic books, or did such a group actually exist in ancient Israel? Is the preference for terms denoting plurality ("disciples"; "school") really warranted, or should we simply attribute the composition of the book to "a scribe who was a disciple of the prophet"? Commentators who have taken up Zimmerli's model are not unaware of these issues (Clements 1982; 1986), and continue to argue that—with certain qualifications—a model in which the prophet's disciples are responsible for the book's composition best accounts for the evidence.

e. The redaction of the book

For the purposes of this discussion, I am using the word "composition" to refer to the *production* of a book, and the word "redaction" to refer to the *subsequent modification* of that book (Fohrer 1983: 139–42). An imprecise analogy to the redaction of prophetic literature can be found in the phenomenon of the modern "study Bible," in which editors have formatted the text and provided section headings, marginal cross-references, and commentary printed under the text. This commentary is intended to explain the text and suggest how a modern reader might appropriate it as scripture. In much the same way, ancient scribes inserted material in a book in order to coordinate it with other books in the growing Israelite scripture collection. They would insert definitions for obscure words and phrases, and attempt to clarify difficult passages for the reader. They would offer responses to ideas in the text from the vantage of their own situation. In short, we can view redactional activity as an early form of textual commentary that becomes part of the text itself.

Literary criticism identifies redaction in texts by the presence of material that causes a lack of *cohesion* (a disruption or irregularity in syntactic or literary features) or a lack of *coherence* (a disruption in outlook or conceptual unity). Features that have been explained as redactional in Ezekiel include shifts in grammatical person and number, repetition, shifts in content or imagery, and shifts in perspective. Of course, identifying material as redactional involves an admittedly subjective element of judgment. We must also face the fact that at times our literary sensibilities may be at odds with what were acceptable conventions in antiquity: some textual features that appear disruptive to a modern reader would no doubt have been unremarkable to ancient authors and readers. Moreover, not even all modern readers agree on what is disruptive and what is not! Nevertheless, our inability to formulate rigid, "objective," and universally applicable criteria for identifying redactional additions does not mean that redaction did not occur. We have good reasons to believe that redactors made modifications to an early book of Ezekiel—not merely because certain literary features of the book are best explained in this way, but because we have actual manuscript evidence that modifications were still being made even after the period under consideration.

Four issues should be kept in mind when attempting to identify redactional insertions in Ezekiel. First, the impact of presuppositions about prophecy and prophetic literature on models of the formation of the book should not be ignored. Older studies often identified redactional additions using criteria that have since been abandoned as anachronistic or misplaced, such as the presence of prose passages (Hölscher 1924: 5–6), any appearance of hope for restoration (Herrmann 1965: 290; Hölscher 1924: 15, 52), or the presence of material reflecting sacral law (Garscha 1974: 303–305). But prophetic speech elsewhere in the ancient Near East is not limited to poetic utterances. And with respect to the issue of whether the oracles of hope can be attributed to the exilic prophet, it seems to me that they can be firmly located in an exilic setting. As Rolf Rendtorff (1991: 214) has argued, "it is highly improbable that we should suppose that none of the proclamation of salvation goes back to the exilic prophet himself, because without it the whole book would fall apart and nothing comprehensible would remain." One of the most fundamental features of the book is its attempt to convince an exilic audience of the possibility of hope for the future. Given Ezekiel's situation, it is extremely likely that he would speak words of both judgment and hope—though for rhetorical reasons it is unlikely that he spoke both together at the same time. Finally, with respect to Ezekiel's legal language, it seems to me that the use of the presence of sacral law as a criterion for redactional activity is due either to an illegitimate idealization and disjunction between the roles of prophet and priest (even though the use of priestly torah by prophets is widely acknowledged), or else an arbitrary decision to stratify material based on purely ordinary differences in form and content.

Second, by formulating criteria for detecting redaction in terms of contextual disruption, we run the risk of demanding an improbable degree of consistency in form and content from the prophet and/or composers of the book. On reflection, however, it is absurd to attribute any and all perceived shifts in form, style, and content to the hand of a later redactor. These features can surely be the product of speakers and authors as well as of redactors.

Third, the unique literary features of the book of Ezekiel make identification of redaction particularly difficult. Paul Joyce (2009: 12) notes that "the nature of the book is such that it is particularly resistant to any straightforward division between primary and secondary material. This is surely not because the whole book is from the prophet Ezekiel ... but rather because of the marked homogeneity of the Ezekiel tradition, in which secondary material bears an unusually close 'family resemblance' to primary." Moreover, expansions of or reflections on surrounding material can occur at every stage of the book's development. This can often lead to confusion in scholarly literature on Ezekiel: does a commentator's use of the term "later addition" mean that the prophet did not orally proclaim a particular unit at the same time as he proclaimed the adjacent unit, the juxtaposition of which occurred only when the book was composed? Or does it mean that the particular unit was never proclaimed by the prophet, but created and inserted by the prophet's disciples during the composition of the book? Or does it mean that the unit in question was an addition to an already-existing book by a subsequent redactor? Because of this potential for confusion, the terms "later" or "addition" should always be accompanied by a statement about the stage of literary development at which the new material was ostensibly added.

A final issue that must be considered is the question of how many layers of redactional activity are present in the book. Here there is a significant difference of opinion between Continental scholarship (which tends to find multiple redactional layers) and non-Continental scholarship (which tends to be skeptical about the existence of multiple layers, and to label attempts to recover them as "overly complex"). This difference of opinion is important, and deserves a full-length treatment that cannot be provided in this volume. Nevertheless, there is one thing that all critical readers should agree on: while it is true that readers will inevitably construe texts in slightly different ways, assigning different levels of significance to what they see, our models of redactional activity must be shaped in light of what we know about scribal practice and book production in antiquity.

f. Examples of redaction in the book of Ezekiel

The following examples are by no means exhaustive, but represent a selection to show the reader how redaction can be identified. For additional examples, see the discussion under the heading "Extension and Coordination" below.

Ezekiel 1.2–3a

One of the clearest examples of redaction can be seen in the first three verses of the book. The book begins (Ezek 1.1) with an ambiguous date formula (the "thirtieth year" of what?) and a first-person reference to seeing "visions of God." However, vv. 2–3 represent an addition: they clarify the ambiguous date in Ezek 1.1 with respect to the rest of the book by supplying a year reckoned from a known event (the exile of King Jehoiachin) derived by working backward from subsequent date formulas. They also provide a third-person introduction to the book that matches those found in other prophetic books (cf. Hag 1.1; Zech 1.1), correlating the book of Ezekiel to a wider corpus of prophetic literature. The first-person reference of v. 1 is continued in vv. 4ff. (it may actually begin in v. 3b, though the textual witnesses differ on this point: v. 3b in the Hebrew Masoretic Text (MT) reads "the hand of Yhwh came upon *him there*," and the Old Greek translation (LXX) reads "the hand of the Lord came upon *me*").

Ezekiel 16.57

Ezek 16.57 makes mention of "the daughters of Edom [*other textual witnesses: "Aram"*] and all those who are around her." But who are "those who are around her"? The next phrase, "the daughters of the Philistines," is most likely a redactional addition that was inserted to answer this question. If the identity of "those who are around her" were known, the phrase would be superfluous. Here we see a redactional concern to identify and clarify. Perhaps this insertion was further motivated by the fact that the oracle against Philistia in Ezek 25.15–17 follows the oracle against Edom in 25.12–14.

Ezekiel 23.48

Ezekiel 23 consists of an allegorical story of two sisters who engage in promiscuous sexual activity and are punished for it. The referents of the allegory, identified in v. 4, are Samaria and Jerusalem, and their downfall at the hand of surrounding countries is attributed to divine judgment. But v. 48 is neither part of the allegory nor its interpretation; it does not refer to Samaria or to Jerusalem, but states that God will "make lewdness cease from the land" so that "all women will take warning and not act in accordance with your lewdness." This reflective, moralizing comment is, to be sure, based on a reading of the surrounding material, but is ultimately motivated by something *outside* the immediate context. And there are two different motivations (and interpretations) that might explain this comment: on the one hand, this redactional insertion could refer to actual women, and if so, would be motivated by a (male) perception and evaluation of female activity in society. On the other hand, the insertion could be an extension of the existing allegory, and the reference to "all women" could metaphorically refer to the political centers of other nations. The motivation for the statement that these other nations should "take warning" (*ysr*) from the lesson of Samaria and Jerusalem could be found in Ezek 5.15, where Jerusalem is told that her destruction will stand as a "mockery and a reviling, a warning (*mwsr*) and a horror, to the nations who are around you."

Ezekiel 28.24, 25–26

Both Ezek 28.24 and 28.25–26 can be explained as redactional additions to the Sidon oracle in Ezek 28.20–23. The Sidon oracle is a short, self-contained unit that begins with a prophetic word formula (v. 20) and command to prophesy (v. 21), followed by a proclamation of God's judgment against Sidon (vv. 22–23), and ending with a recognition formula. Ezek 28.24 is clearly not part of the earlier self-contained unit. However, v. 24 has been composed in relation to it: the verse consists of theological reflection on the statements of judgment against surrounding nations. V. 24 interprets judgment on the nations as deliverance for Israel—an interpretation that is not present in any of the oracles about the nations in Ezek 25–32. It promises deliverance for Israel from "the ones all around who scorn them," picking up the language of Ezek 16.57. V. 24 is therefore either a reflective and interpretive comment inserted during the composition process, or it is a later redactional addition.

But vv. 25–26 are a further addition: the end of v. 26 repeats in almost verbatim fashion the end of v. 24 and signals the insertion of new material within the created frame (this framing repetition is an editorial technique known as *Wiederaufnahme*). The inserted material links the judgment on the nations even more closely to the restoration of Israel by using language taken from elsewhere in the book: it explicitly mentions the return from exile and the "manifestation of God's holiness" as a result of that return (cf. Ezek 20.41; 36.23; 39.27). It describes living on the land "which I gave to my servant, to Jacob" (cf. Ezek 37.25). It uses the stereotypical "build houses, plant vineyards" language (cf. Deut 28.30; Jer 35.7; Amos 5.11; Zeph 1.13) to describe future restoration (cf. Isa 65.21; Amos 9.14). Most importantly, it links "living securely" (twice in v. 26) to the judgment of the nations—undoubtedly a major concern of the post-exilic community. How after all was it possible for Israel to "live securely" in the land—as promised elsewhere (Ezek 34.25, 27, 28; cf. Lev 26.5)—if there were still threats from surrounding nations? This sudden intrusion of material about the restoration of Israel and its accompanying circumstances in a context about judgment of surrounding nations *could* be a compositional feature of the early book of Ezekiel. However, given the other contexts this passage is referencing, many believe it is more likely to be a redactional addition.

Ezekiel 38–39

The Gog-oracles in Ezek 38–39 form a self-contained unit; its beginning is marked by a prophetic word formula (Ezek 38.1) and its end is signaled by the date formula beginning a new section in Ezek 40.1. The first clue that these chapters are a later addition with respect to the rest of the book lies in Ezek 38.17, which states that Gog was spoken of "in former days by my servants the prophets of Israel." The reference here seems to be drawing on the "foe from the north" described in Jer 6.22–23; and indeed, many words from this passage appear here in Ezekiel: "remotest parts" (Jer 6.22; Ezek 38.6, 15), "north" (Jer 6.22; Ezek 38.6, 15); "rouse oneself" (Jer 6.22; LXX Ezek 38.14 [MT has "know"]); "come" (Jer 6.22; Ezek 38.14); "ride horses" (Jer 6.23; Ezek 38.15). Similarly, the language and sequence of imagery from Jer 49.30–33 (and Isa 10.3, 6–7) is picked up in Ezek 38.8–13. Ezek 38–39 therefore evinces a temporal stance long after the time of Jeremiah and his contemporary Ezekiel (Cooke 1936: 414). The eschatological outlook of these chapters is also unique in Ezekiel, as can be seen by the temporal markers in Ezek 38.8, 16 (which never appear elsewhere in the book).

The comprehensive treatment of these chapters by William Tooman shows that Ezek 38–39 consists of a pastiche of locutions taken from other books and from passages elsewhere in Ezekiel which are transformed to create new images and arguments. To list but a few examples (besides the ones from Jeremiah listed above): the locutions in Ezek 38.4 are derived from Ezek 23.12, 24; 29.4, and the list of names in Ezek 38.2, 5–6 is taken largely from the list of trading partners in Ezek 27 (supplemented by selections from the table of nations in Gen 10). An inversion of Ps 79.1–4 provides the conceptual background to Ezek 39. More specifically, Ezek 39.6 uses the refrain of Amos 1.4, 7, 10, etc., and Ezek 39.17 picks up the language of Ezek 39.4 (which is itself taken from Ezek 29.5) but reworks it with the imagery of Isa 34.6–7. Ezek 39.29 is a conflation of Ezek 37.14 with Joel 3.1–2 [ET 2.28–29]. Tooman (2011: 271) concludes that the redactor is coordinating the book of Ezekiel with other literature in the developing Israelite scripture collection:

> This coordination was motivated by a desire to fill certain gaps in Ezekiel (regarding the vindication of Israel and the ultimate fate of the nations) and to extend or adjust certain themes in the book (e.g., purity of the land, transformation of Israel). In effect, the author of GO [the Gog oracles] sought to supplement Ezekiel and the entire prophetic corpus, contributing to existing prophecy by delineating the time and circumstances of Israel's vindication.

Redaction in Ezekiel 40–48

The presence of these chapters at the end of the book raises a number of issues: on the one hand, the placement of Ezek 40–48 is logical insofar as the restoration of the temple and return of the divine presence are themes that are only briefly mentioned earlier in the book (Ezek 20.40-41; 37.27-28). On the other hand, it is precisely the fact that these themes are only briefly mentioned earlier that suggests to some that material in Ezek 40–48 may be an editorial addition to the book. Ezek 40–48 are clearly composite, but did the material originate in entirety from the exilic prophet, or is some of it from a later hand? As we might expect, some hold that all the material comes from the prophet (Greenberg 1984; Haran 1979), while others see a core of Ezekielian material (mostly chs. 40–43) that was expanded by later redactors (Gese 1957; Konkel 2001; Tuell 1992). These latter scholars detect tensions in the text that they feel are best accounted for by a model of sequential editorial activity. For example, Ezek 40.45-46 with its "some priests for temple, other priests for altar" scheme seems to some to conflict with Ezek 44.13, where the Levites, whose job it is to minister in the temple, are explicitly prohibited from "functioning as priests" (Gese 1957: 66; Levenson 1976: 129–32).

g. The transmission and textual witnesses of the book of Ezekiel

The process described above, whereby material was added to clarify or extend the text in new ways, continued long after the book was composed and can be seen in the extant textual witnesses (cf. Stromberg 2008). Both the Hebrew evidence (medieval Masoretic manuscripts and the fragments found in the Judaean desert, which both represent the same textual family) and the ancient Greek translation (LXX) and later revisions made to it provide evidence of this. And there are enough differences between the Hebrew and Greek witnesses that they constitute two different textual families. Emanuel Tov (2012: 299–301) notes that the Old Greek translation of Ezekiel represents a Hebrew parent text that is 4–5 percent shorter than the Hebrew Masoretic text. According to Tov, "this shorter text was slightly expanded in M+ [*combined evidence of Masoretic Text, Targum, Syriac Peshitta, and Vulgate*] by various types of elements: exegesis, harmonization, emphasis, parallel words, and new material.... Most of the plus elements are explicative-exegetical" (Tov 2012: 299). The examples listed below show the nature of and motives for some of the editorial additions to the book of Ezekiel.

To explain an obscure word (Ezek 8.11)

Ezek 8.11 (LXX)	Ezek 8.11 (MT)
And seventy men of the elders of the house of Israel—and Jaazaniah son of Shaphan was standing in their midst—were in front of them, and each had his incense burner in hand, and the vapor of incense was rising.	And seventy men of the elders of the house of Israel—and Jaazaniah son of Shaphan was standing in their midst—were standing in front of them, and each had his incense burner in his hand; and the fragrance of *the cloud of* incense was rising.

The original Hebrew text described what was rising from the burning incense as "fragrance," a word that occurs only one time in the Hebrew

Bible. While the Greek translator correctly guessed its meaning and translated it more or less appropriately as "vapor," the scribe who copied the Hebrew text lying behind the MT wanted to be absolutely certain that the readers of his Hebrew text would understand this obscure word, and inserted the explanatory word "cloud" next to it.

To clarify a phrase by borrowing from another text (Ezek 8.10)

Ezek 8.10 (LXX)	Ezek 8.10 (MT)
And I entered, and I looked, and behold, empty detestable things and all the idols of the house of Israel inscribed on it all around.	And I entered, and I looked, and behold, every—*a pattern of creeping things and beasts*—detestable thing and all the idols of the house of Israel inscribed on the wall all around.

Leaving aside the issue of the difference between LXX's "empty" and MT's "every," MT-Ezekiel has inserted a phrase clarifying the meaning of "detestable things and idols." The word for "idol" used here is the term *glwlym*. According to the following examples, the word seems to have been used to refer to free-standing humanoid statutes of deities: God will "place your corpses on the corpses of your idols" (Lev 26.30); they are made of "wood and stone, silver and gold" (Deut 29.16 [ET v. 17]); they can be "broken and destroyed" (Ezek 6.6); they are "made" (Ezek 22.4). But how can a free-standing statute be "inscribed on a wall" (Ezek 8.10)? And what kind of "detestable thing" is the prophet speaking of? The text represented by MT-Ezekiel clarifies by inserting a phrase taken from Deut 4.17–18, explaining that Ezekiel is speaking of pictures or patterns (*tbnyt*) of creeping things and beasts that have been carved on the wall.

To coordinate one text-segment with another

Both LXX-Ezekiel and MT-Ezekiel reveal a continuing scribal tendency to coordinate the vision reports even more closely than they already have been (see the discussion below). For example, the phrase "like the sound of Shadday" in MT Ezek 1.24 is an insertion based on Ezek 10.5, and the clauses "he took me up and he lifted me" in LXX Ezek 2.2 are an insertion based on Ezek 3.14.

To coordinate the book of Ezekiel with another book (Ezek 7.19 to Zeph 1.18)

Ezek 7.19 (LXX)
Their silver will be thrown into the streets, and their gold will be despised. Their appetites will not be satisfied and their stomachs will not be filled, because it was the test of their iniquity.

Ezek 7.19 (MT)
They will throw their silver into the streets, and their gold will be treated as an unclean thing. *Their silver and their gold will not be able to deliver them on the day of the wrath of Y*hwh. They will not satisfy their appetite and they will not fill their stomachs, because it was the stumbling-block of their iniquity.

Setting aside minor translational differences, the significant difference is that MT-Ezekiel contains an entire clause not present in LXX-Ezekiel. This additional material is a scribal addition which was taken from Zeph 1.18, "Both *their silver and their gold will not be able to deliver them on the day of the wrath of Y*hwh, and in the fire of his jealousy all the land will be consumed, for an ending—a terrifying one!—he will make of all the inhabitants of the land." The scribe recognized the finality of the judgment described in Ezek 7, and was reminded of another text describing a similar final judgment (Zeph 1.14–18). By inserting a line from Zephaniah in the text of Ezekiel, the scribe was arguing that the judgment described in Ezekiel was the same terrifying "Day of Yʜwʜ" described in the book of Zephaniah.

Another example is the statement "that which you find, eat" in MT Ezek 3.1; this is an addition (absent in the Old Greek) that coordinates the section describing Ezekiel's call to Jer 15.16, a text that reflects on the call of the prophet Jeremiah. Yet another example occurs in MT

Ezek 6.5a. The clause "I will put the corpses of the sons of Israel before their idols" is an interpolation from Lev 26.30 (which was already being used as the source text for the composition of Ezek 6.1–7). This interpolation makes it clear that "your slain" (Ezek 6.4b) and "your bones" (Ezek 6.5b) are not referring to literal "mountains" (the addressees of the oracle, Ezek 6.2–3), but to people.

To widen the scope of the text's argument

Ezek 39.28 (LXX)
And they will know that I am the Lord their God when I am *revealed to* them among the nations.

Ezek 39.28 (MT)
And they will know that I am Yнwн their God, when I *exiled* them to the nations; *and I will gather them to their land; and I will leave none of them there any longer.*

Setting aside the interpretive differences between the two textual witnesses (*hglwty* as "my being revealed to" vs. "my exiling"), MT-Ezekiel contains an addition that envisions a comprehensive return of the global diaspora. While this draws on existing passages depicting a far-reaching return (cf. Ezek 20.40–41; 34.12; 39.25), the idea that none will be left among the nations is given a unique articulation here (Mackie 2014: 119–21).

To coordinate a text with other passages in light of a relevant topic

The descriptions of Ezekiel's visionary experience of the divine presence sparked an immense interest in readers of the book. This interest can be seen in later texts that reflect developing Jewish speculation about the heavenly realm and the angelic beings who inhabit it, such as 1 Enoch 14, 71 and 4Q403, 405 (Songs of the Sabbath Sacrifice). But this interest is already reflected in the textual transmission of the book of Ezekiel itself. For example, the description of the "wheels" (*'wpnym*) in MT Ezek 10 contains expansions in vv. 12, 14 (based on material in the earlier vision of Ezek 1) that make it clear that these should be understood as angelic entities and not mere mechanical structures (Halperin 1976). A similar interest can be seen in an addition in LXX Ezek 43.3, which states that the vision which Ezekiel saw by the Chebar canal (Ezek 1) was a "vision of the Chariot." The word "Chariot" was beginning to be used as a technical term for either the wheels-plus-platform-plus-throne structure associated with the cherubim (as in Ben Sira 49.8), or for angelic beings themselves (as in 4Q405 20.ii.3).

Two "variant literary editions"? The case of Ezekiel 36.23b-38

A final example concerns the highly debated case of Ezek 36.23b-38 and the manuscript Papyrus 967. This Greek witness is notable for several reasons: first, it is dated to the late second or early third century CE, making it one of our oldest Greek witnesses. Second, while Joseph Ziegler placed great emphasis on Codex B when producing the Ezekiel volume for the Göttingen edition of the Septuagint, other text critics have argued that Papyrus 967 is just as important as a witness to the Old Greek. Third, Papyrus 967 alone out of all Greek witnesses (along with the Old Latin Codex Wirceburgensis) lacks Ezek 36.23b-38, and it is this feature which has aroused particular attention for scholars of the book of Ezekiel. Some have argued that the absence of these verses is due to paraplepsis by homoioteleuton: the scribe's eye skipped from "... that I am Yhwh" in v. 23a to "... that I am Yhwh" in v. 38, leaving out the intervening verses (Filson 1943). But since most agree that vv. 23b-38 are far too much material to be lost via paraplepsis, some have argued that the absence of these verses was caused by the loss of a page in the *Vorlage* (parent text) of Papyrus 967. Both of these explanations presume that the presence of vv. 23b-38 constitutes the original reading. In fact, it is sometimes argued that the preceding section (vv. 16–23a) makes no sense without the following verses, inasmuch as it raises the problems of the exile of the people and damage to God's reputation and therefore requires the solution supplied in vv. 23b-38 (Block 1998: 340–41).

However, according to others (Crane 2008; Lilly 2012; Lust 1981, 2003), the difference between the textual witnesses cannot be explained by accidental omission. For these scholars, Papyrus 967 represents a shorter version of the book of Ezekiel, and the Hebrew (MT-Ezekiel, the Masada Ezekiel scroll) and other Greek witnesses (LXX^{A,B}, etc.) represent a more developed version. Thus we have two "variant literary editions" of the text of Ezekiel—an assessment which is further supported by the fact that in Papyrus 967, ch. 36 of Ezekiel is followed by chs. 38–39, with ch. 37 placed afterward. Furthermore, the translational features of Ezek 36.23b-38 in the other Greek witnesses differ from what we see in the surrounding material, and these verses appear to have been secondarily supplied from the Hebrew in a manner similar to what we find in the early Greek recensions. Finally, it is argued that vv. 23b-38 in the Hebrew text display the same features of editorial expansion that we have commented on above. For example, we see the use of themes and locutions borrowed from elsewhere in the book ("show myself holy," Ezek 20.41 > Ezek 36.23b; "gather you from the peoples/lands," Ezek 11.17; 20.34, 41; 34.13 > 36.24; "bring them to their land," Ezek 34.13 > 36.24; gift of new heart/spirit with resulting obedience, Ezek 11.19–20; 37.14 > Ezek 36.26–27; the covenant formula, Ezek 11.20 > 36.28; the reference to being "clean" and "saving," Ezek 37.23 > 36.29; the reference to "remembering" and "loathing," Ezek 20.43 > 36.31; "not for your sake," Ezek 36.22 > 36.32; the reversal of famine, Ezek 34.27, 29 > 36.29b). We see the extension of the argument in a new direction (the reversal of waste places into rebuilt and inhabited places, Ezek 36.33–36). These verses also contain linguistic features that do not appear elsewhere in Ezekiel, as well as locutions that are characteristic of the book of Jeremiah (e.g., "the land which I gave to your fathers," Jer 30.3 > Ezek 36.28; "build and plant," Jer 26.4; 31.4–5, 28; 42.10 > Ezek 36.36).

Still other scholars have argued that there is simply not enough evidence to make a final decision as to whether the shorter or longer form of Ezek 36 is original. They hold that the absence of Ezek 36.23b-38 in a single Greek witness constitutes a problem for the textual history of the Greek text alone—one which might simply be ascribed to accidental omission. The nature of the Hebrew text is another matter: its features could be explained by ascribing it to the school of Ezekiel as an editorial expansion that brings together the descriptions of restoration found elsewhere in the book (Flanagan 2009; Zimmerli 1983: 245-46).

3. Compositional and redactional techniques in the book of Ezekiel

In this section, I will examine the compositional and redactional techniques at work in the book of Ezekiel—that is, the choices involving the creation of form and content that resulted in the shape and argument structure of the book. In the previous chapter I limited the discussion to issues of genre, imagery, and distinctive language. But we must now consider how units of prophetic material were created, where these units were placed, and how these units were related to each other.

a. The placement of the date formulas

One of the most obvious compositional techniques in the book of Ezekiel is the placement of date formulas at the beginning of certain oracles. Opinions on the authorship of the date formulas have varied; Hölscher (1924: 108, 126) claimed they were later additions, whereas Cooke (1936: xix) argued for their genuineness. The facts that dates are tied to specific oracles, and that these oracles are not always placed in chronological order, suggest that the date formulas were attached to oracles before they were joined together into a book (rather than being added to an already-existing book). It seems possible that when the book was formed, the dated oracles were the "backbone" around which the other oracles were inserted. In a number of cases, the positioning of both dated and undated oracles was motivated by content rather than by chronology. For example, the latest-dated oracle in the book, Ezek

29.17-20, is placed with the Egypt material because it concerns the fate of Egypt.

The use of these date formulas creates an emphasis on the problems of exile and the fall of Jerusalem, provides an authentication of the prophetic word, structures the text-segments in the book, and contributes to the creation of a narrative sequence. First, the date formulas are directly related to two of the most significant arguments in the book: that exile is punishment for rebellion against God, and that the fall of Jerusalem is necessary and unavoidable. With the exceptions of the formulas in Ezek 1.1 and 24.1 (on the latter, see 2 Kgs 25.1), all the dates given are calculated from the first Judean exile to Babylon in 597 BCE. Indeed, the formulas in Ezek 1.2; 33.21; 40.1 make explicit reference to the exile. Moreover, a number of date formulas are strategically tied to notices about the siege and fall of Jerusalem (Ezek 24.1-2; 25-27 [cf. 3.26-27]; 33.21-22; 40.1). The result for the reader, then, is a constant reinforcement of these twin arguments. The book presents time itself in terms of the problems of exile and the destruction of the city (Mayfield 2010: 92-93).

Second, as Zimmerli (1979: 112-13) suggests, the date formulas are attempts to authenticate the prophetic word. This is most clear in Ezek 24.1-2, where after the date formula, Ezekiel is told to "write for yourself the name of the day, this very day"—the reference being the beginning of the siege of Jerusalem. We see earlier and less formulaic attempts to authenticate prophetic oracles in Isa 8.1-4 and Hab 2.2-3. In both cases, the prophet is instructed to "time stamp" a statement about the future so that when it comes to pass, the prophet may be acknowledged to have spoken accurately. Zimmerli also notes that in prophetic material earlier than Ezekiel, the use of date formulas is sporadic (e.g., Isa 6.1; 14.28), whereas in Jeremiah they occur more frequently and are more elaborate (e.g., Jer 25.1; 28.1; 32.1; 36.9; etc.), and in later prophetic literature a detailed and formulaic convention is even more widely used (Hag 1.1, 15; 2.1, 10, 20; Zech 1.1, 7; 7.1).

Third, the date formulas aid in creating the argument structure of the book by separating or bringing together the surrounding text-segments and by providing a structure that creates cohesion (Mayfield 2010: 85, 97). In Ezek 24–25, for example, very diverse material is brought together: a parable of a boiling pot and its interpretations (Ezek 24.3-14); a report of a sign act about Ezekiel's reaction to the death of his wife and its interpretation (Ezek 24.15-24), including a note about the arrival of a survivor (24.25-27; note the link of v. 25 to vv. 16, 21); and a collection of oracles against Ammon, Moab, Edom, and Philistia (Ezek 25.1-7, 8-11, 12-14, 15-17). All of these are placed after the notice of the beginning of the city's siege in Ezek 24.1-2, and all have been related to it. The parable of the boiling pot interprets the siege as punishment for bloodshed and moral uncleanness (Ezek 24.7, 12-14), and the sign act is a symbol of the shock at the news of the destruction (Ezek 24.21-24). The notice about the arrival of a survivor (Ezek 24.25-27, picked up in 33.21-22) authenticates Ezekiel's message about the impending fall of Jerusalem. Finally, the oracles against the nations address the problem of their scornful joy at the fall of the city (Ezek 25.3, 6, 8) and their unfair advantage over the helpless survivors (Ezek 25.12, 15). As Mayfield (2010: 161ff.) notes, the three major units (parable, report of sign act, oracles against the nations) have been juxtaposed on the basis of a common theme (the destruction of the city), and are temporally related to the notice about the beginning of the siege in different ways. The first two units anticipate the siege, though with an increasing sense of inevitability; the third looks back at it retrospectively, but also looks forward to hope for God's judgment on these nations.

Fourth, the use of date formulas provides a narrative sequence for the book. This results in a rarity: whereas most books in the prophetic corpus are composite collections of poetic speeches that have been editorially arranged, Ezekiel is a *story*—lacking, admittedly, the plot dynamics found in the book of Jonah (another rarity in the prophetic corpus), but a story nonetheless. But what is so significant about the fact that Ezekiel is a story? One function of narrative is that it creates a linkage of cause and effect with a rhetorical force that goes significantly beyond mere statement of fact. Those who undergo a traumatic experience are desperate to find an explanation for their suffering—and a negative explanation is typically better than no explanation at all. For Ezekiel, human behavior and disaster can be conveniently correlated, and this seems to explain why he uses narrative: to provide an interpretation of the exile for his community. Ezekiel's explicit references to knowing the reason for the disaster (Ezek 6.10) and extensive use of causal language (Ezek 5.7, 9, 11; 13.8, 22; 16.36, 43; 21.29 [ET v. 24]; 22.19; etc.) are in line with the narrative connection of cause and effect.

Thomas Renz (1999: 132–41) discusses other functions of the narrative shape of Ezekiel, all of which have to do with its rhetorical effect on the reader: the first-person narrative mode reinforces the reliability of the prophetic voice; the divine assessment of human behavior is given priority; and Ezekiel is portrayed as the passive recipient of God's speech (which in turn compels the passivity and receptivity of the audience to the message of the book). Yet another function of narrative is that it provides movement—in this case, movement from disaster to restoration, since the earlier parts of Ezekiel's story primarily contain descriptions of accusation and judgment, and the latter parts descriptions of hope. But this narrative movement does not merely *describe* hope; it is meant to *create* hope in readers while they are construing the storyline in their heads. Renz (1999: 130) describes the shift in the book as having an epideictic function: "both sections advocate in effect the same values, the first [chs. 1–33] in a mostly negative way using 'legal' material to dissociate Israel from her past, the second [chs. 34–48] in a mostly positive way using 'political' material to associate the community with the Israel of the future."

Another way in which the narrative sequence created by the date formulas points to hope can be found in Ezek 40.1, which reads "in the twenty-fifth year of our exile, on the tenth day of the month." To understand the significance of this date formula, it is necessary to turn to Lev 25.8–22, which mandates the regular counting of "seven weeks of years," i.e., forty-nine years, with the fiftieth year being consecrated as a "Jubilee" year of economic and agricultural liberation. As Zimmerli

(1983: 346; cf. 344–47) argued, the mention of the "twenty-fifth year" in Ezek 40.1 (and the curious occurrences of the number twenty-five and its multiples in the following chapters) "can be understood as the halfway point with regard to the coming great liberation by Yahweh." In fact, the "liberation" mentioned in Lev 25.10 is explicitly referenced in Ezek 46.17. Why the occurrence of "the beginning of the year, on the tenth day of the month" in Ezek 40.1? For Zimmerli, Ezekiel is referencing the month Tishri—mentioned in Lev 25.9 as the "tenth day of the seventh month" on which the Jubilee is proclaimed at the Day of Atonement—as the first month of the year. In this way the dating formula in Ezek 40.1 references traditional calendrical systems with their notions of sacred time, and creates hope for liberation in the near future.

b. Content placement across the book

As I noted above, the date formulas result in chronological movement through the creation of a plot line. But there are other kinds of movement as well: as many readers have noted, there is an shift in content in the book, moving from (mostly) "judgment on Israel" (chs. 1–24) to "judgment on the nations" (chs. 25–32) to "hope for Israel" (chs. 33–48). This can only be the result of a deliberate compositional placement of units. According to Renz (1999: 230–31), this content shift actually creates a coherent argument that has a rhetorical function for the readers of the book of Ezekiel:

> At first, the readers were only asked to see the end of Jerusalem as the result of her sin, then they were asked to "judge" Jerusalem, and with Jerusalem their own rebellious behavior. In the oracles against the nations the readers were invited to see the same pattern of rebellion against Yahweh at work which had brought Jerusalem to its end. The readers are encouraged to see that rebellion against Yahweh reduces Israel to the level of other nations and does not have a future, since Yahweh will destroy pride against him everywhere. Thus they will realise that assimilation into other

nations will only continue the rebellious history of the past and consequently will not open up a future for their community. Chs. 33–48 then show that the beginning and end of New Israel is the acknowledgement of Yahweh's kingship which has the promise of transformation.

The shift in content from mostly negative (cf. Ezek 2.10, where Ezekiel eats a scroll containing "lamentations, mourning, and woe") to positive revolves around the fall of the city of Jerusalem. Chs. 1–24 contain for the most part oracles that look forward to the destruction of the city (note the statements in e.g. Ezek 4.1–3; 5.1–2; 11.1–12; 17.16–17; 21.7 [ET v. 2]; 22.2–3; 23.22; 24.6), and chs. 25–48 contain oracles that presume or respond to the destruction of the city (note the statements in 25.3; 26.2; 33.24; 35.5, 12, 15). This bifurcation is formed by the note about the beginning of the siege of the city in Ezek 24.1–2 and the note about the arrival of an escapee from the destruction of the city (Ezek 24.25–27; 33.21–22).

However, although it is true that there is to a large extent a content shift as described above, this should not obscure the fact that the book contains descriptions of hope before ch. 33 (e.g., Ezek 11.17–21; 14.11; 16.60–63; 17.22–24; 20.33–38, 39–44; 28.24, 25–26; 29.21a) and descriptions of judgment on the nations after chs. 25–32 (e.g., Ezek 35). How do we explain the placement of these units? While some of these may be later redactional insertions to an existing book of Ezekiel (see e.g. the discussion of Ezek 28.25–26 above), others are compositional: that is, descriptions of hope have been deliberately placed after and in response to descriptions of judgment when the book was put together. As I noted above, the placement of a message of hope immediately after accusation and judgment would have been both confusing and rhetorically counterproductive at the level of oral proclamation. These are most likely designed as "reader management" devices: that is, they break up the unrelenting accusations and judgments by giving the reader enough positive descriptions to encourage continued reading, and they point to solutions for the problems being raised in the book.

It is important to note that these brief notices of hope are not random occurrences, but are deliberately placed as responses to issues in the local context. For example, Ezek 11.16 (the assurance of God's presence with the exiles) counters the marginalization of the exilic community by the Jerusalemites described in v. 15. However, a further response was felt to be necessary: a more extensive statement of restoration has been included in vv. 17–21. But this is part of a larger compositional strategy that reflects on the future of Israel. In Ezek 9.8, the prophet responds to the vision of the destruction of Jerusalem by crying out to ask whether God is "destroying the remnant of Israel." The only response from God (9.9–10) is that judgment is warranted—which does not really answer Ezekiel's question. The prophet asks the same question again in Ezek 11.13 after a vision of the death of a prominent (and idolatrous) Jerusalemite. The entire following unit in Ezek 11.14–21 was placed in its location as a response to Ezekiel's question, arguing that the true "remnant of Israel" is the exilic community of 597 BCE—not the idolatrous inhabitants of Jerusalem.

The other statements of hope have a similar relationship to their contexts. In the statement of hope in Ezek 14.11, we see an instance of later theological reflection on the ultimate purpose of the punishment described in vv. 1–10. Such a reflection arises from the perspective of the book as a whole. In Ezek 20.33–38, 39–44 we see two different expressions of hope. The first unit, vv. 33–38, responds to the exile and potential for assimilation to foreign nations described in v. 32 by envisioning restoration as a new exodus and journey through the wilderness in which sinners are purged out before entry into the land. The second unit, vv. 39–44, responds to the problem of idolatrous worship described throughout the chapter (vv. 7–8, 16, 24, 28–32) by envisioning a pure people and restored cult in the future. Likewise, the oracle against Edom in Ezek 35 is deliberately juxtaposed to the oracle of hope addressed to the mountains of Israel in Ezek 36 because of the issue of safety in the land (see the discussion below). In all these examples, we can see a compositional strategy in which units were deliberately placed to serve as solutions to problems.

c. Placement of vision reports

Another compositional strategy of placement can be seen in the location of and relationship between the vision reports. There are three main visions (Ezek 1.1–3.14; 8.1–11.25; 40.1–48.35), the first and third of which bracket the entire book, and two subsidiary visions (3.22–27; 37.1–14) inserted between these three. The visions are linked to each other not only by shared vocabulary, but also by explicit statements referencing the content and location of the earlier visions and the movement of the divine presence out of and into the envisioned temple. These visions and the compositional links between them can be outlined as follows:

1.1–3.14	First main vision (by Chebar canal)
3.22–27	Subsidiary vision: in the plain (*bqʻh*)
	3.22 > 1.3 ("hand of Yhwh upon" Ezekiel)
	3.23 > 1.1, 3; 1.28 (Chebar; Glory of Yhwh; "fell on my face")
	3.24 > 2.2 ("spirit entered me and made me stand on my feet")
8.1–11.25	Second main vision (in the prophet's house)
	8.1 > 1.3 ("hand of Yhwh upon" Ezekiel)
	8.2 > 1.26–27 (radiant humanoid figure)
	8.3 > 1.1 ("visions of God")
	8.4 > 3.22, 23 explicit reference to earlier vision in the plain (*bqʻh*)
	10.1 > 1.26 (throne on platform over cherubs)
	10.5 > 1.24 (sound of wings)
	10.9–22 > 1.4–21 (description of cherubs and wheels)
	10.15, 20, 22 > 1.1 explicit references to earlier vision
37.1–14	Subsidiary vision: in the plain (*bqʻh*)
	37.1 > 3.22 ("hand of Yhwh upon" Ezekiel)
	37.1, 2 > 3.22, 23; 8.4 (location is the *bqʻh*, "plain," used only in these passages)

	37.10 > 2.2; 3.24 (language of "spirit entering" and "standing on feet" used earlier for the prophet is used here of the revived dry bones)
40.1–48.35	Third main vision (location not reported)
	40.1 > 1.3 ("hand of Yhwh upon" Ezekiel)
	40.2 > 1.1 ("visions of God")
	43.2, 4 Glory of the God of Israel comes from the east, enters temple by east gate > 10.19; 11.23 Glory of the God of Israel exits temple and leaves temple mount by the east
	43.2 > 1.24 (" like the sound of many waters")
	43.3a > 9.10 explicit reference to earlier vision
	43.3b > 1.1 explicit reference to earlier vision
	43.3 > 1.28 ("fell on my face")
	43.5 > 3.12, 14; 8.3 ("spirit lifted me")

What functions do the placement of and relationships between these visions play in the book as a whole? As Davis (1989: 11) observes, "one central image serves the threefold function of prophetic validation, theodicy, and promise." The three main vision reports are connected by the shared theme of divine presence and absence. The first vision is a legitimation of the prophet and a guarantee that Yhwh can be present even in exile; the second is an argument that because the temple has been profaned, Yhwh is actively working for its downfall (though he has been functioning as a sanctuary for the exiles); the third is an argument that in the future, God will return to a restored temple, to be on earth again with his people (Ezek 43.7, 9). The first subsidiary vision comments on the nature of the people and on the prophet's task; the second subsidiary vision attempts to convince the people that national restoration is possible through God's intervention.

d. Placement of the "watchman" sections

The placement of the "watchman" sections (Ezek 3.16–21; 33.1–9) also plays an important role in the shape and argument of the book. It seems likely that the material in Ezek 3.16b-21 was not originally part of the surrounding context, but was composed for it: one can read seamlessly from v. 16a to v. 22 (note the MT plus "there" in v. 22, inserted to refer back to v. 15) without the intervening verses. The watchman material in Ezek 3.16b-21 is built from the watchman material in Ezek 33.1-9 (the following verses in 33.10-20 are in turn built from ch. 18, though no hint of this material can be seen in ch. 3). Both Ezek 3 and 33 state that Ezekiel has been appointed by God as a watchman (Ezek 3.17; 33.7), and both place the same emphasis on prophetic accountability: if Ezekiel warns the people, he will live; if he fails to warn them, he will die.

But there are also important differences between the two sections. First, Ezek 33.1-9 contains an introduction that states the argument in hypothetical and non-metaphorical terms (vv. 2-6, a city watchman before an impending battle) before restating it in non-hypothetical and metaphorical terms (vv. 7-9, the prophet as metaphorical watchman). Ezek 3.16b-21 lacks any such explanatory introduction. Second, Ezek 33.1-9 contains two scenarios (the wicked are not warned, or are warned, vv. 8-9), whereas Ezek 3.16b-21 contains four scenarios (the wicked are not warned, or are warned, vv. 18-19; the righteous are not warned, or are warned, vv. 20-21). Third, in Ezek 33, the warning of the watchman section is placed in context of the following argument (vv. 10-20) that if people repent, God will respond positively to them. Here the prophet argues that God responds to people "in the present," picking up the argument of Ezek 18.21-22, 24. Of course, whether this *theoretically* possible change on the part of the people to which God will respond positively is presented as *actually* possible or plausible in the rest of the book is another matter! In the four scenarios presented in Ezek 3, no change on the part of the wicked is envisioned as possible. This is in keeping with the immediately preceding context, where Ezekiel is told that the people will not listen (Ezek 3.7) and that they are stubborn and rebellious (Ezek 3.7, 9).

The watchman material in Ezek 3, then, has been placed here to clarify the nature of the prophet's commission: he is to speak God's message and warn the people without expecting any response to his words. His function as a watchman in Ezek 3 is not to create repentant people, but to exculpate God from the potential charge that he did not warn the guilty people of their impending doom. The placement of the watchman material in Ezek 33 serves a different purpose, namely, to introduce the words attributed to the exiles in 33.10 and the following description of how God responds to change in vv. 11–20. Moreover, the placement of the entire section immediately before the report of the city's fall (Ezek 33.21) functions at the book level by depicting the inhabitants of the city as those who refused to take warning and were justly punished.

e. Placement of the "muteness" imagery

The references to the restriction and non-restriction of speech in Ezek 3.24–27; 24.25–27; 33.21–22 (and Ezek 16.63; 29.21) play an important role in the shape of the book, linked as they are to Ezekiel's call, the siege of Jerusalem, and the arrival of a refugee after Jerusalem's fall. Yet the meaning of these passages constitutes one of the most difficult problems in the book. Why is restriction attributed first to a divine command to Ezekiel in 3.24, then to an unspecified "they" in v. 25? Do these verses represent Ezekiel's withdrawal from the people, or their resistance to him, or both? Does 3.25 have anything to do with vv. 26–27? If according to 3.26 God prevents Ezekiel from speaking, how do we explain the remainder of the book, in which Ezekiel is repeatedly told to speak? Is this muteness absolute, or sporadic? Is it a restriction of speech per se, a restriction of content, or a restriction on independent speech? Is Ezekiel prevented in 3.26 from being a "person who reproves" or a "person who arbitrates" (*'yš mwkyḥ*)? If the former, does 3.27 clarify by restricting his reproof of the people to that which he receives from God alone (as opposed to independent reproof)? If the latter (cf. Ezek 14.13–14, but also 22.30!), why is 3.27 necessary at all? How could a refugee from fallen Jerusalem arrive in Babylon on the same day as the city's fall (24.26), resulting in the end of Ezekiel's muteness?

If Ezekiel has been under some kind of speech restriction from 3.26 onward, or from 24.1–2 onward, why the reference in 33.22a to God's hand being upon him in the evening? How (if at all) do the references to speech in 16.63 and 29.21 relate to the other passages?

One way of understanding these verses is offered by Zimmerli, who argues that the earliest material consists of Ezek 3.24b (in which Ezekiel's shutting himself in his house signified the siege of Jerusalem) and Ezek 33.21–22a (in which Ezekiel was speechless in the evening due to a visionary experience, but could speak in the morning by the time a refugee from the city arrived). This was subsequently expanded by the placement of 3.25–27; 24.25, 27; 33.22b in the book, and the earlier imagery was turned into an argument that the prophet's speech was restricted between the fall of the city and the arrival of a refugee as a sign act for the people. Even later additions were made in 24.26 (to link ch. 24 more tightly with ch. 33), and in 29.21. These verses remain obscure, though many attempts have been made to explain them (Glazov 2001: 223ff.; Sherlock 1983; Wilson 1972). Whether Zimmerli's reconstruction is correct or not, the following seems clear: the material in Ezek 3.26–27; 24.27; 33.21–22 has been woven into a framework within the narrative of the book that highlights the divine control of Ezekiel's prophetic function and the significance of the fall of Jerusalem for the exiles. Moreover, the present shape of the text is due to the compositional thematic linking of two different kinds of restriction, one non-verbal (Ezek 3.24–25) and the other verbal (Ezek 3.26–27).

f. Juxtaposition and linking of units

Another compositional technique relating to placement is the juxtaposition of units on the basis of shared content or theme, further reinforced by the use of shared linking words and phrases. For example, we see two originally separate units juxtaposed on the basis of a concern for the status of prophecy in Ezek 12.21–25 and 12.26–28. But these are part of an even larger cluster of units brought together by a shared theme. As Greenberg (1983: 6) noted, all of the material in Ezek

12.21–14.10 is concerned with prophecy and the issue of its failure, its delay, its misrepresentations, and with those who inquire of prophets.

Likewise, thematic concerns are given priority over chronological concerns in the placement of units in the oracles against the nations: all the Egypt material has been placed together in chs. 29–32. This means that even though the unit in Ezek 29.17-20 is given the latest date heading, it is included with the other earlier-dated Egypt material. This also explains the placement of the Tyre material (chs. 26–28) before the collection of Egypt oracles, and the placement of the news of Jerusalem's fall (33.21-22) after them, resulting in the out of sequence date formulas in 26.1 (in relation to 24.1 and 29.1) and 33.21 (in relation to 32.1). Block (1998: 4–5) detects additional compositional arrangement in these oracles: the total number of nations included is seven (Ammon, Moab, Edom, Philistia, Tyre, Sidon, Egypt); there are seven oracles about Egypt headed by the Prophetic Word Formula (Ezek 29.1, 17; 30.1, 20; 31.1; 32.1, 17); there are seven date notices within the oracles against the nations (Ezek 26.1; 29.1, 17; 30.20; 31.1; 32.1, 17); the placement of the oracle of hope in Ezek 28.24-26 occurs in the middle of the material, creating two sections of similar length on either side (Ezek 25.1–28.33 and 29.1–32.32).

Both Greenberg (1983: 25–26) and Block (1997: 23) have drawn attention to the juxtaposition of units to create two adjacent "panels," often appearing with a final "coda" that re-states and combines their themes. One example is found in Ezek 13, which consists of a unit condemning "the prophets of Israel" (Ezek 13.2-16) juxtaposed to a second unit condemning "the daughters of your people who are prophesying (*mtnb'wt*)" (Ezek 13.17-23). These two juxtaposed units have been compositionally linked together by shared words and phrases: forms of the root *nb'* ("to prophesy") followed by "from their own heart" (vv. 2, 17); "envision falsehood" (*ḥzh sw'*, vv. 6, 7, 9, 23; note variation in v. 8); "(practice) divination" (*qsm*, vv. 6, 7, 9, 23; note variation in v. 8); "a lie" (*kzb*, vv. 6, 7, 8, 9, 19). The curious thing about the juxtaposition of these units is the difference between the actions described in them: the male prophets in the first unit are depicted as proclaiming a message ostensibly from God (Ezek 13.2, 6, 7, 10), whereas the female figures in the second unit are depicted as apparently manufacturing and employing devices, the use of which has beneficial effects for some and detrimental effects for others. Stökl (2013) reconstructs the practices of these female "prophets" as interaction with the dead, which reflects a distinction between (to use Stökl's terms) "intuitive divination" practiced by the male figures in the first unit and "technical divination" practiced by the female figures in the second unit. If, as Stökl suggests, the women in the second unit are not "prophets" in the same sense that the men in the first unit are, why are these two groups juxtaposed? Whatever the social realities behind the text, the composition as we currently have it has combined the two groups because it understands both to be misrepresenting and usurping the proper function of Yhwh. The first group claims to speak for Yhwh and give messages of peace when he did not speak (vv. 6, 10); the second group—whose activity is interpreted through the grid and borrowed language of Ezek 3.17–21—disheartens the righteous even though Yhwh has not done so (v. 22). Both can therefore be juxtaposed as "false prophets" who misrepresent the God of Israel.

Another example is found in two juxtaposed poems in Ezek 19, both of which relate the recent history and downfall of the monarchy (v. 1, the "princes of Israel"). The first poem uses the central image of a lioness (Ezek 19.2–9), and the second poem uses the central image of a vine (Ezek 19.10–14). Both recount the initial proud and majestic state of the monarchy (vv. 2–3, 6–7, 10–11) and its subsequent ruin (vv. 4, 8–9, 12–14) in language appropriate to each image. While the two poems use very different images and emphasize different details (e.g., the transition from one king to another in vv. 4–5), they depict the same disastrous end. Both poems refer to the monarchy as "your mother" (vv. 2, 10); both are likewise termed a "lament" (vv. 1, 14). Similarly, the oracle of judgment against the southlands is linked to the following oracle of the flashing sword by the repeated phrase "from south to north" (Ezek 21.3, 9 [ET 20.47; 21.4]), and the statement in the first oracle that a fire will burn "every green tree and every dry tree" (21.3 [ET 20.47]) is paralleled by the statement in the second oracle that Yhwh will "cut off both righteous and wicked" (21.8 [ET v. 3]).

The two juxtaposed oracles against the king of Tyre, Ezek 28.1–10 and 11–19, are similarly linked by identical words. In both oracles, it is said that the king's "heart was proud" (Ezek 28.2, 5, 17) as a result of his success in "trade" (vv. 5, 16). In the first oracle, strangers will draw their swords against the "beauty of [the king's] wisdom" and profane his "splendor" (v. 7); in the second, the king is accused: "by your beauty, you corrupted your wisdom for the sake of your splendor" (v. 17). In the first oracle, the king's splendor will be "profaned" (v. 7) by strangers; in the second, the king will be "profaned" (v. 16) by Yhwh because the king "profaned" (v. 18) his own sanctuaries.

A final example can be found in Ezek 35.1–36.15, which consists of two sections: the first addressed to "Mt. Seir" (35.2–15), and the second to the "mountains of Israel" (36.1–15). Each is introduced by an address and command to prophesy (35.2; 36.1). But although they have introductions that mark each as a self-contained unit, Zimmerli (1979: 232) argues that these two sections "[are] to be regarded as a homogenous unit" and "have been put together in a precise, logical relationship." What then holds these two units together? First, as Zimmerli notes, they have both been placed under a single messenger formula (35.1), a formula that does not appear again until the next major unit (36.16). Second, these two units 35.2–15 and 36.1–15 are held together by shared subject matter (the land of Israel) and argument (God will protect the land of Israel from surrounding nations who wish to possess it). The first section proclaims judgment on Edom for desiring the land of Israel; the second section proclaims reassurance to Israel that surrounding nations will not possess the land and that the exiles will be gathered home. Third, the two units have been linked together by a large number of shared keywords: "mountains of Israel" (35.12; 36.1, 4, 8); "mountains, hills, valleys, ravines" (35.8; 36.4, 6 [the last two words have been inverted in ch. 36]); forms of the root "to be desolate" (*šmm*, 35.3, 4, 7, 9, 12, 14, 15; 36.3, 4); "waste" (*ḥrb*, 35.4; 36.4, 10); "cities" (35.4, 9; 36.4, 10); "everlasting" (35.5 of enmity; 35.9, of desolation;

36.2, of heights of Israel); forms of the root "to possess" (*yrš*, 35.10; 36.2; 3, 5, 12); "inheritance" (*nḥlh*, 35.15; 36.12); "envy/zeal" (*qn'h*, 35.11; 36.5, 6); "Edom, all of it" (35.15; 36.5); forms of the root "to rejoice" (*śmḥ*, 35.14, 15; 36.5). But the repeated keywords do not simply create cohesion through shared content. They are also used to create an argument expressed through reversals: because Edom rejoiced that Israel was "desolate" and "waste" (35.12, 15; 36.3, 4), God will make Edom "desolate" and "waste" (35.3, 4, 7, 9, 15). Because the "cities" of Israel have become a prey to surrounding nations (36.4), Edom's "cities" will become desolate (35.4, 9) and God will restore the "cities" of Israel (36.10). The "mountains, hills, ravines, and valleys" of Israel will be restored (36.4, 6), but "mountains, hills, valleys, and ravines" of Edom will be filled with the slain (35.8). The "envy" of Edom for the land of Israel (*qn'h*, 35.11) will be confronted by the "zeal" of YHWH for his people (*qn'h*, 36.5, 6). Zimmerli (1983: 234) rightly concludes that the compositional placement of the Edom oracle in Ezek 35.1–15 (rather than with the rest of the oracles against the nations) must be explained in relation to 36.1–15: "From this point of view it also becomes clear why these Edom-oracles have not been put alongside 25:12–14. Structurally they have acquired in chapter 35f another meaning and have become pre-oracle motivation for the proclamation of salvation."

g. Other instances of linked units

In the examples above, we saw that units of similar theme were not only juxtaposed, but also linked to each other by means of repeated locutions. This compositional technique of linking also occurs in adjacent units which are thematically dissimilar: for example, the end of the tour of abominations in the temple is linked to the following vision of destruction by the repeated locution "cry out in my hearing with a loud voice" (Ezek 8.18; 9.1). The story of Israel as a foundling child and faithless wife (Ezek 16) and the fable of the eagles and vine (Ezek 17) are linked by the locution "despised the oath, broke the covenant" (Ezek 16.59; 17.16, 18, 19). The report of the sign act prohibiting mourning in

Ezek 24.15-24 and the announcement of the end of the prophet's muteness in 24.25-27 are linked by repeated vocabulary in vv. 16, 21, 25.

We also see the use of repeated locutions to create connections between non-adjacent units. I noted above the example of Ezekiel's repeated question in Ezek 9.8 ("Ah, Lord Yhwh! Are you destroying the entire remnant of Israel?") and 11.13 ("Ah, Lord Yhwh! Are you making a complete end of the remnant of Israel?"), a repetition which creates a conversation about whether the future of Israel lies with Jerusalem or with the exiles. We also see a link across sections in Ezek 21.13-18 [ET vv. 8-13] and 21.33-37 [ET vv. 28-32], with the repetition of "a sword, a sword...polished...slaughter...in order to be lightning" (21.14-15 [ET vv. 9-10]; 21.33 [ET v. 28]). The refrain "I will bring you to/you will come to a dreadful end, and you will be no more ... forever" occurs across sections in the collection of Tyre oracles (Ezek 26.21; 27.36; 28.19), as does the phrase "perfect in beauty" (27.3; 28.12). The locutions "slain by the sword" (Ezek 31.17; 32.20-26, 28-32) and "uncircumcised" (31.18; 32.19, 21, 24-30, 32) link together two non-adjacent oracles against Egypt, as do the phrases "on the open field ... beasts of the earth ... birds of the sky" (29.5; 32.4). Finally, we see the same language used for Egypt and other nations in Ezek 32.18-32 as we did in Ezek 26.20, an oracle against Tyre. This compositional technique of employing repeated locutions creates cohesion across both adjacent and non-adjacent units and invites the reader to see the similarities in argumentation.

h. Wordplay

The book of Ezekiel contains various forms of wordplay, including paronomasia, clusters of repeated words, metathesis, and so forth. Some of these are used in passing; they enhance the rhetoric of an argument, but do not really contribute to the composition of larger text-segments. An example of this kind of wordplay can be found in Ezek 20.29. In Ezek 20, the prophet details the history of Israel's apostasy from the exodus out of Egypt onward, examining the behavior of the generation in Egypt and in the wilderness as well as the behavior of the second generation in the wilderness. In vv. 27–29, the pattern of Israel's apostasy is shown to have continued even when they entered Canaan. These verses utilize Deuteronomistic-sounding expressions to argue that when the people's ancestors entered the land, they offered illicit sacrifices at "every high hill and leafy tree" (v. 28; cf. Deut 12.2; 1 Kgs 14.23; 2 Kgs 16.4; 17.10; cf. Ezek 6.13), sacrifices which were a "provocation" (v. 28; cf. 1 Kgs 15.30; 21.22; 2 Kgs 23.26). In v. 29, Yhwh is said to have accused them using a string of similar-sounding words: "What (*mh*) is the high place (*hbmh*) where you are entering (*hb'ym*)?" In the following sentence, the author cannot resist remarking on his own pun: "And that is why its name is called "high place" (*bmh*) until this day!"

But wordplay can also operate within and contribute to the composition of an entire text-segment. For example, in Ezek 12.1–13 we find the repeated use of and punning on the words "eyes" and "to see." The pun created here involves both the literal meaning "to see" as well as the figurative meaning "to comprehend." The unit begins with Yhwh's remark that Israel "has eyes to see, but does not see" (Ezek 12.2). Ezekiel is then commanded to perform a sign act depicting the deportation of the citizens of Jerusalem "before their eyes" (2x, v. 3). When confronted with this sign act, Yhwh says, perhaps they will "see" (v. 3). Ezekiel is told to act like a deportee, carrying out his baggage "in their eyes" (2x, v. 4). He must dig through a wall "in their eyes" (v. 5) to represent captives being taken through the breached walls of Jerusalem. And he must go through the hole in the wall, carrying his baggage on his shoulder "in their eyes" (vv. 6, 7) at night. But the prophet is also told to cover his face so that he may not "see" (v. 6) the land; by doing so, he represents the "prince" (i.e., King Zedekiah) who will be deported, covering his face so that he may not "see" (v. 12). Commentators have interpreted this last action variously as an expression of the prince's shame or grief, or as an argument that the prince would never again see the land (cf. Jer 22.10–12). An additional comment in v. 13 states that the prince will be caught in God's net and taken to Babylon, but "will not see it"—a reference to the fact that after the Babylonians captured Zedekiah, they blinded him and took him in chains to Babylon (2 Kgs 25.6-7). These repetitions of the words "eyes" and "to see" highlight the contrast between the intransigence of Ezekiel's audience and the fact that the prophet visually depicts his arguments and interprets them for those watching. It also highlights the fate of Jerusalem's king, perhaps implying that losing one's sight (literally, by being blinded) is a fitting punishment for refusing to "see" (that is, to comprehend).

Another example of wordplay at the text-segment level occurs in MT Ezek 36.12-15. The oracle in which these verses occur is addressed to the "mountains of Israel" (vv. 1, 4, 8). This oracle reverses many of the earlier judgments in the book, looking forward to the fertility of the land, the return of its people, and the restoration of waste places. It also reverses a locution taken from Lev 26.22 ("I will send among you wild animals, and they will bereave you") that was used earlier in Ezek 5.17; 14.15. Here in Ezek 36.12-13, it is claimed that while the land itself (not simply wild animals!) once "bereaved" (*škl*) its inhabitants, it will no longer do so. In this way the passage affirms that the punishments for covenant violation in Lev 26 have in fact been experienced, and that restoration is now possible. However, in MT Ezek 36.14-15, the word "to bereave" (*škl*) undergoes metathesis; it is now argued that the land "will no longer cause the nation to stumble (*kšl*)." The effect of the *škl/kšl* wordplay is to argue that the particular sin in which Israel "stumbled"— namely, illicit worship on the mountains (vv. 1, 4, 8; cf. Ezek 6.2-7, 13; 18.6, 11, 15; 22.9)—will no longer be practiced. It should be noted that the LXX reflects a somewhat different textform here, one which consistently reads "to bereave" in vv. 12-14, and lacks the clause "and your nation you will no longer cause to stumble" in v. 15; in v. 14 of the MT, the verb "to stumble" has a corresponding *Qere* reading of "to bereave."

One final example is that of a repeated keyword which, unlike the repeated words noted earlier in this chapter, does not have a linking function. Instead, this repeated word thematizes some of the main problems in the book—and is also used to describe the solution to these problems. The word in question is the verb "to be distant" (*rḥq*). The first occurrence is in Ezek 8.6, set in a vision report in which Yhwh shows Ezekiel the "great abominations that the house of Israel is doing here, so as to be distant (*lrḥqh*) from my sanctuary." This ironic comment explains that while the people are physically present at Yhwh's sanctuary, they are in reality spiritually "distant." Many commentators and translations take this verse to mean that Israel has driven Yhwh away (i.e., "distanced" him) from his own sanctuary; but the infinitive verbform as vocalized here is a stative verb referring to the *people's* distance (which is also how the Old Greek translation renders it). This spiritual distance is one of the main problems that Ezekiel must grapple with. The next occurrence is found in Ezek 11.15, where the Jerusalemites are quoted as saying to the exiles of 597 BCE, "Be distant (*rḥqw*) from Yhwh; the land has been given to us as a possession!" This marginalization of the exiles by those who remained in the land is another problem. A third problem is articulated in Ezek 44.10, where the subject of the restoration of cult personnel is raised. The Zadokite priests are commended and enfranchised, but the Levites are condemned for an incident in which they "were distant" (*rḥqw*) from Yhwh and went astray with idols.

The "distance" of people from temple (in a metaphorical sense), of exiles from their heritage, and of cult personnel from their God—all these are emblematic of the crisis confronting Israel in the sixth century. How then can this "distance" be overcome? In Ezek 11.16, Yhwh admits to the exiles that while he has "distanced them (*hrḥqtym*) among the nations," he has nevertheless been a sanctuary to them in exile, and will in the future gather them back to the land (v. 17). This reference simultaneously acknowledges the problem of exile while attempting to alleviate the problem. And in Ezekiel's vision of a restored temple, he hears Yhwh saying (Ezek 43.9) that if the people "make distant" (*yrḥqw*) their "whoring" and the corpses of their kings, then he will reside in their midst forever. Israel in the land and Yhwh in their midst, dwelling in a purified temple—this is the future for which Ezekiel hopes, and he shares this with his community to give them hope.

i. Extension and coordination

As I noted above, Zimmerli was able to identify and describe a process of editorial extension (*Fortschreibung*) at work in the book of Ezekiel, whereby a literary insertion picks up and develops the surrounding material in a further direction or in a new way. A clear example can be found in Ezek 17.22-24. The preceding verses contain an allegorical fable of a vine and two eagles (vv. 1-10), followed by its interpretation (vv. 11-21) describing the exile of King Jehoiachin and eventual downfall of unfaithful King Zedekiah. These verses form a self-contained and coherent unit; they are introduced by a prophetic word formula and a command to speak (vv. 1, 2), and they conclude with a recognition formula (v. 21) which stands before a messenger formula introducing the following section (v. 22a). But the following section, vv. 22-24, reverses the tragedy of the monarchy detailed in the preceding verses. It picks up the following locutions from the preceding verses: "take" (vv. 3, 5 > v. 22); "top of a cedar" (v. 3 > v. 22); "pluck off the top of its shoots" (v. 4 > v. 22); "transplant" (v. 8 > vv. 22, 23); "to produce branches and lift up fruit" (v. 8 > v. 23; note the inversion!). It depicts a series of reversals: in vv. 22-24, the plucked twig grows into a full cedar (unlike the earlier section, where the plucked twig of v. 4 did not grow, and the planted seed of vv. 5-6 became a low vine—signifying its status as a vassal). In vv. 22-24, the one who carries out the planting is God (a reversal of the figures of the two eagles in the preceding section, who represent Babylon and Egypt respectively). In vv. 22-24, the plucked twig is planted on the "high mountain of Israel" (a reversal of the exilic destination of the plucked twig in v. 4), a locution appearing elsewhere in the book only in Ezek 20.40. The two restoration passages are thus coordinated together. Whereas it was the fate of the unfaithful vine to dry up and wither (vv. 9, 10), the destiny of the cedar in vv. 22-24 is to grow so large and be so fertile that birds will nest in it. The unit ends in v. 24 with a theological reflection on the God who makes reversals possible; it also picks up the language of "green tree and dry tree" from Ezek 21.3 [ET 20.47] and reverses the fate of the people described there. To sum up: vv. 22-24 represent an editorial reflection on and extension of the preceding material. They never existed as an independent unit, but were composed in relation to the preceding material. They reverse the tragedy in the preceding material (and in other passages) into hope for the monarchy in the future, and are coordinated with other passages in the book that describe hope.

Similar instances of extension and coordination can be found in Ezek 34. Here vv. 1–10 represent the base unit, identifying a problem and presenting the solution: the shepherds of Israel have been mistreating the flock, so God will rescue his flock by removing the bad shepherds. But this unit has been extended by the addition of vv. 11–16, which address two issues that are not dealt with in the preceding argument, namely, the fact that the flock has been scattered, and the question of who will now care for the sheep. In vv. 11–16, we see these concerns met with the argument that God himself will search out and gather his flock, and that he himself will be their shepherd. Ezek 34.11–16 also pick up the following locutions from the preceding unit: "scattered" (vv. 5–6, 12); "seek" (vv. 10, 11–12); "deliver" (vv. 10, 11–12); "search" (vv. 6, 16); "feed the flock" (vv. 2–3, 13–15); and almost the entirety of v. 4 is repeated in v. 16. Moreover, the scope of restoration has been widened from simple deliverance of the flock from the shepherds (v. 10) to the gathering of the wider diaspora (vv. 11–12, "seek … and deliver them from all the places where they were scattered"). Another editorial extension occurs in vv. 23–24; these are distinct from the immediately preceding unit vv. 17–22 (clearly marked off by an inclusio). But vv. 23–24 actually represent an extension of the earlier vv. 11–16. They take up the earlier claim that God will be the shepherd who feeds the flock (vv. 12–15) by arguing that he will do so by appointing *David* as shepherd to feed the flock (v. 23). Moreover, vv. 23–24 are drawing on Ezek 37.24–25, because the reference to "one shepherd" in Ezek 34.23 is inexplicable without reference to the discussion in ch. 37. So not only does Ezek 34.23–24 extend the idea of God as shepherd to the idea of God's agent David as shepherd, it does so by coordinating the picture of restoration in ch. 34 to the picture of restoration in ch. 37. As I noted above, it is often difficult to determine whether these editorial extensions and coordinations occur at the compositional or the redactional level: Zimmerli (1983: 220, 222) ascribes these verses and their editing to Ezekiel, whereas Anja Klein (2008: 409) ascribes them to later redactors.

j. Text referencing as a literary technique

Many commentators have remarked on Ezekiel's numerous allusions to other texts, and some have found the command in the prophet's commission report ("eat this scroll," Ezek 3.1) suggestive in light of this. While I think it likely that Ezekiel the prophet spoke to his community, and that in doing so he would have referenced traditional material, I also think it is necessary to consider references in the book of Ezekiel to earlier texts under the rubric of compositional strategy. If (as I have argued above) the book of Ezekiel is not a mere transcript of speech, then the text referencing we are confronted with should be understood as a literary phenomenon. Ezekiel's allusions to earlier texts exhibit various modifications of the source material to fit a new context. We see the conflation of locutions borrowed from one text with locutions from another text, or with material taken from elsewhere in Ezekiel. We see the prophet and his editors interacting with arguments from other texts, or simply borrowing imagery from those texts in order to create new arguments. The creative use of earlier texts and the strategic integration of borrowed material into a new Ezekielian context are factors that have contributed to the growth process, shape, and function of the book.

The book of Ezekiel makes use of a great deal of older traditional material. For example, while the prophet did not have the Pentateuch in the shape that we do—the combination of diverse narrative, poetic, and legal materials we now have is a product of theological reflection that reached its current form after the exile—he does know much of the material that appears in the Pentateuch. Ezekiel knows Adam/Eden traditions (Ezek 28.11–19); he knows traditions about Abraham and the land (Ezek 33.24); he knows the story of Sodom from Gen 18–19 (his reference in Ezek 16.49-50 to Sodom's social injustice is likely an interpretation of the word "outcry" in Gen 18.20, based on the use of this word in Exod 22.22-24); he knows the story of the exodus from Egypt and the journey through the wilderness to Canaan (Ezek 20.5-28). In some cases, the form of the traditions Ezekiel knows—or the manner in which he chooses to present them!—differs in significant ways from the form of the traditions now preserved in the Pentateuch (see e.g. Ezek 16.3, which emphasizes Israel's Canaanite origins; or Ezek 20.5-10, in which Israel is said to have committed apostasy while still in Egypt).

It is in keeping with the book's presentation of Ezekiel as a former Jerusalemite priest that we see in it an intimate knowledge of Israel's legal traditions as well. This is not to say that all legal traditions in the Pentateuch appear in the same form in Ezekiel (for some interesting differences, see particularly the description of the temple and its laws envisioned in Ezek 40-48). But many locutions or instructions peculiar to legal material now attested in the Pentateuch appear also in Ezekiel, for example, Ezek 20.12 (// Exod 31.13); Ezek 20.37 (// Lev 27.32); Ezek 22.26 (// Lev 10.10 + 20.25; 22.26); Ezek 28.12-13 (// Exod 28.15-21); Ezek 44.17-19 (// Exod 28.42 + Lev 16.4, 23); Ezek 44.20 (// Lev 21.5); Ezek 44.21 (// Lev 10.9); Ezek 44.22 (// Lev 21.13-15); Ezek 44.23 (// Lev 10.10); Ezek 44.25 (// Lev 21.1-4); Ezek 44.28 (// Num 18.20); Ezek 44.29 (Num 18.9, 11, 13, 14 + 15.21); Ezek 44.31 (// Lev 22.8); Ezek 46.7 (// Lev 5.11; 14.21, 22, 30-32; 27.8; Num 6.21); Ezek 47.22 (// Lev 19.34; 25.45-46).

Ezekiel also knows earlier prophetic traditions. He repeats what appears to be an older prophetic description of Assyria and its downfall (Ezek 31.3-17) and then applies it to Egypt (31.2; cf. v. 18, "This is Pharaoh and all his horde"). He uses the motif of Egypt as an unreliable support (Ezek 29.6-7), a motif that also occurs in earlier prophetic material (Isa 36.6). Most commentators agree that Ezekiel's metaphor of Israel as a sexually promiscuous woman (Ezek 16) was influenced by similar imagery in Hosea. There are so many similarities between Jeremiah and Ezekiel in language and theme that it is reasonable to believe there was some kind of contact between the two: perhaps they read reports of each other's messages sent from their respective locations (cf. Jer 29.1-3, 15, 24-29), or perhaps the schools of disciples who composed the words of the two prophets into books (and their subsequent redactors) utilized each other's material. Examples of these similarities include e.g. Ezek 2.8-3.3 (// Jer 1.9; 15.16); Ezek 3.4, 8-9 (// Jer 1.7-8, 17-19); Ezek 7.26 (// Jer 18.18); Ezek 13.2, 6-8 (// Jer 14.14-15); Ezek 13.10 (// Jer 6.14; 8.11); Ezek 14.12-21 (// Jer 15.1-3); Ezek 16, 23 (// Jer 3.6-10); Ezek 18.1-4 (// Jer 31.29-30); Ezek 24.15-23 (// Jer 16.1-9); Ezek 34.1-16, 23 (// Jer 23.1-6); Ezek 36.24-28, 33-38 (// Jer 32.37-40; 33.6-12).

These similarities can be discussed from different standpoints, for example, in terms of a tradition's "influence on" a prophet, or a prophet's "dependence on" earlier tradition. Such a discussion properly lies in the realm of tradition history or the history of ideas. But what I am interested in for the purposes of this chapter is compositional technique—that is, how the author uses and transforms earlier texts as part of a compositional strategy. To do this, we need to have something very close to what Ezekiel had access to. However, the complex composition history of Jeremiah and the Pentateuch problematizes our ability to speak with confidence about the precise shape of what Ezekiel had access to and how he used and transformed it.

Additional complications arise when we consider relationships between texts: are the similarities between the material in the book of Ezekiel and other biblical books due to coincidence, to how people usually speak, to a particular shared social setting, or to literary dependence? And if due to literary dependence, what is the direction of dependence? And is the dependence manifested in an unconscious assimilation and expression of the earlier text's content, or in a deliberate and strategic use of a particular literary context? For example, we find in Ezek 6.13 and 20.28 (note the expansions in the MT) locutions that are very similar to what we see in Deut 12.2. But is Ezekiel alluding to the actual context of Deut 12.2 and transforming its instruction into an accusation? Or is this simply the use of what has become traditional religious language, attested in other texts as well (e.g., 1 Kgs 14.23; 2 Kgs 16.4; 17.10; Jer 3.6, 13; 17.2–3; Hos 4.13)? In the following discussion, I will provide four examples of text-referencing in Ezekiel that illustrate both the role that allusion to earlier texts plays in the argument structure of the book as well as the difficulties encountered in this kind of analysis.

Gen 49.10 in Ezek 21.32 [ET 21.27]

There is a passage in Ezekiel that contains material very similar to what we see in Gen 49.10. The Blessing of Jacob (Gen 49.1–28) in its present form plays an important role in a higher-level editorial layer of the Pentateuch, displaying as it does a pro-Judahite and eschatological orientation and a connection to other texts (cf. Gen 49.1, 8–12 // Num 24.7–9, 14, 17; note the use of the temporal formula "in the latter days [*bʾḥryt hymym*] in the narrative frame of both contexts). Nevertheless, many commentators agree that the earliest form of the poem is to be dated to the monarchic period, if not earlier. The example discussed below has been extensively analyzed; notable and recent treatments include Moran (1958), Steiner (2010, 2013), and Frolov (2012).

Gen 49.10	Ezek 21.32 [ET 21.27]
The scepter will not depart from Judah, nor the staff from between his feet, *until he comes to whom it belongs* (?) [*ʿd ky ybʾ šylh* (Ketiv)/ *šylw* (Qere)], and the obedience of the peoples is his.	A ruin, a ruin, a ruin I will make it!—also, such has never happened—*until he comes to whom belongs* [*ʿd bʾ ʾšr lw*] the judgment, and I will assign it.

The meaning of Gen 49.10 is infamously obscure: is *šylh* / *šylw* to be understood as the toponym "Shiloh," as a relative plus suffixed preposition ("which belongs to him"), or as an alternative vocalization of the noun "tribute" plus the suffixed preposition "to him"? This obscurity is further compounded by the ambiguity of the word *ʿd* "until" (and its relation to the following word *ky*). However this verse should be construed, what does seem clear is that in context of Gen 49.8–12 it is a positive statement about the supremacy of Judah. But how does Ezekiel use this verse?

Ezek 21.30–31 [ET vv. 25–26] viciously attacks King Zedekiah ("and you, O profaned, wicked prince of Israel!"), announcing his day of punishment and the removal of his crown. This announcement of doom culminates in v. 32 [ET v. 27] with Ezekiel's use and reversal of imagery from Gen 49.10. The points of lexical contact between the two texts are clear: the *'d ky* of Genesis corresponds to the *'d* "until" of Ezekiel; the same verb *bw'* ("to come") occurs in both, though in different tenses; and the mysterious *šylh / šylw* of Genesis corresponds to Ezekiel's *'šr lw* "which belongs to him." Whereas Gen 49.10 has a positive function in the context of vv. 8–12 (and in context of the entire poem, identified as a "blessing" in v. 28), Ezekiel lifts the words out of their local context and assigns a very different referent to them, reversing the statement of Judah's supremacy into a statement of doom for the Judahite King Zedekiah. In Ezekiel, the "coming one" is the Babylonian King Nebuchadnezzar, to whom God has assigned the power of judgment, judgment of a kind that has never happened before. Note that Ezekiel also seems to be alluding to the blessing of Judah and using its vocabulary for his lament over the monarchy in Ezek 19 (cf. the shared vocabulary in Gen 49.9–11 and Ezek 19.2, 3, 5, 6, 10, 11, 14). Such intertextual reversals of hope to doom are attested as a technique in other prophetic texts as well (cf. Isa 2.4 in Joel 4.10 [ET 3.10]).

Deut 4.28, 34 in Ezek 20.32–34

The book of Deuteronomy in its present form is a complex text with a lengthy composition history. On the one hand, most scholars would agree that the compositional process extended into the post-exilic period. On the other hand, most would also agree that the book is built from pre-exilic material that existed in written form. Proceeding from these starting points, a number of studies have examined the possibility that Ezekiel used some form of Deuteronomy (see e.g. Ganzel 2010; Levitt Kohn 2002). The example I will discuss below has been analyzed in more detail by Rom-Shiloni (2005).

Deut 4.28, 34	Ezek 20.32-34
And there you will <u>serve</u> gods—the work of human hands, *wood and stone*—which cannot see and cannot hear and cannot eat and cannot smell.	And the thought that comes to your mind will never come about—that which you are saying: "Let's be like the nations, like the clans of other lands, <u>ministering</u> to *wood and stone*!"
Or has any god attempted to come take for himself one nation from the midst of another with trials, signs, and wonders, and with war, and *with a strong hand and an outstretched arm*, and with great terrors, like all that Yhwh your God did for you in Egypt before your eyes?	As I live—utterance of Lord Yhwh—*with a strong hand and an outstretched arm* and with outpoured wrath I will be king over you! And I will bring you out from the peoples, and I will gather you from the lands among which you have been scattered *with a strong hand and an outstretched arm* and with outpoured wrath.

The locution "wood and stone" (used for images of deities) occurs in Deut 4.28; 28.36, 64; 29.16; 2 Kgs 19.18 [// Isa 37.19]; Ezek 20.32; Dan 5.4, 23. The locution "with a strong hand and an outstretched arm" occurs in Deut 4.34; 5.15; 7.19; 11.2; 26.8; 1 Kgs 8.42 [// 2 Chr 6.32]; Jer 21.5 (note swapping of adjectives and reversal of imagery!); 32.21; Ezek 20.33, 34; Ps 136.12. The frequency and distribution of these locutions and the books in which they appear indicate that the locutions are Deuteronomic in origin. The fact that they occur together in proximity only in Deut 4 and Ezek 20 suggests the possibility of literary dependence.

In Deut 4 and 28, the first locution appears in an argument that idolatry is covenant violation (Deut 4.23, 25; 28.15) that will result in exile into foreign countries (4.27; 28.36a, 64–65) where the Israelites will worship other gods. This may be seen as a punishment in kind: "if you really want to worship other gods that badly, then worship them you shall!" But the rhetoric of Deuteronomy does not only attempt to compel covenant loyalty through threats. In the second locution we see positive imagery, recounting how Yhwh has liberated the people from slavery in Egypt ("with a strong hand and an outstretched arm") in an attempt to emphasize the uniqueness and beneficial nature of their relationship.

If a relationship between Ezekiel and some form of Deuteronomy is plausible (given the points of contact discussed in Levitt Kohn 2002 and Ganzel 2010), and if we grant that Ezekiel had access to these two Deuteronomic locutions, how then is he using them? First, he places Deuteronomy's image of idolatry as punishment for covenant violation into the mouths of his contemporaries as an expression of their intent. He also changes the verb "serve" (*'bd*) into the term "minister to" (*šrt*), insinuating that the exiles desire to take on a priestly function in idolatrous worship. He then polemicizes against this idea by denying that it will ever happen. For Ezekiel, who lives in exile, worshipping other gods "like the nations" is equivalent to assimilation—and this he argues against in the strongest possible terms, for to assimilate would mean the end of Israel as an entity. But to simply deny that such idolatrous worship will occur is not enough; Ezekiel must also create hope for the future in a positive way. He does this by emphasizing God's sovereignty and by using Deuteronomy's locution of liberation from Egypt. By alluding to the exodus tradition, he suggests to his audience that what happened once may also happen again: a return from exile is possible. But each time Ezekiel uses this Deuteronomic locution of liberation, he includes the additional non-Deuteronomic element "with outpoured wrath" (vv. 33, 34). This is a frequent and distinctive expression for divine judgment in the book (Ezek 7.8; 9.8; 14.19; 20.8, 13, 21; 22.22; 30.15; 36.18). The apparently incongruous combination of positive and negative imagery is clarified by the following verses (vv. 35–38), in which the envisioned return is also a process of purging the rebels out of Israel along the way—an allusion to older wilderness traditions (v. 36). This example demonstrates how Ezekiel can shape borrowed material and integrate it into his own argument.

Zeph 3.3-5, 8 in Ezek 22.25-31

Ezekiel 22 contains three sections, each introduced by a prophetic word formula (vv. 1, 17, 23): an accusation against the "bloody city" that catalogues her misdeeds and concludes with a short statement of judgment (Ezek 22.1–12, 13–16), a two-part statement of accusation and judgment expressed in image of smelting impure metal (Ezek 22.17–22), and a final two-part statement of accusation and judgment that identifies the agents who are committing evil (Ezek 22.23–31). It is this last section that we will investigate here (see also Fishbane 1985: 461–63).

Zeph 3.3-4, 8	Ezek 22.25-31
Her officials in her midst are roaring lions.	Whose princes[LXX] *in her midst are like a roaring lion*, tearing prey: they eat people;
Her judges are *wolves* of the evening, they leave no bone to gnaw until morning.	they take treasure and precious things, they multiply her widows in her midst.
Her prophets are reckless, treacherous men.	*Her priests do violence to* my *instruction*,
Her priests profane what is holy, they do violence to instruction.	and *they profaned my holy things.* They do not distinguish between the holy and the profane, and they do not make known the difference between unclean and clean. And they hide their eyes from my sabbaths, and so I was profaned in their midst.

	Her officials in her midst are like *wolves* tearing prey, in order to shed blood, to destroy people, in order to seize unjust gain. And *her prophets* smear whitewash for themselves, seeing empty visions and divining a lie for themselves, saying "Thus says Lord Y<small>HWH</small>" when Y<small>HWH</small> did not speak. The people of the land practice extortion and rob; and they oppress the poor and needy, and they extort the alien without justice.
Therefore, wait for me—utterance of Y<small>HWH</small>—for the day when I arise as a witness, because it is my decision to gather nations and to assemble kingdoms,	And I sought among them a man who would repair the wall and stand in the breach before me on behalf of the land, so that I would not destroy it, but I found no one.
to pour out upon them my indignation, all the heat of my anger, because all the land will be consumed in the *fire* of my zeal.	So *I poured out my indignation upon them*, I finished them off with the *fire* of my wrath; I have placed their way on their head—utterance of Lord Y<small>HWH</small>.

Ezekiel has borrowed Zephaniah's four-element list (officials, judges, prophets, priests) and many of the surrounding locutions, but has expanded it to a five-element list (princes, priests, officials, prophets, people of the land), modifying it, and supplementing it with material from the local context and from elsewhere in the book. This use of Zeph 3 may have been triggered by the occurrence of "A city!" in Ezek 22.3, for the unit in Zephaniah that Ezekiel borrows from begins with the phrase "Alas, the fouled, defiled, oppressing city!" (Zeph 3.1).

The changes that Ezek 22 contains are in accordance with the argument in context and with Ezekiel's lexical preferences. For example, the expansion of list elements shows that he wishes to make an even broader accusation than Zephaniah, indicting not just the leadership (vv. 25–28) but also the common person (v. 29). Note that the MT of Ezek 22.25a reads "a conspiracy of its prophets" (*qšr nby'yh*)—probably a misreading of "whose princes" (*šr nśy'yh*, cf. LXX)—anticipating v. 28 and introducing confusion, because prophets are not known for doing what is described in v. 25. Instead of using Zephaniah's civil categories "officials" and "judges," Ezekiel uses "officials" and "princes." This can be explained on the one hand by the fact that the book of Ezekiel never critiques or even mentions "judges," and on the other by the fact that the book is well-known for its critique of the monarchy (for which Ezekiel uses the term "prince" in preference to "king"). Instead of Zephaniah's rather abstract "what is holy ... instruction" (Zeph 3.4bc), Ezek 22 specifies that the priests damage "*my* instruction ... *my* holy things" (Ezek 22.26ab). The latter is a technical term for priestly sacred donations (cf. Lev 22.2–16); it occurs with the first-person possessive pronoun only in Ezek 22.8, 26; 44.8, 13. Ezekiel has also inverted the order of the clauses in Zeph 3.4bc, a common way to mark literary dependence (Lyons 2007).

Ezekiel has supplemented the list with terms taken from the immediately preceding oracles in ch. 22. Note the sources of the following terms: v. 25 "widows" (v. 7); v. 26 "my sacred donations" (v. 8), "my sabbaths" (v. 8); v. 27 "to shed blood" (vv. 6, 9, 12), "seize unjust gain" (vv. 12, 13); v. 29 "extort the alien" (v. 7); v. 31 "fire of my wrath" (v. 21). This has the effect of tying together the three units of the chapter into a cohesive whole. But Ezekiel has also supplemented the list with material from elsewhere in the book and from other texts. Note the sources of the following locutions: v. 25 "tearing prey, eating people" (Ezek 19.3, 6); "widows" (Ezek 19.7); v. 27 "tearing prey" (Ezek 19.3, 6); v. 28 (taken in entirety from Ezek 13.6, 7, 10); v. 30 (created from Ezek 13.5); v. 31 "finished them off" (a variation on "finished off my anger on them," Ezek 5.13; 6.12; 7.8; 13.15; 20.8, 13, 21); "I have placed their way on their head" (Ezek 19.10; 11.21; 16.43). The use of locutions from Ezek 13 and 19 is deliberate, referencing the earlier condemnation of false prophets and the lament over Israel's monarchy, respectively. The reference to prophets who "smear whitewash" (Ezek 22.28) is incomprehensible without a prior knowledge of the extended metaphor in Ezek 13.10–15. The accusation in Ezek 13.5 that the prophets have not performed their proper function of "repairing damage" to Israel is given a distinctly intercessory twist in Ezek 22.30, and the image is heightened by having Yhwh himself unsuccessfully search for a person who would repair the damage. And what was merely an image of royal power in the international sphere in Ezek 19.3, 6, 7 ("he learned to tear prey, he devoured people . . . its widows") is here transformed into an accusation that the "people" and "prey" that Jerusalem's rulers have "torn" and "devoured" are her own citizens (Ezek 22.25 "in *her* midst . . . *her* widows"). Ezekiel's expansion of Zephaniah's list with the fifth element "people of the land" brings to mind the earlier two-element list "prince . . . people of the land" (Ezek 7.27; MT adds "king" here). And to describe priestly misdeeds in v. 26, Ezekiel brings in the description of priestly function from Lev 10.10 ("to distinguish between holy and profane, and between unclean and clean"), though he uses the syntax of Lev 20.25 (*hbdyl byn . . . l* rather than *hbdyl byn . . . wbyn*).

This passage illustrates a number of compositional techniques: borrowing from and referring to other texts, supplementation, modification. But to what end? As I noted above, these compositional techniques result in the integration of separate units into a cohesive whole in ch. 22, and draw on earlier arguments in the book to enhance the argument made here. The borrowing and expansion of Zephaniah's list format results in an effect similar to that of a merism: it represents the totality of offenders. Ezekiel, who often employs lists in this way (Ezek 5.1–2, 12; 6.12; 7.15, 26, 27; 14.21; 33.27), reuses and modifies Zephaniah's list here to devastating effect.

The Use of Lev 17–26 (The "Holiness Code") in Ezekiel

Scholars have long been aware of the large number of locutions that are common to both Ezekiel and the material in Lev 17–26 (traditionally called the "Holiness Code," or "H"). It has also been accepted that the nature of the shared locutions indicates a literary relationship between these two texts. But the direction of literary dependence is disputed, with some ascribing chronological priority to H (e.g., Driver 1891: 138–43; Lyons 2009: 61–67, 114–39) and others to Ezekiel (e.g., Nihan 2007: 543–45; Wellhausen 1885: 378–84), and still others claiming that there is mutual literary dependence (e.g., Zimmerli 1979: 47, 51–52). While the direction of dependence cannot be determined from every occurrence of shared locutions, in the three following examples Ezekiel is evidently the borrowing text. In Ezek 7.12–13, we see a reference to the "buyer" (*qwnh*) who will not rejoice and the "seller" (*mwkr*) who will not mourn or "return" (*šwb*) to the "thing sold" (*mmkr*). These four words occur together only here and in Lev 25.25–28. The passage in Ezekiel is incomprehensible (what is being bought and sold, and why would the seller return to it?) without a knowledge of the land redemption laws in Lev 25, suggesting that it presumes the existence of this material as a source text. In Ezek 34, we see a reference to the "shepherds of Israel" who have been mistreating the flock. The list of their misdeeds includes the locution "rule with harshness" (*rdh bprk*), which occurs only in Lev 25.43, 46, 53; Ezek 34.4. When Ezekiel uses the expression, he glosses the rare word "harshness" with the more common word "force" (*ḥzqh*), resulting in the syntactically awkward but semantically comprehensible statement "with strength you ruled them and with harshness." This interpretive expansion suggests that Ezekiel is the borrowing text. Finally, Ezek 34.26 refers to "rain" in the singular ("I will send rain in its time"), but continues with the comment "They shall be rains of blessing." The incongruous slip into plural indicates dependence on Lev 26.4 ("I will give your rains in their time").

But if Ezekiel is borrowing locutions from the Holiness Code, how and why is he using them? The answer lies in his rhetorical situation: Ezekiel uses H to describe the invasion and exile, to explain why there was an invasion and exile, and to describe hope for future restoration beyond the exile. First, Ezekiel borrows H's laws and transforms them into accusations. For example, the locution "my statutes ... my ordinances, by which a man will live if he does them" occurs only in Lev 18.5; Ezek 20.11, 13, 21 (note unique variations in Ezek 20.25; 33.15); Neh 9.29. In Lev 18 this locution functions as a command; in Ezek 20.21 this locution has been transformed into an accusation that the people did *not* "walk in God's statutes or keep his ordinances, by which a man will live if he does them." Similarly, the list of accusations in Ezek 22.7–12 is largely made up of material taken from the instructions in Lev 18.7 (cf. Lev 20.11), 9 (cf. 20.17), 15 (cf. 20.12), 17, 19, 20 (cf. 20.10); 19.3, 13, 16, 30; 20.9; 22.15; 25.36.

Second, Ezekiel borrows H's conditional (cf. Lev 26.14, "if") covenant punishments and transforms them into descriptions of current or imminent judgment. For example, the punishments of bereavement by wild animals, destruction of cattle, punishment by sword, plague, and famine, and a desolated land in Lev 26.22, 25–26, 33 are borrowed for use in Ezek 14.13–21. That these are not simply generic terms for what usually happens during invasion and siege is illustrated by the presence of the rare expressions "to break the staff of bread" (occurring only in Lev 26.26; Ezek 4.16; 5.16; 14.13; Ps 105.16) and "wild animals will bereave" (occurring only in Lev 26.22; Ezek 5.17; 14.15). Whereas in Lev 26 these punishments have a pedagogical function and are intended to turn the offender back to God (cf. v. 23), in Ezekiel they have no such function: judgment has arrived, and repentance is not expected. The same combination of locutions for punishment from Lev 26 also appears in Ezek 5.12; 6.12; 33.27, where they are structured in various ways to emphasize the totality of judgment.

Third, Ezekiel borrows H's conditional (cf. Lev 26.3, "if") covenant blessings and transforms them into unconditional promises of blessing in the future. The density of these clustered locutions in both source text (Lev 26.3–13) and target text (Ezek 34.25–30) is striking, showing Ezekiel's use of a specific literary context: "rain in its time" (Lev 26.4; Ezek 34.26); "the land will give its produce, and the tree of the field will give its fruit" (Lev 26.4; Ezek 34.27); "live securely" (Lev 26.5; Ezek 34.25, 28); "peace" (Lev 26.6; Ezek 34.25); "no one who terrifies" (Lev 26.6; Ezek 34.28); "I will finish off wild animals from the land" (Lev 26.6; Ezek 34.25); "slave/to enslave" (Lev 26.13; Ezek 34.27); "break the bars of the yoke" (Lev 26.13; Ezek 34.27); the Covenant Formula (Lev 26.12; Ezek 34.30). But even more striking is the fact that the covenant envisioned in Ezekiel is unconditional, and that the conditional blessings of H have been transformed into guarantees to fit this new outlook.

Fourth, Ezekiel affirms H's laws as "statutes of life" (Ezek 33.15; cf. Lev 18.5), presenting them as authoritative instruction. In ch. 18, Ezekiel argues that people are evaluated by God on the basis of their own righteousness or wickedness, not by the behavior of their ancestors. In this chapter, descriptions of good and evil behavior in the case studies created by Ezekiel (righteous father, wicked son, righteous grandson) are built from instructions contained in the Holiness Code: e.g., Ezek 18.6, 11, 15 (cf. Lev 18.19–20; cf. 20.10); Ezek 18.8, 13, 17 (cf. Lev 25.36). Ezekiel takes up H's connection between obedience and life (Lev 18.4–5) and creates the same connection in his own argument (Ezek 18.9, 17, 21).

4. Conclusion

In this chapter I have described several different models for the composition and redaction of the book of Ezekiel. I have also given examples of the strategies of placement, juxtaposition, linking, editorial extension, and intertextual referencing that resulted in the formation and subsequent growth of the book. These strategies produced the literary cohesion and coherence that commentators have found so striking. But the book of Ezekiel is also a remarkable case study in the textualization of prophecy. What we see at all levels of the book's formation and transmission is a process of extension and linking, both internally and to other legal and prophetic texts—the same process that lies behind what would eventually become the formation of a scripture collection beginning in the Second Temple period. As Anja Klein (2010: 581–82) has noted, "prophecy in the Book of Ezekiel is to a high degree prophecy continued: Existing prophetic texts are referred to and interpreted in the course of the book . . . . the book as a whole seems to be designed as an ideal compendium of prophetic tradition. As such, it both fulfils and concludes Old Testament prophecy."

Further reading

For surveys of scholarship on the book of Ezekiel, see Darr (1994); Levitt Kohn (2003); Pohlmann (2006); Olley (2011).

3

Israel, Yhwh, Land, and Temple

In this chapter I will explore some of the main themes and arguments in the book of Ezekiel. Because of this largely thematic approach, I will not in every case attempt to distinguish between the oldest material in the book and later expansions to it. I have chosen the topics of Israel, Yhwh, land, and temple to guide this thematic exploration for two reasons: first, these four topics are intimately related in the argument structure of the book of Ezekiel. To understand any one of these topics requires an understanding of the others. Second, these topics represent the main concerns of Ezekiel, and it is the way these topics are dealt with in the book that so often strikes the modern reader as strange or even offensive. For example: How do we explain Ezekiel's pessimism about the people, and the seemingly endless accusations detailing their "abominations"? Why is there such an emphasis on "shame"? Why does Ezekiel so often describe Yhwh as an enraged deity? What lies behind Ezekiel's conviction that a return to the land is possible, and why the lengthy discussion of architectural details at the end of the book? The answers to these questions can be traced to Ezekiel's rhetorical setting: he is attempting to address the problems and questions caused by the trauma of deportation, and create hope for his community.

1. Ezekiel's depiction of Israel

a. The identity of "Israel"

Who is "Israel" for Ezekiel? As we can see from the use of the phrase "my people" in the book of Ezekiel (e.g., Ezek 13.9–10; 21.17 [ET

21.12]), the entity "Israel" is conceived of as people who are in some way uniquely affiliated with the deity Yhwh. He is depicted as one who "chose" Israel and swore an oath to them with the words "I am Yhwh your God" (Ezek 20.5). It is true that the relationship between these two parties is described as threatened, and perhaps for a time even non-existent (cf. Ezek 16.59); but the book hopes for a restoration in which Yhwh is fully recognized as Israel's God and they are recognized as his people (Ezek 11.20; 14.11; 37.23, 27). The book of Ezekiel, then, assumes a shared history between Yhwh and Israel that began in the distant past and that functions as the grounds for certain obligations between them (Ezek 16; 20).

This definition of Israel in terms of a relationship with Yhwh has implications for how other nations are depicted in the book. The distinction between Israel and (for example) Edom or Moab is not merely sociopolitical and geographical, but conceived of in religious terms. This is of course true in other Israelite prophetic books as well. But as I noted before, one characteristic of the book of Ezekiel is that other nations are not included in its hope for a restored Israel, and there is no notion of "global" or "universal" restoration in Ezekiel. This may be due to the fact that the book was composed so close to the trauma of exile that there was not yet a sufficient reflective distance to raise questions about the scope of restoration.

But if Israel is conceived of as distinct *from* other peoples, does Ezekiel also conceive of distinctions *within* "Israel"? There are in fact several distinctions which he presents, and one which he creates. First, there are passages in the book that presume a historic distinction between two Israelite kingdoms, northern and southern (governed respectively by the cities of Samaria and Jerusalem). For example, in ch. 16 Jerusalem is compared with Samaria and Sodom (depicted metaphorically as her two sisters, Ezek 16.46). The argument of Ezek 16.44–52 is that Jerusalem is so wicked that even Samaria and Sodom appear righteous in comparison. Yet in a startling reversal, Ezek 16.53–55 makes the argument that Samaria and Sodom will be restored. The rhetorical strategy used here seems to be inviting the exiles to hypothetically conceive of a restoration for Sodom and Samaria, then to claim that if this is conceivable, they should have no reason to doubt a restoration for Jerusalem—which, from the exiles' perspective, is the issue of contention. In another reversal (v. 61), Jerusalem will in the future receive Samaria and Sodom not as sisters, but as "daughters" (on this difficult verse, see Block 1997: 518). Whatever this means, it suggests a reversal of earlier political conditions.

The distinction between northern and southern kingdoms is also presumed in Ezek 23. Here Israel's history is told using an extended metaphor of two promiscuous sisters named Oholah and Oholibah, who represent the cities of Samaria and Jerusalem. Ezekiel argues that despite the destruction of Samaria by Assyria (interpreted as divine judgment, Ezek 23.9-10), the citizens of Jerusalem were undeterred and did not change their behavior (vv. 11-18). Just as Samaria was destroyed, Jerusalem therefore will also be destroyed (vv. 31, 32-34). Unlike Ezek 16, this chapter does not end on a note of hope for restoration for the two kingdoms.

We see another explicit reference to the two kingdoms in Ezek 35.10, where Edom is quoted as saying about Israel, "The two nations and two lands belong to me, and we will possess it!" But it is not until Ezek 37 that we see the historic distinction of the two kingdoms presented as a problem to be solved by reunification. In Ezek 37.15-22, Ezekiel the prophet is told to perform a sign act using two sticks. On one he is to write "For Judah and for the sons of Israel associated with him," and on the other he is to write "For Joseph (the stick of Ephraim) and all the house of Israel associated with him." The prophet is then told to hold them so that they appear to be a single stick (v. 17), and interpret the sign act as a statement that God will reunify the tribes of Israel (vv. 18-19). This is further clarified in vv. 20-22 by the argument that God will reconstitute the exiles in the land of Israel as a single national entity with one king over them. The national unity hoped for in Ezek 37 is also reflected in the idealized tribal land distribution in Ezek 47.

An examination of the terms for expressing national/geopolitical identity also yields information about the prophet's political outlook.

First, Ezekiel shows a marked preference for the term "House of Israel" (occurring roughly eighty times, over half the occurrences in the entire Hebrew Bible). His use of this term in the face of the exilic experience constitutes an argument that there could still be a "House of Israel" in the future. Second, Ezekiel uses the word "Israel" far more often than he uses the word "Judah" (in MT Ezekiel: "Israel," 186 times; "Judah," fifteen times). Third, these two words are rarely used in Ezekiel to refer to separate and opposed kingdoms, as they are in, for example, 2 Kgs 3.9; Jer 3.8. For example, Ezekiel uses "Israel" to refer to the geopolitical entity ruled by King Zedekiah (Ezek 21.30 [ET 21.25]), which a few verses earlier was referred to as "Judah, in which Jerusalem is fortified" (21.25 [ET 21.20]). The terms "House of Judah" and "House of Israel" are used without distinction in Ezek 8.6, 10–12, 17 to refer to citizens of Jerusalem, and the terms "elders of Judah" and "elders of Israel" are used without distinction in Ezek 8.1; 20.1, 3 to refer to certain exiles who come to the prophet. Ezek 12.19 refers to the "inhabitants of Jerusalem on the land of Israel." Even in Ezek 9.9; 25.3; 27.17, where "Israel" and "Judah" are mentioned side by side, commentators have argued that these are not opposed as two different entities (cf. Friebel 1999: 214–15). One exception to this pattern of usage seems to be Ezek 4.4–6, where it appears that an original reference to "Israel" (with no distinctions in mind) was expanded into a two-part sign act referring to the iniquity of the north and the punishment of the south.

Another important distinction within "Israel" evident in the book of Ezekiel is the one that is made between the exiles of 597 BCE (Ezekiel's community) and the citizens of Jerusalem before its destruction in 587 BCE. The book of Ezekiel (and the book of Jeremiah) reflect the sudden emergence of *two* Israelite communities: one in the land, and one in Babylon. The existence of two communities threatened the ability of each one to define itself as "Israel," the exclusive recipient of YHWH's favor. As Dalit Rom-Shiloni (2013: 2, 139–97) has noted, Israel's pre-exilic traditions about judgment for covenant violation did not anticipate the possibility of a partial deportation. As a result, both the

Jerusalemites and the exiles of 597 used earlier traditions in creative ways in order to face this unprecedented state of affairs.

The stance taken by the Jerusalemites can be seen in Ezek 11.15, where they are quoted as saying to the exiles of 597, "Be distant from Yhwh; the land has been given to us as a possession!" In the context just before this we find another land claim: the Jerusalemites are saying, "This city is the pot and we are the flesh!" (Ezek 11.3; cf. vv. 1–12). Yet another quote expressing a claim to the land by those who survived the destruction of Jerusalem in 587 BCE can be seen in Ezek 33.24; here they employ traditions about the promise of land to the patriarchs to justify their claim. All of these passages testify to a conflict between those who remained in the land and the exiles of 597 BCE over which group was to be understood as "Israel"—and who, by extension, had a justifiable claim to the land.

Numerous arguments in the book of Ezekiel must be understood as counter-claims that favor the exiles over and against those who remained in the land. For example, in a direct response to the marginalization of the exiles quoted above (Ezek 11.15) we find statements of hope addressed to the exilic community that Yhwh has been present with them (v. 16), that Yhwh will gather them out of exile and repatriate them in the land (vv. 17–18), and that they will be spiritually transformed and reconstituted as the people of Yhwh (vv. 19–20). In contrast, the fate of the Jerusalemites is obliquely laid out in v. 21: "as for those whose heart goes after their detestable things and their abominations, I will place their actions on their heads." The book of Ezekiel consistently argues that God will not turn back from his decision to destroy Jerusalem as punishment for its actions (Ezek 5.8–11; 7.9; 8.18; 9.5–7, 10; 24.14). The fates for covenant violation envisioned in earlier priestly traditions—sword, famine, wild animals, pestilence, scattering (Lev 26.22, 25, 26, 33)—are applied by Ezekiel to those in the land to argue for their complete destruction (Ezek 5.1–2, 12; 6.11–12; 7.15; 14.12–21; 33.27). Of course, the reader knows that there were in fact survivors of the destruction of Jerusalem. This reality is reflected in the book as well, which grudgingly accounts for the survivors by arguing that they were left over only as witnesses that Jerusalem deserved its fate (Ezek 6.8–10; 7.16; 12.16; 14.22–23).

There is, then, a significant distinction between the Jerusalemites and the exiles of 597 BCE in the book of Ezekiel. Yet this distinction should not be pressed too far. While the *addressees* of most of these oracles are Jerusalem and the land of Israel, the *audience* of these oracles consists of the exiles. Both the Jerusalemites and the exiles alike are addressed as "House of Israel" (6.11; 11.5, 15; 12.9; 20.31). The exiles are accused of the very same things as those who remained in Jerusalem (e.g., rebellion, Ezek 5.5–6; 12.2–3; idolatry, Ezek 8; 14.1–3; 20.30, 39). And it is the exiles of 597 BCE—the former elites of Jerusalem—who would have crafted and supported the foreign policies that are so harshly critiqued by the prophet in Ezek 16 and 23. So while according to Ezek 11 the Jerusalemites and the exiles may not share the same future, they certainly share the same past. The indictments of Jerusalem are therefore indictments of the exiles as well, and the judgment of Jerusalem explains the exiles' condition.

And there is an even more significant distinction in the book of Ezekiel than the ones mentioned thus far: a distinction that is created between the "Israel-of-the-past-and-present" (that is, all those who are identified as "rebellious," who along with their ancestors have transgressed against Yhwh), and the "Israel of the future" (which will consist of those who have been transformed by Yhwh so as to walk in his statutes)—or, to use the terminology of Renz (1999: 176), a distinction between "Old Israel" and "New Israel." So while there is to be sure a distinction made between the Jerusalemites and the exiles, Renz (1999: 93) points out that

> the inhabitants of Jerusalem are not the bad part of Israel compared to which the exiles are the good part, but the Jerusalemites stand for the past and for the rebelliousness of the exiles themselves. . . . It is thus a matter of making the exiles realise the nature of their association with the Jerusalemites and engaging them in a process of dissociation from the Jerusalemites at the same time.

In the following sections, I will describe the language and arguments Ezekiel uses to create this distinction between Israel's past/present and its future.

b. The accusations directed at Israel

One of the notable features of the book of Ezekiel is the amount of negative language describing the behavior of the prophet's contemporaries and their ancestors. In some cases, specific kinds of behavior are listed; in other cases, more general terms are employed. For example, one of the most common accusations in the book is that Israel has "rebelled" (*mrh*, Ezek 5.6; 20.8, 13, 21) or that they are a "rebellious house" (*byt mry*, Ezek 2.5–8; 3.9, 26, 27; 12.2, 3, 9, 25; 17.12; 24.3; 44.6). This is often used without specifying in what way or against what standards Israel has rebelled. Another general accusation is that Israel has "acted unfaithfully" (*m'l*, Ezek 14.13; 15.8; 20.27; 39.23, 26). The specific accusations of worshiping other deities, child sacrifice, and political alliances with other nations are summed up in the general accusation that Israel has "broken the covenant" (Ezek 16.59). Ezekiel also makes heavy use of the term "abomination" (*tw'bh*, forty-three times) to describe the people's actions. While in some instances this word is used with specific reference to illicit worship (e.g., Ezek 5.11; 6.9; 8.6, 9, 13, 15, 17; 11.21), in others it is simply a general reference for behavior that Ezekiel finds abhorrent (e.g., Ezek 5.9; 7.3, 4).

Three of the expressions mentioned above—"rebellion," "acting unfaithfully," and "breaking the covenant"—are accusations that presume a relationship between Yhwh and Israel. This relational emphasis is also apparent in passages which argue that Yhwh takes Israel's behavior personally. In his speeches, Yhwh says that Israel has rebelled "against me" (Ezek 2.3; 20.8, 13, 21), that they are not willing to listen "to me" (Ezek 3.7), and that they did not walk in "my statutes" (Ezek 5.7; etc.). Yhwh claims that "I was broken by their wanton heart" (Ezek 6.9). Finally, Ezek 16 describes Yhwh as an aggrieved husband whose wife (Jerusalem) has cheated on him. This heavy use of relational language—in which it is claimed that Israel's crimes are not victimless, but that Yhwh himself has been injured—is a rhetorical attempt to evoke strong emotions and personally involve Ezekiel's audience.

The specific kinds of behavior that are condemned in the book can be categorized according to the social spheres in which they occur. In the familial and civic sphere, the prophet accuses his contemporaries of "violence" (Ezek 7.11, 23; 8.17; 12.19; 45.9) and "bloodshed" (Ezek 7.23; 9.9; 16.38; 22.2–4, 6, 9, 12, 13, 27; 23.37, 45; 24.6–9; 33.25; 36.18; note the expression "the bloody city"). As I noted in Chapter 1, this accusation stems from a specifically priestly ideology. Ezekiel also speaks of murders carried out by the upper-class citizens of Jerusalem (Ezek 11.6–7). And in Ezek 22 he piles accusation upon accusation, naming violence practiced by leaders (vv. 6, 27), mistreatment of parents (v. 7), abuse of aliens, orphans, and widows (vv. 7, 29), incest, adultery, and rape (vv. 10–11), and economic offences such as bribery, charging exorbitant interest, extortion, and robbery (vv. 12–13, 29). In Ezek 34, we see a critique of two groups, the "shepherds of Israel" (vv. 2–6, presumably, Israel's political leaders; cf. 2 Sam 5.2; Isa 63.11) and the "fat sheep" (vv. 17–21; presumably, the upper class). The former are condemned for enriching themselves at the expense of the "flock" (i.e., the people of Israel) and failing to care for them; the latter are condemned for eating and drinking the best and spoiling what remains for others, and for shoving aside the weaker sheep.

In the religious sphere, the prophet accuses his contemporaries of abandoning or being negligent in the proper worship of Yhwh. Above all this takes the form of worshipping other deities, typically referred to with the pejorative terms "detestable things" (*šqwṣym*, Ezek 5.11; 7.20; 11.18, 21; 20.7, 8, 30; 37.23) or "detestable turds" (*glwlym*, typically translated "idols"; Ezek 6.4–6; 8.10; 14.3–7; 20.7–8; 22.3; etc.); note also references to the images of deities (Ezek 7.20; 8.3, 5, 12; 16.17). But it is not always the case that these other deities are being worshipped to the exclusion of Yhwh. In Ezek 14.1–5 the prophet castigates those who attempt to consult Yhwh while simultaneously "lifting up idols in their hearts." Likewise, in Ezek 23.39, the prophet accuses people of "slaughtering their children to their idols" and then entering YHWH's sanctuary "on the same day."

Accusations that the people have worshipped other deities are scattered throughout the book, but can also be clustered, as we see in Ezek 8. In this vision report, the reader is told of "abominations" in the Jerusalem temple, which include a prominently displayed image (v. 5; according to some, a statue of the goddess Asherah), "loathsome" pictures inscribed on walls (v. 10), the worship of the deity Tammuz (v. 14), and the worship of the sun (v. 16; cf. 2 Kgs 23.11). Such accusations explain another accusation, namely, that the people have "defiled YHWH's sanctuary" (Ezek 5.11; 23.38, 39) or have "defiled YHWH's holy name" (Ezek 20.39; 43.7–9) with their practices. Ezekiel also claims that they have practiced illicit worship at rural sanctuaries (Ezek 6.3–6, 13; 20.28–29; cf. 22.9 "eat on the mountains"), and have "profaned" YHWH's sabbaths (Ezek 20.13, 16, 21, 24; 22.8; 23.38). Most of the material in Ezek 40–48 is a response to perceived past abuses to the sanctity of the temple, temple practice, cult personnel, and land. Israel's priests are accused of failing to teach and maintain proper distinctions (Ezek 22.26), and various divinatory practices are condemned for being "false" and misrepresenting YHWH (Ezek 13.1–16, 17–23; 22.28). A more controversial accusation is Ezekiel's claim that Israel has practiced child sacrifice (Ezek 16.20–21, 36; 20.26, 31; 23.37, 39). Setting aside the question of evidence for when and how widely child sacrifice was practiced in the ancient Near East, we can at least say that it was believed to be practiced in Israel (cf. Deut 12.31; 2 Kgs 3.26–27; 17.17, 31; Jer 7.30–31; 19.4–5). In this claim, then, Ezekiel is not unique.

In the political sphere, Ezekiel critiques Israel's foreign policies. What is noteworthy here is the extent to which the political and religious spheres coincide. For example, when King Zedekiah's doom for rebelling against Babylon is anticipated in Ezek 17, his rebellion is depicted not only as breaking a covenant with Babylon (vv. 15–18), but also as breaking a covenant with YHWH (v. 19)—possibly because Zedekiah's oath to Babylon would have been sworn in the name of YHWH. And critiques of Israel's political relations with Egypt, Assyria, and Babylon

(Ezek 16.15, 26, 28–34; 23.5–21) are juxtaposed with accusations of cultic impropriety (Ezek 16.16–25; 23.7). Both are presented under the metaphorical vocabulary of "lewdness" (Ezek 16.27; 23.21, 27), "fornicating" (e.g., Ezek 16.15–17, 26, 28; 23.3, 5, 19; etc.), "whoring" (e.g., Ezek 16.15, 20, 22, 25, 26; 23.8, 11, 14, 27; etc.), and "committing adultery" (Ezek 16.32; 23.37). Thus political alliances (which are also spoken of non-metaphorically in Ezek 17.15; 29.6–7, 16) are depicted as instances of religious unfaithfulness to Yhwh in the same way as the abandonment of Yhwh in favor of other deities.

What are the sources of this accusatory language? In many cases, Ezekiel is drawing on traditional material. For example, the list of accusations in Ezek 22.7–12 seems to be mostly based on instructions in the Holiness Code (cf. Lev 18.7, 9, 15, 17, 19, 20; 19.3, 13, 16, 30; 20.9; 22.15; 25.36). Ezekiel's accusation that the people were given Yhwh's "statutes ... and ordinances, by which a man will live if he does them" (Ezek 20.11) but rejected them (Ezek 5.6, 7; 20.13, 21) borrows the wording of Lev 18.5. The accusations aimed at the "shepherds of Israel" in Ezek 34 are remarkably similar to those found in Jer 23.1–5. Critiques of alliances with surrounding nations can be found in earlier prophetic accusations (Isa 20.1–6; 30.1–5; 31.1–3; Jer 2.14–19, 36–37; Hos 7.11–13; 8.9–10; 12.2 [ET v. 1]). Among these, we also see Hosea and Jeremiah using the "adulterous wife" motif to accuse Israel of religious unfaithfulness (Jer 2.20–25; 3.1–13; Hos 1.2; 2.10–15 [ET vv. 8–13]).

But it would be a mistake to imagine that Ezekiel is simply parroting earlier expressions and mindlessly recycling earlier imagery. What we find in Ezekiel is the creative reuse of earlier material in rhetorically significant ways. For example, the "adulterous wife" imagery that appears in earlier prophetic material is intensified by Ezekiel, who has multiplied sexually explicit terminology and imagery beyond anything found in Hosea. It is taken to grotesque extremes in Ezek 16 and 23, and can be understood as an attempt to shame his audience. The fact that they are not ashamed is itself a further accusation. And within these two chapters we find other rhetorical strategies to heighten his accusations: first, the ascription of Canaanite ancestry to Jerusalem (Ezek 16.3, 44–45) in order to both accuse its citizens (v. 44, "like mother, like daughter") and to justify their punishment (cf. Lev 18.26–30; 20.23; Rom-Shiloni 2013: 165–69); second, the "guilty by association" tactic of naming the metaphorical sexual partners—i.e., political allies—of Samaria and Jerusalem (Ezek 16.26, 28–29; 23.5-7, 16–17), who subsequently retaliated against them; third, the argument that Jerusalem does what even prostitutes would not do—that is, actually pays her "lovers" to come (Ezek 16.33–34); and fourth, the compare-and-contrast tactic of asserting that Jerusalem is so bad that Sodom and Samaria appear righteous by comparison (Ezek 16.44–52).

Additional rhetorical strategies to heighten the effectiveness of Ezekiel's accusations can be found in Ezek 20, the recounting of Israel's history. Here Ezekiel omits any positive behavior from Israel's history, which denies his audience any leverage by which they could hope to claim divine favor. He locates the origins of their apostasy at the very beginning of their history, even before they leave Egypt (Ezek 20.8). According to Ezekiel, there never was a time when the people were innocent. He mentions Yhwh's gracious intention for Israel at the beginning of the story (Ezek 20.5–6) in order to depict their subsequent actions as an ungrateful response (note the same strategy in Ezek 16.1–14; Hos 11.1–4; Amos 2.9–11). He frames the story of Israel's history as multi-generational apostasy, then accuses his contemporaries of acting in the very same way as their ancestors (Ezek 20.30). The effect is to depict his contemporaries as incorrigible, stuck in a pattern of behavior, without any hope for change in the present (Ezek 20.39).

But to what end? What is the point of this litany of accusations? Ezekiel is actually doing two things. First, he is attempting to explain the fall of Jerusalem and the exilic condition. The way in which he does this is to create a firm connection between actions and consequences, which means that he must convince his audience of their guilt and their responsibility for the disaster. Of course, it is true that according to Ezekiel, Yhwh himself is responsible for the disaster (cf. Ezek 11.16, "I made them distant among the nations"; 14.22, "the calamity which I brought against Jerusalem"; 24.21, "I am about to profane my sanctuary"); in this way Ezekiel argues that the defeat of Israel by Babylon cannot be interpreted as a defeat of Yhwh by Babylonian deities. In fact, he claims that the Babylonians are brought by Yhwh himself (Ezek 7.21, 24; 16.37; 23.22). But moving beyond the issue of agency, it is the *reason for* the disaster that Ezekiel ascribes to Israel's actions: it was the punishment they deserved (Ezek 9.8–10; 14.23). This explains his rhetoric of equivalency: "I will judge you *according to* your ways" (Ezek 7.3, 8, 9; 24.14); "I will deal with them *according to* their way, and judge them *according to* their judgments" (Ezek 7.27); note that this argument also exonerates Yhwh from charges of arbitrariness or injustice. Second, Ezekiel not only explains the disaster, but also attempts to create hope for a future in which the problem of Israel's behavior has been solved. The accusations, then, are the grounds from which Ezekiel makes his arguments about spiritual transformation in the future. The solution ("they will walk in my statutes and keep my ordinances," Ezek 11.20) is explicitly framed as a reversal of the problem ("they rebelled against my ordinances, and they did not walk in my statutes," Ezek 5.6; 20.13; etc.).

c. Incorrigibility, initiative, and the question of repentance

If Ezekiel's accusations reveal his diagnosis of Israel's problem, what is his solution? One might expect the prophet to urge them to change their behavior. It is commonly supposed that this was in fact the function of a prophet; after all, we see such language in the mouth of Ezekiel's contemporary Jeremiah (Jer 3.12; 4.1–2; 7.1–7), and Zechariah's description of earlier prophets quotes them as saying, "Turn from your evil ways and your evil deeds!" (Zech 1.4). But the situation is more complex than this. The prophet Ezekiel not only seems to be extremely pessimistic about the possibility that Israel would respond and change, he actually seems to doubt their very ability to do so.

Examples of this pessimism include the following: the book repeatedly makes the claim that Israel is "rebellious" (Ezek 2.3, 5–8; 3.9; 12.2–3; etc.), that the people are stubborn (Ezek 2.4; 3.7), and that they have a "heart of stone" (Ezek 11.19; 36.26). The desired outcome of Ezekiel's activity seems to be less about changing the people's behavior (cf. Ezek 2.5a, "whether they listen or whether they refuse") and more about vindicating the outcome of prophecy (v. 5b, "they will know that a prophet has been in their midst"). In fact, God explicitly tells Ezekiel that "the house of Israel will not be willing to listen to you, because they are not willing to listen to me" (Ezek 3.7). When Ezekiel's function is described in terms of a watchman who warns of an approaching threat, the four scenarios envisioned (Ezek 3.18-21) omit the possibility that a wicked person might turn from his sin. The watchman metaphor is framed in terms of Ezekiel's culpability, which suggests that its purpose is to defend Yhwh from the charge that he never warned the people of impending disaster. And any chance of a reprieve for the city of Jerusalem is immediately ruled out: Yhwh will not "have pity or compassion" (Ezek 5.11; 7.4, 9; 9.5, 10; 24.14), even when its inhabitants cry out (Ezek 8.18); the vision about Jerusalem's destruction "will not be revoked" (Ezek 7.13), and no intercession would be accepted even if Noah, Daniel, and Job were present to attempt it (Ezek 14.13-21).

When the prophet recounts Israel's history to his audience, he depicts Israel as apostate from the beginning (Ezek 20.8) and describes a recurring pattern of rebellion in subsequent generations (Ezek 20.10-29)—a pattern that his own generation also displays (Ezek 20.30). He concludes his "history lesson" with the comment, "Go on, serve your idols!" (Ezek 20.39a), suggesting a belief that change is not possible in the present, but only in the future (vv. 39b-44). One place in the book points to a complete rupture of the relationship between God and people: "I will do with you just as you have done, you who have despised the oath so as to break the covenant" (Ezek 16.59). This is reminiscent of Hos 1.9, where the symbolic name of Hosea's child ("Not my people") indicates that the "marriage relationship" between Yhwh and Israel is over. Finally, the description of the exiles' reaction to Ezekiel's words gives no indication that they will respond by changing their actions. To them, the prophet is a source of entertainment, a maker of clever allegories (Ezek 21.5 [ET 20.49]) and a singer of love songs (Ezek

33.30–32). People come to listen, "and they hear your words, but they do not do them" (Ezek 33.31, 32).

The passages listed above seem to reflect a belief that the people are incorrigible—that they are not only unwilling to respond, but are actually unable to change. This lack of any expectation for a positive response from the people has as its counterpart the argument that a change in the people's moral disposition can only come about through Yhwh's unilateral initiative, an argument expressed in the following passages:

> I will give them one heart, and I will put a new spirit within them; and I will remove the heart of stone from their flesh, and I will give them a heart of flesh, in order that they will walk in my statutes and keep my ordinances and do them. And they will be my people, and I will be their God.
>
> (11.19–20)

> And I will remember my covenant with you in the days of your youth, and I will establish for you an eternal covenant. Then you will remember your ways, and you will be ashamed when I take your older and younger sisters and give them to you as daughters.
>
> (16.60–61)

> And I will establish my covenant with you, and you will know that I am Yhwh, in order that you will remember and be ashamed, and never again open your mouth because of your disgrace, when I make atonement for you for all that you did—utterance of Lord Yhwh.
>
> (16.62–63)

> And I will take you from the nations and gather you from all the lands, and I will bring you to your land. And I will sprinkle clean water on you, and you will be clean from all your uncleannesses, and I will cleanse you from all your idols. And I will give you a new heart, and I will put a new spirit within you, and I will remove the heart of stone from your flesh and give you a heart of flesh. And I will put my spirit within you, and I will make you walk in my statutes, and you will keep and do my ordinances.
>
> (36.24–27)

These descriptions of restoration are unconditional; they are not depicted as a response to a prior act of repentance by Israel. Moreover, when the motive for Yhwh's restorative action is stated, it is described as a self-interested concern for his reputation: "And I had concern for my holy name, which the house of Israel had profaned among the nations where they had entered" (Ezek 36.21); "Not for your sake am I acting, O house of Israel; rather, for the sake of my holy name" (Ezek 36.22; cf. v. 32). This is in keeping with the motivation behind Yhwh's actions as presented in Ezekiel's historical review (Ezek 20), where Yhwh repeatedly decided not to destroy Israel because his reputation was at stake.

It therefore comes as a surprise to find three explicit appeals to repent in the book of Ezekiel:

> Therefore, say to the house of Israel, "Thus says Lord Yhwh: Repent and turn away from your idols, and turn your faces from all your abominations."
>
> (14.6)

> Therefore, I will judge each one of you according to his ways, O house of Israel—utterance of Lord Yhwh. Repent and turn away from all your transgressions, so that iniquity will not become a stumbling-block for you! Cast away from yourselves your transgressions by which you have transgressed, and make for yourselves a new heart and a new spirit! Why would you die, O house of Israel? For I do not take pleasure in the death of one who dies—utterance of Lord Yhwh. So repent and live!
>
> (18.30–32)

> And you, son of man, say to the house of Israel: "This is what you have said: 'Our transgressions and our sins are upon us, and we are rotting in them; how can we live?'" Say to them: "As I live—utterance of Lord Yhwh—I do not take pleasure in the death of the wicked, but rather, when a wicked man repents from his way, so that he lives. Repent, repent from your evil ways! For why would you die, O house of Israel?"
>
> (33.10–11)

There are considerable differences of opinion as to the function of these passages and how they relate to the rest of the book. For example, James Robson would agree that "a self-initiated response to Yahweh is inconceivable, and future salvation seems to be the work of Yahweh alone." Robson believes, however, that the offers of repentance are real, and that they are directed to the exilic readers of the book (as opposed to the audience of the speaking prophet). Moreover, the statements about salvation through divine initiative and the calls to repent "provide complementary perspectives on the same event, albeit with divine initiative working through *rwḥ* ["spirit"] enabling a response impossible for the inveterately rebellious nation" (Robson 2006: 233, 275).

For Moshe Greenberg (1983: 341), the call to repentance in Ezek 18.30–32 is a real offer in which Ezekiel ascribes to human capacity the ability to "make for oneself a new heart and a new spirit." But this is Ezekiel's argument in this chapter alone, because here he is attempting to prevent despair and motivate the people to accept responsibility (in the latter, at least, Greenberg thinks Ezekiel was in part successful, because of the quote in Ezek 33.10). But what about the other passages? "Elsewhere the prophet enlarges on the people's incorrigibility (e.g., chs. 16; 20), while in 11:19 and 36:36 it is expressly God who will create a 'new heart and new spirit' in the redeemed of the future." For Greenberg, then, it is because of rhetorical exigency that Ezekiel "vacillates between calling on the exiles to repent and despairing of their capacity for it" (Greenberg 1997: 737; cf. 735–38).

Thomas Raitt explains the tensions in Ezekiel as the result of a "developmental sequence" in Ezekiel's message, moving from "strong words of judgment with words of hope or calls to repentance" to a stage where "the failure of the people to repent is given as one of the grounds for punishment" to a stage where we see "a radical and unqualified message of salvation" (Raitt 1977: 36). For Raitt, it was the people's failure to repent that prompted Ezekiel's harsh messages of judgment, and it was the disaster of exile and the complete breakdown of the relationship between God and Israel that enabled Ezekiel to make proclamations of unconditional salvation.

Jacqueline Lapsley explains Ezekiel's calls to repentance and statements about divine initiative not in terms of a tension between divine sovereignty and human responsibility, but as stemming from a cultural shift in views about human moral agency and capacity. The differences are

> symptomatic of a tension in inherited cultural understandings of human nature, and, for Ezekiel, of an underlying discomfort with the prevailing view of the moral capabilities of the people.... The idea that the people were capable of understanding their moral failings and transforming themselves simply could not bear the weight of what Ezekiel saw as the history of failure and present of exile and destruction.

Ezekiel's goal, then, is "not to bring about a change in the people's behavior in the present, but to instill a particular kind of knowledge in them in the future." This new knowledge is associated with a new moral self that Yhwh alone can bestow (Lapsley 2000: 106, 120, 159).

For Paul Joyce, "Israel's obedience will be the result rather than the cause of deliverance, part and parcel of the restoration and certainly not a condition upon which it depends." Joyce explains the calls to repentance as rhetorical devices with a twofold function. First, they underscore Israel's responsibility: "[B]y emphasizing the demand of Yahweh, the call to repentance underlines the fact that Israel has had every warning and is wholly to blame for the crisis which is even now engulfing her." Second, the calls to repentance are an argument that disaster "is not what Yahweh would wish for Israel." In other words, they are statements about divine openness, not articulations of expectations about Israel's ability or willingness to change. Ezekiel's statements about divine initiative and human responsibility are so deeply shaped by his "radical theocentricity" that there are places in the book in which the latter is subsumed under the former (Joyce 1989: 126, 57, 128).

The five positions listed above are just a small sample of the ways in which readers have attempted to make sense of the relationship between Yhwh's involvement in restoration and human moral capacity as presented in the book (see also Renz 1999: 80–84, 112–13; Schwartz 1994; Strine 2012). To further complicate matters, we find occasional variations in how restoration is described. The sequence of events leading to transformation is usually: gathering from the nations > entering the land > transformation/acceptance (e.g., Ezek 11.17–20; 20.40–43; 36.24–27; 37.21–23). But in Ezek 37.14, the gift of God's spirit is mentioned *before* entry into the land is mentioned. And in Ezek 20.34–38, we see the following sequence: gathering from the nations > entering the wilderness > making the people "enter into the bond of the covenant"/"purging the rebels and transgressors" > entering the land. If the "rebels and transgressors" are purged, who are the non-rebellious exiles who remain? Doesn't Ezekiel claim throughout the book— indeed, throughout the preceding verses!—that his contemporaries *are* rebels? How then did they become non-rebellious, when did their moral transformation take place, and why were others not transformed? Finally, in Ezek 14.4–5, 10–11 we find an argument that the goal of divine punishment is to ensure obedience—without any mention whatsoever of internal transformation! Do these passages represent different stages in Ezekiel's thought? Different strategies for different occasions? Different redactional perspectives? Should some (e.g., Ezek 14) be understood ironically—that is, as non-solutions? And do all these passages represent real differences in outlook, or are some of them complementary? Commentators have given different answers to these questions, and uncertainties remain.

d. What does Ezekiel hope for Israel to become?

If one of the main problems described by the book of Ezekiel is the incorrigibility of Israel, both past and present—resulting in the further problems of deportation, a defiled land, and damage to God's name (cf. Ezek 36.17–20)—then what is the solution? It might be helpful at this point to demonstrate just how diverse models for restoration (and their accompanying assumptions about human moral capability) could be in ancient Israel. For example, the outlooks of at least some passages in

Deuteronomy display pessimism about the possibility of perfect covenant faithfulness: they claim that the people will inevitably rebel, suffer the consequences, and go into exile (Deut 4.25-28; 30.1; cf. 31.16-18, 20-21, 29). But if they repent (Deut 4.29-30; 30.2), then God will bring them back out of exile and enable them to love him so that they will obey (30.3-8). A similar model can be seen in the Deuteronomistic History, where Solomon's temple dedication prayer petitions God to respond positively when his exiled people repent and cry out in supplication to him (1 Kgs 8.46-50).

We see something similar in Lev 26, though expressed in different terminology. The first part of Lev 26 lists blessings for covenant obedience (vv. 3-13), then punishments for covenant violation (vv. 14-39). The consequences of covenant violation are largely the same in both Deut 28 and Lev 26, and escalate in severity: infertility of land, plagues, famine, invasion by enemies, death and deportation. However, while Deut 28 depicts these as "curses," Lev 26 depicts them as restorative punishments, designed to discipline the people back to God (vv. 18, 23-24, 27-28). But if these do not work, what then? According to the model of restoration outlined in Lev 26.40-42, if the people "confess their iniquity ... or then humble their uncircumcised heart, and make amends for their iniquity," then Yhwh will remember his covenant with the patriarchs and remember the land. The retrospective comment in v. 44 claims that even when the people were in exile, God did not in fact reject or loathe them so as to destroy them or break his covenant with them. In the models for restoration described above, then, humans are able to make positive moral decisions and initiate changes in their behavior.

But Ezekiel's model of restoration is quite different than these, for he is extremely pessimistic about the possibility that his contemporaries are either willing or able to repent. This explains his argument about Yhwh's unilateral initiative in restoration. And even supposing that the people did repent and return, what would prevent them from rebelling against Yhwh, going into exile, and profaning Yhwh's name yet again? Because the book of Ezekiel hopes for the permanent restoration of

Yhwh's reputation and a permanently obedient people permanently living in a cleansed land with Yhwh in their midst (Ezek 11.17-20; 36.22-36; 37.23, 25-28), its model of restoration must of necessity be different. Because a change initiated by the people does not seem to be a viable option (according to evidence both past and present, cf. Ezek 20), and in order to prevent any future apostasy and exile, Ezekiel offers a radical solution: Yhwh will take the initiative to perform an ontological transformation of the people (a "new heart," a "heart of flesh," Ezek 11.19; 36.26), enable obedience ("so that they may walk in my statutes," 11.20; "I will put my spirit within you and make you walk in my statutes," 36.27), and forge an unbreakable relationship (an "eternal covenant," 16.60; 37.26).

This radical model of restoration can be compared to what we see in Jer 31.31-34, where it is said that Yhwh will make a "new covenant" in which obedience and knowledge of God are guaranteed by means of the internalization of Yhwh's law; or in Jer 32.40, where the "eternal covenant" that Yhwh will make guarantees that he will not turn back from doing good to Israel, and their obedience will be guaranteed by the internalization of the fear of Yhwh. On the one hand, Ezekiel uses the language of transformation in a way that Jeremiah does not, and it is Yhwh's spirit (not Yhwh's law, as in Jeremiah) that is internalized in Ezekiel. On the other hand, both Jeremiah and Ezekiel hope for a different kind of covenant, and argue that obedience will be guaranteed. This explains why—in contrast to the covenant described in Lev 26—there are no punishments in the covenant Ezekiel envisions. It is for the same reason that we see the conditional covenant blessings of Lev 26.4-6, 12, 13 transformed by Ezekiel into unconditional guarantees of blessing in a "covenant of peace" (Ezek 34.25-28, 30). Restoration of the people's spiritual condition therefore goes hand-in-hand with a return from exile to a restored land.

It is important to understand that Ezekiel's model of restoration is an attempt to solve not only current problems (the apostasy of the people, invasion and exile, the insults of the nations, damage to God's reputation), but also to prevent these problems from ever happening again in the future. This explains Ezekiel's language of permanence: the people will "never again profane [Yʜᴡʜ's] holy name" (Ezek 20.39; 43.7); there will "never again be a prickly thorn or painful briar among all those around them" (28.24); they will "never again be prey" (34.22, 28); "never again be consumed by hunger" (34.29); "never again experience the insults of the nations" (34.29; 36.15); "never again experience the disgrace of famine" (36.30); "never again be two nations, and never again be divided into two kingdoms" (37.22); "never again defile themselves with their idols, detestable things, and transgressions" (37.23). The land will "never again" bereave its people of children, devour them, or cause them to stumble (36.12, 14, 15). Finally, God will "never again hide his face from them" (37.29).

The book of Ezekiel uses the following distinctive expressions to describe restoration (note the clustering of these expressions in Ezek 11; 16; 20; 34; 36; 37):

- "gathering" from exile (Ezek 11.17; 20.34, 41–42; 28.25; 34.13; 36.24; 37.12, 21; 39.27): this is a reversal of the punishment that Yʜᴡʜ would scatter the people among the nations (cf. Ezek 6.8; 11.16; 12.15; 20.23; 22.15; 36.19), a locution taken from Lev 26.33. The people's return to the land of Israel is necessary to protect God's reputation (Ezek 36.16–24). As I noted above, a gathering of the people out of exile and into the land seems to be the first event in the sequence of restoration. But it is not enough to return to the land; the people must be enabled to obey (Ezek 11.20; 36.27) so that they can remain in the land.
- "a single heart" (MT Ezek 11.19): this term indicates single-minded or shared purpose (cf. Jer 32.39; Ps 86.11; 1 Chr 12.39 [ET v. 38]; 2 Chr 30.12). Both Ezek 11.19 and Jer 32.39 describe this as the gift of God. In the immediate context, it stands in contrast to what is described in Ezek 11.21, "a heart that goes after detestable things and idols." In the wider context, it stands in contrast to what is described in Ezek 6.9 ("their whoring heart") and 14.3 ("taking up idols in their heart"). The Old Greek translation preserves a different reading here, reflecting a Hebrew word which differs by

only one letter; many commentators have argued that this reading is original, and the MT is secondary. It reads "a different heart" (*lb 'ḥr*) instead of "a single heart" (*lb 'ḥd*). This is perhaps a more straightforward term for the transformation envisioned in this passage.

- "heart of flesh" (Ezek 11.19; 36.26): in both passages, this is described as a reversal of the people's current condition of having a "heart of stone." The people are, in a sense, subhuman and in need of a heart transplant (compare 1 Sam 25.36–37, where in the morning after his drunken party, Nabal receives unwelcome news, and "his heart died within him, and he became like a stone"). The replacement of a "heart of stone" with a "heart of flesh" points to a transformation in which the people become truly human and receptive to God. This stands in contrast to their current state, in which the people are described as "hard of heart" (Ezek 2.4; 3.7).
- "new heart and new spirit" (Ezek 11.19; 36.26): the word "heart" is used elsewhere to describe the center of cognition, intention, and emotion (e.g., Gen 6.5; 1 Sam 1.8; 1 Kgs 3.9; Isa 10.7; Prov 18.15); the word "spirit" can refer to one's attitude or emotional state (Num 5.14; 14.24; Isa 65.14; Ezek 3.14). What is envisioned here is a transformation of disposition. To use the terminology of Lapsley (2000: 103–106, 186), Yhwh will create a new moral identity within the people.
- "my spirit" (Ezek 36.27): in some texts, God's spirit is associated with animation (individual, Ezek 3.24; Ecc 12.7; national, Ezek 37.14); in others, with divine empowerment or extraordinary ability (cf. Exod 35.30–35; Isa 11.1–5; Zech 4.6–7; Dan 5.14); in still others, with righteous action (Ps 143.10). Commentators differ as to the precise nuance of its meaning in Ezek 36.27; does this refer to a new animating principle, a new ability, a new impulse for righteousness, or a new identity shaped by very mind of God? But all would agree that here it is the gift of God's spirit that enables obedience: "I will put my spirit within you, and I will *make* you walk in my statutes and keep and do my ordinances." While other

prophetic texts (e.g., Isa 32.15–20; Joel 3.1 [ET 2.28]) reflect a hope for the outpouring of God's spirit, these texts lack Ezekiel's distinctive language of internalization.

- "remember" (Ezek 16.61, 63; 20.43; 36.31): memory is described as a moral faculty in several passages. In his extended metaphor of Jerusalem as Yhwh's wife, Ezekiel claims that she "did not remember" the earlier days when Yhwh rescued her (Ezek 16.22, 43; note that in Ezek 23.19, what she *did* "remember" was her earliest habits of "whoring"). This failure to remember is a moral defect. It is only in the future, when Yhwh transforms Israel, that she will be able to "remember" (Ezek 16.61, 63; 20.43; 36.31).
- "be ashamed" (Ezek 16.54, 61, 63; 36.32; 43.10–11)/"loathe yourselves" (Ezek 6.9; 20.43; 36.31): like memory, shame is also treated as a moral faculty in Ezekiel (Lapsley 2000: 126–56). Indeed, memory and shame are closely linked in the book (cf. Ezek 6.9; 16.61, 63; 20.43; 36.31). Currently, the people lack the capacity to feel shame; this is demonstrated by their lack of any response to the sexually explicit language Ezekiel uses to characterize them in chs. 16 and 23. In his extended metaphors, Ezekiel claims that they do what even prostitutes would not do (Ezek 16.31–34), that Jerusalem has a perverse sexual appetite for her bestial lovers (23.20), that she debases herself even with low-class drunkards (23.40–44). "Be ashamed!" says Ezekiel (16.52)—but they are not, and cannot be, ashamed. It is only when the people are transformed and given a new heart that they will be able to look back at what they have done, recognize their actions for what they were, and be horrified. The ability to feel shame, therefore, is a positive development; it will show in truth that they have been given a new moral identity. But the restoration of the people will also include the removal of another kind of disgrace—namely, that which was caused by the mockery of surrounding nations (Ezek 34.29; 36.6–7, 15).
- "eternal covenant" (Ezek 16.60; 37.26)/"covenant of peace" (Ezek 34.25; 37.26): for a covenant to be "eternal," it must be unbreakable;

for a covenant to be unbreakable, human obedience must be guaranteed—and this is precisely what the book of Ezekiel argues for. Earlier notions of a conditional covenant, with blessings and curses or punishments contingent on human behavior (e.g., Lev 26.3, 14; Deut 28.1, 15), are replaced in Ezekiel with the idea of an unconditional covenant where blessings will be guaranteed (Ezek 34; 36). And since the people will be transformed, covenant punishments or curses are omitted as unnecessary. It is fitting, then, for such a covenant to be called a "covenant of peace."

The restoration described in the book of Ezekiel includes other elements as well: the people will be cleansed (Ezek 36.25, 29; 37.23); God himself will atone for them (Ezek 16.63); the land will be cleansed (Ezek 11.18) and made fertile (Ezek 34.26–27, 29; 36.9–11, 29–30, 33–38); God will rescue his flock Israel from hostile shepherds and belligerent sheep (Ezek 34.1–22); Israel will be reconstituted as a nation (Ezek 37.1–14); the nation will be reunified under a single Davidic king (Ezek 37.15–22, 24; cf. 17.22–24); the people will live securely, in safety from enemies (Ezek 28.24–26; 34.25, 27–28; 39.26); they will offer pure offerings (Ezek 20.40); and Yhwh will once again live with his people, in his sanctuary (Ezek 37.26–28; 43.7, 9). But what is Yhwh's motivation for transforming "Old Israel" into "New Israel" (to use Renz's terminology)? Or to ask the question more broadly: what is the nature of the God depicted in Ezekiel?

2. Ezekiel's depiction of God

For reasons of space, the following discussion cannot be a comprehensive treatment of Ezekiel's theology. What I will do is show how the depiction of Yhwh in the book relates to Ezekiel's attempt to explain the trauma of exile and provide hope for his audience. The section below will explore the book's theocentricity and its description of Yhwh's harshness, kindness, and absence or presence.

a. The "radical theocentricity" of the book of Ezekiel

Paul Joyce (1989: 105) has demonstrated that the book of Ezekiel displays "evidence of a distinctive emphasis on the absolute centrality of Yahweh and his self-manifestation, a radical theocentricity which is of an order difficult to parallel anywhere in the Old Testament." This radical theocentricity is perhaps most evident in the literary shape of the book, which is framed as a story about Yhwh's speech to Ezekiel and which gives prominence to Yhwh's voice above all other voices. But the book's theocentricity is also revealed by the repeated use of three distinctive expressions. First, the Recognition Formula ("They/you will know that I am Yhwh"), which appears some seventy times in the book, is used to argue that both Israel and the nations will come to a new and accurate knowledge of God, either through God's judgment (on Israel, Ezek 11.12; on the nations, Ezek 25.17) or through God's deliverance of Israel (Ezek 16.62; 36.23).

Second, the expression "for the sake of my [holy] name" (Ezek 20.9, 14, 22, 44; 36.22, 32; cf. 36.23; 39.7, 25) reveals the motivation behind Yhwh's behavior: he acts out of self-interest, in order to preserve or restore his reputation. In Ezekiel's summary of Israel's history, he describes Yhwh repeatedly refusing to destroy Israel because Yhwh is concerned about what the surrounding nations might think (Ezek 20.8-9, 13-14, 21-22; cf. Exod 32.10-14; Num 14.11-19). In Ezek 36, Israel's exilic condition is causing the nations to believe that Yhwh is unable to properly care for his people (Ezek 36.19-20). This is damaging Yhwh's reputation, which he will restore by bringing Israel out of exile (vv. 21, 23-24). The motivation behind this action is explicitly contrasted with the possibility that he might be restoring Israel because they deserve to be restored: "it is not for your sake that I am acting, O house of Israel, but for the sake of my holy name, which you profaned among the nations which you entered" (Ezek 36.22; cf. v. 32).

A third expression that points to the centrality of Yhwh in the book of Ezekiel is the statement that Yhwh will "manifest his holiness" (Ezek 20.41; 28.22, 25; 36.23; 38.16, 23; 39.27). It is not simply the case that Ezekiel believes Yhwh to be holy; rather, Ezekiel believes that Yhwh's holiness must be recognized as such. This is a vindication of Yhwh, because the behavior of his people has impugned his sanctity (Ezek 20.39; 36.20–21). This emphasis on the recognition of Yhwh's reputation and sanctity also explains the numerous references to the publically observable nature of his actions: "I will perform judgments among you *in the sight of the nations*" (Ezek 5.8); "I acted for the sake of my name, so that it should not be profaned *in the sight of the nations*" (by not destroying Israel, Ezek 20.9, 14, 22); "I will manifest my holiness among you *in the sight of the nations*" (by bringing Israel out of exile, Ezek 20.41; 28.25; 36.23; 38.23; 39.27).

Finally, the theocentricity of the book is revealed in the plot line: Yhwh will get what he wants, one way or another. He will be king over his rebellious people (Ezek 20.33), he will bring them out of exile (Ezek 11.17), he will compel their obedience (Ezek 11.19–20; 36.27), and he will live in their midst as their God (Ezek 37.27). He will permanently solve the problem of international hostility against Israel by coercing the shadowy figure named "Gog," enticing Gog and his coalition armies into the apparently undefended land of Israel in order to destroy them there (Ezek 38–39). Again, Yhwh's motive in protecting Israel is so that his holiness, greatness, glory, and reputation might be known (Ezek 38.16, 23; 39.7, 13, 21–22).

b. Understanding the harshness of Ezekiel's God

The modern reader may find the book's theocentricity disturbing, especially when coupled with Ezekiel's language of divine rage and human shame, and the absence of certain words (e.g., "love," "kindness," "graciousness," and "redemption") to describe Yhwh's actions. This may be compounded by the deterministic imagery of Yhwh forcibly removing the people from exile (Ezek 20.32–34) and compelling them to obey (Ezek 36.27). As a result, some have concluded that Ezekiel's God is not only egocentric, but that he restores his people out of spite: he will bring them out of exile, but neither he nor the people will be happy about it (Schwartz 2000). This is, perhaps, an understandable conclusion. But I think it is possible to demonstrate that Ezekiel's harsh language—so foreign to the sympathies of modern readers—is actually part of his rhetorical strategy, a carefully crafted response to his audience and their exilic situation.

It may be useful here to contrast Ezekiel's rhetorical strategy with that of another exilic prophet—the voice we hear in Deutero-Isaiah (Isa 40–55; cf. Albertz 2010). The exiles quoted in this text doubt that Y$_{HWH}$ sees their situation so that he might rescue them from it (Isa 40.27–28). The prophet must therefore comfort them by convincing them that they are forgiven and that Y$_{HWH}$ is on their side (Isa 40.1–2, 10–11; 41.8–18). The timidity of the people explains the repeated reassurance "Don't be afraid!" (Isa 40.9; 41.10, 13, 14; 43.1, 5; 44.2). And the prophet must also convince them that Y$_{HWH}$ (as opposed to other gods) has the ability to bring them out of exile, typically by pointing to Y$_{HWH}$'s power and wisdom in creation (Isa 40.12–26; 41.1–4; 44.24–28). The prophet's message can be summed up as follows: "I have blotted out your transgressions like a mist, and your sins like a cloud; return to me, because I have redeemed you!" (Isa 44.22).

Ezekiel's situation is different: he is still trying to explain the trauma of the recent deportation and the destruction of Jerusalem, and the language of a harsh deity plays an essential role in his attempt to explain the disaster. Why did the exile happen? Because Y$_{HWH}$ was angry at Israel. Why was Y$_{HWH}$ so angry? Because Israel rebelled against him. This is spelled out clearly in the book:

> And those of you who escape will remember me among the nations where they have been taken captive, how I was broken by their whoring heart that turned away from me, and their eyes that whored after their idols. And they will be loathsome in their own sight for the evils that they have done, for all their abominations. And they will know that I am Y$_{HWH}$; I did not speak in vain that I would do this disaster to them.
>
> (Ezek 6.9–10)

> Now the end is upon you, and I will send my anger into you, and I will judge you according to your ways, and I will place all your

abominations upon you. My eye will not have pity on you and I will not have compassion, because I will place your ways upon you and your abominations will be in your midst. And you will know that I am Yhwh.

(Ezek 7.3–4)

Therefore, thus says Lord YHWH: Because you forgot me, and you tossed me behind your back, you also will bear the consequences of your lewdness and your whorings.

(Ezek 23.35)

And the nations will know that the house of Israel went into exile because of their iniquity, because they acted unfaithfully against me; and I hid my face from them, and I gave them into the hand of their foes, and all of them fell by the sword. I dealt with them according to their uncleanness and according to their transgressions, and I hid my face from them.

(Ezek 39.23–24)

Ezekiel argues that because earlier attempts at cleansing Israel failed, a final judgment is necessary (Ezek 24.13). There must be a complete break with the past: "Thus says Lord Yhwh: I will do with you just as you have done, you who have despised the oath so as to break the covenant!" (Ezek 16.59). For Ezekiel, an outpouring of divine anger at an incorrigible people is the only way to explain the disaster of exile and the destruction of Jerusalem.

But it is not simply Ezekiel's situation that is different from what we see in Deutero-Isaiah; the problems posed by Ezekiel's audience are also different. Ezekiel is faced with his contemporaries' belief that Yhwh has forsaken the land and therefore cannot see in order to condemn people's actions (Ezek 8.12; 9.9), and their belief that they are being punished not for their own sins, but for those of the previous generation (Ezek 18). It seems likely, then, that the prophet is deliberately avoiding the language of a comforting and redeeming deity because this would not serve his rhetorical purposes. According to Ezekiel, the people have not even acknowledged their guilt. How could they possibly respond to an offer of forgiveness if they do not accept that they are guilty? Because the prophet is intent on forging a link between actions and consequences, he apparently feels that an emphasis on the language of divine love would disrupt this attempt. But this is a tricky balancing act indeed: the prophet must simultaneously explain the exile by convincing his audience of their guilt, justify Yhwh's involvement in exile, prevent a despair that could lead to fatalism, decry the temptation to assimilate, and provide some reason for his audience to believe that they might survive as the people of Yhwh.

c. The kindness of Ezekiel's God?

As I have argued above, the God of Ezekiel is described as a harsh deity. But a close reading of the book reveals something more complex than harshness alone. It is actually possible to observe how the prophet moves between the twin poles of Yhwh's harsh judgment and his compassion. First, Yhwh's repeated statement "My eye will not have compassion, and I will not spare" (Ezek 5.11; 7.4, 9; 8.18; 9.10) makes little sense unless one expects Yhwh's fundamental orientation to be one of compassion. It is divine judgment that must be explained as the aberration, and this Ezekiel does by arguing that it was brought about by another aberration—the people's rebellion. Second, L.-S. Tiemeyer (2006) has noted an intriguing theme in certain texts: Yhwh's impulse to forgive is believed to be so great that if he is asked to forgive, he is practically bound to do so. The only way, then, for Yhwh to successfully judge offending humans is to prevent intercession, a motif we see in Exod 32.10 (though here Moses disregards Yhwh's instruction and intercedes anyway, vv. 11–14); Jer 7.16; 11.14; 14.11–12; Amos 7.7–8; 8.1–2 (here Yhwh preempts the prophet's intercession, unlike the earlier successful incidents of 7.1–3, 4–6). Tiemeyer argues that this theme is also present in Ezekiel, which explains why Yhwh appoints Ezekiel as a watchman, but controls his mouth to prevent him from intervening (Ezek 3.26b) in a way that would motivate Yhwh to forgive. It is because Yhwh forces Ezekiel to ingest a scroll of woe

(Ezek 2.8–3.3) and rigidly controls his speech (3.26–27) that we see proclamations of unavoidable and certain destruction from the prophet (e.g., Ezek 7.1–4; 8.18; 24.14). It is only after Yhwh accomplishes the destruction of Jerusalem that Ezekiel's mouth is opened (Ezek 33.21–22). Thus Yhwh's comment in Ezek 22.30 ("I sought for someone among them who would build up the wall and stand in the gap before me on behalf of the land, so that I would not destroy it, but found no one") is somewhat ironic; Yhwh has sealed the mouths of his prophets, the only people who might have done this very thing!

But the book also contains more overt descriptions of Yhwh's compassion. While Ezekiel describes Yhwh as acting out of self-interest and concern for his reputation, this does not mean that Yhwh is uncompassionate: Ezek 39.25 argues in one breath that Yhwh will "be jealous for his holy name," and in the other that he will "have compassion" on Israel (note that Isa 40–48, well-known for its emphasis on divine compassion, also describes Yhwh as acting out of self-interest in Isa 43.25; 48.9, 11). The book does not present a mean and vindictive deity when it describes Yhwh as "broken" by the people's actions (Ezek 6.9), argues that he "has been a temporary sanctuary" for the exiles (11.16), claims that he will "rescue" his people from those who harm them (13.21, 23; 34.10, 22; cf. 34.1–9, 17–19), and describes him as a shepherd who cares for his people (34.10–16). The notion of a heartless deity is hard to square with the depiction of Yhwh in Ezek 18.32; 33.11 as one who "does not take pleasure in the death of the wicked" and who wishes his people to repent. The idea that Yhwh restores the people out of spite does not fit with the extravagant picture of restoration as a "covenant of peace" that guarantees security and fertility (Ezek 34.25–31; 36.34–38), or with the imagery of the tree of life and water of life (Ezek 47.1–12). And the description of Yhwh's motive for restoring Israel in Ezek 16.60 ("I will remember my covenant with you in the days of your youth") comes arguably close to nostalgia. Here the author's belief in the relational impulse that led Yhwh to rescue the abandoned child Israel (16.6–7) and enter into a covenant with her (vv. 8–14) is the grounds for the hope that YHWH will be impulsively moved to enter into a relationship with restored Israel.

Most of the passages listed above refer to YHWH's care for Israel in the present and the future. But Ezekiel also makes reference to YHWH's care for Israel in the past: YHWH rescued Israel as a foundling child (Ezek 16.6), multiplied Israel and gave her extravagant gifts (16.7–14), and spied out a good land to give to his people (20.6). While it is true that the function of these passages in their contexts is to demonstrate Israel's obligation to God and to justify God's punishment of Israel for rebelling against him, and while it is true that one should not over-romanticize the marriage metaphor in Ezek 16, these passages do depict YHWH's concern for and kindness to Israel.

One passage that often comes up when discussing the nature of Ezekiel's God is Ezek 20.25-26: "And also, I gave them statutes [ḥqym] that were not good, and judgments [mšpṭym] by which they could not stay alive. And I pronounced them defiled on account of their gifts—when they offered every firstborn—in order that I might make them desolate, in order that they might know that I am YHWH." The majority of commentators have argued that v. 26 is an explanation of v. 25—in other words, that Ezekiel is describing child sacrifice to YHWH as a command that YHWH himself gave Israel in order to punish them (see Cooke 1936: 218; Greenberg 1983: 368-70; Zimmerli 1979: 411-12). Certainly there were Israelites who believed that YHWH desired child sacrifice (cf. Jer 7.31); and it is true that Ezekiel describes a God who takes a hand in the actions of the wicked in order to ensure their judgment (Ezek 14.9-10). However, a few recent commentators have argued that Ezekiel's "not-good statutes" do *not* refer to child sacrifice. First, as Kelvin Friebel (2005) notes, there is nothing in the syntax of v. 26 to suggest that it should be understood as the result of v. 25 rather than simply as the next negative event in the sequence of Israel's misdeeds. Second, whatever the "not-good statutes" might be—for Friebel, these refer to decrees of punishment; for Block (1997: 640), Ezekiel is reasoning backwards from effect to cause, and leaves the referent undefined—the use of the plural suggests that something other than a "decree" of child sacrifice is in mind. The use of the two-part plural expression "statutes ... and judgments, by which they could not stay alive" is clearly an ironic reversal of Lev 18.5, a passage which Ezekiel has already alluded to in this chapter (Ezek 20.11, 13, 21). Third, while Ezekiel is using a locution for "firstborn" which also occurs in Exod 13.12–13 (the laws of the firstborn), this does not necessarily mean he is describing child sacrifice to Yhwh. After all, he specifically identifies these "gifts" and "offerings" (Ezek 20.26) with the worship of deities other than Yhwh (v. 31). Moreover, this is consistent with every other accusation he makes about child sacrifice (Ezek 16.20–21, 36; 23.37, 39). So while the God of Ezekiel does deal out harsh punishments, Block and Friebel make a plausible case that a command of child sacrifice is not one of these.

Just as Ezekiel's harsh depiction of Yhwh serves a crucial rhetorical function for his situation, his depiction of the kindness of Yhwh also serves a rhetorical function. First, the statements about Yhwh's kindness in the past create an argument about the enormity of Israel's guilt: Yhwh cared for them, and they should have responded in gratitude and obedience, but instead they rebelled against him. Thus their punishment is deserved. Second, the statements about Yhwh's restoration of Israel in the future are attempts to prevent despair and create hope. A clear example of Ezekiel's rhetorical strategy can be found in the vision report in Ezek 37. The dry bones that Ezekiel sees represent his contemporaries, who are quoted as saying, "Our bones are dried up, and our hope is lost, we are completely cut off." As Michael Fox (1980) has demonstrated, the vision report of dry bones coming to life is crafted in such a way as to spark the imaginations of Ezekiel's audience, and to dare them to believe that national restoration is a possibility.

d. The presence and absence of Yhwh

As one might expect in an exilic composition, one of the most important themes in the book of Ezekiel is that of Yhwh's presence and absence (cf. Joyce 1996; Kutsko 2000). We see this from the fact that the book begins with an argument that the presence of Yhwh may be experienced even in exile. Ezekiel's term for manifestation of the deity that he encounters in Babylon is the "Glory of Yhwh" or "Glory of the God of Israel" (cf. Ezek 1.28; 3.23; 8.4; 43.2–4). This term for the Divine Presence is reminiscent of Israel's wilderness traditions, which recount Yhwh's "Glory" journeying with the people from Egypt to Canaan (Exod 16.10; 24.16-17; 33.18-23 [in these first three examples, apart from a sanctuary]; 40.34; Lev 9.23; Num 14.10; 16.19). The use of this term for Yhwh's presence points to its mobility—which, as Kutsko (2000: 152) points out, "furnishes the means to bridge the gap between the Temple and exilic experience."

We see the issue of Yhwh's presence raised again in Ezek 8.12; 9.9, where the citizens of Jerusalem are claiming, "Yhwh does not see us; Yhwh has forsaken the land!" As the vision report makes clear, however, Yhwh is present to see. Ironically, it is the people who are "distant" (Ezek 8.6) from Yhwh's sanctuary, even as they enter it to profane it with their practices. The matter of Yhwh's presence is taken up again in Ezek 11.14-21, a passage that has been set into its present context in order to create an argument about who constitutes "Israel" (cf. 9.8; 11.13). In response to the Jerusalemites' marginalization of the exiles (Ezek 11.15, "Be distant from Yhwh; the land has been given to us as a possession!"), Ezekiel is to tell the exiles that while Yhwh has "made them distant among the nations," he has nevertheless been among them even in exile as a "sanctuary" (v. 16). The way in which he has been a sanctuary is qualified by the word $m'ṭ$, which some commentators understand as an adverb of time (i.e., "I have been a *temporary* sanctuary," or "I have *for a little while* been a sanctuary"; cf. Job 24.24). This would reflect the argument (expressed in v. 17) that their exile is only a temporary condition. Other commentators take it as an adverb of degree (i.e., "I have been a sanctuary, *albeit in small measure*"; cf. 2 Kgs 10.18; Zech 1.15). This would depict the exilic experience as a time of judgment in which God's presence may nevertheless be encountered.

Another passage relating to the issue of Yhwh's presence is the vision report in Ezek 8–11. This has commonly been interpreted as a vision of Yhwh abandoning his temple so that it may then be destroyed by the Babylonians (Block 1997: 274–76; Greenberg 1983: 195–201). To support this interpretation, commentators point to the descriptions of the Divine Presence, arguing that it moves from above a cherub inside the most holy place to the threshold (Ezek 9.3), then to its mobile throne-platform (10.18–19), then to the east gate of the temple (11.1), then finally to a position outside the city (a mountain on its east side, 11.22–23; note that this pattern of movement seems to be reversed in Ezek 43.1–2, 4–5). According to this interpretation, Ezekiel believes that Yhwh's city and temple are inviolable as long as he is in residence (cf. Mic 3.11b; Ps 46). But after he abandons them, they can be destroyed. This logic can be seen in Jer 12.7, and other ancient Near Eastern texts do in fact describe deities abandoning their temples before they are destroyed (cf. Bodi 1991: 183–218).

William Tooman (2009) has recently challenged this understanding of Ezek 8–11, arguing that the vision does not depict a "temple abandonment" that allows its destruction, but rather a visitation of Yhwh for its destruction. He points out that the Divine Presence has *already* been depicted outside the temple—first in Ezek 1, when it initially appears to the prophet in Babylon, then also in Ezek 8.2 (in language identical to the description of Glory of Yhwh in 1.27) when it transports Ezekiel in a vision to Jerusalem (note also Yhwh's claim in Ezek 11.16 that he "has been a temporary sanctuary" for the exiles in Babylon). Furthermore, Ezekiel does not in fact depict the Divine Presence inside the most holy place in the vision report: the prophet's guided tour begins *outside* the sanctuary, at the entrance of the north gate of the courtyard (cf. Ezek 8.4, "the glory of the God of Israel was there"). The alternation between the singular "cherub" (Ezek 9.3; 10.2, 4, 7) and plural "cherubs" (10.3, 5, 15, 18, etc.) is curious, but provides no reason (*contra* Greenberg) to imagine that two different referents are envisioned, one (the singular) inside the most holy place and the other (the plural throne-bearers) outside. After all, according to 1 Kgs

6.23–28, there were *two* cherub-statues in the inner sanctum. So Yhwh has not moved from the inner sanctum to the threshold so as to abandon his temple, but has momentarily dismounted from his mobile throne-platform to the threshold (Ezek 9.3) so that the "man dressed in linen" can take fire from under the throne-platform (10.2, 7). And while it is true that in his vision Ezekiel sees the Divine Presence exiting the city (Ezek 11.23), this is not an argument that Yhwh is "abandoning" his city and temple so that they may be destroyed. Rather, the vision depicts Yhwh leaving the temple and city after coming in order to destroy them himself. The focal point of the vision is the destruction scene in which Yhwh calls for slaughter to begin in the temple and move throughout the city (Ezek 9.1–7), a scene which causes the prophet to ask whether Yhwh is destroying the whole remnant of Israel (9.8). This is consistent with other statements in the book where the destruction of city and temple is attributed to Yhwh himself (Ezek 14.21; 24.21). Finally, the book of Ezekiel overtly interprets this not as a vision of divine abandonment, but as a vision of divine visitation for destruction: "like the vision I saw when he came to destroy the city" (Ezek 43.3).

As Ezekiel describes it, the presence of Yhwh cannot be constrained or contained; he is neither limited to the land of Israel, nor is he driven away from it. Ezekiel argues against the claim of the Jerusalemites that Yhwh has forsaken the land (Ezek 8.12; 9.9). He comforts his fellow-exiles by describing his own vision of Yhwh in Babylon (Ezek 1–2), and tells them that Yhwh has been a sanctuary for them in exile (11.16). He argues that Yhwh is present in the land of Israel even when Edom thinks that it has been abandoned and is ripe for the plucking: "You said, 'The two nations and two lands will be mine, and we will possess it!'—*even though I was there*" (Ezek 35.10; cf. v. 12). The hope Ezekiel offers his audience is a vision of a restored temple, a permanent physical dwelling place for Yhwh in the midst of his people (Ezek 37.26–28; 43.7, 9). It is fitting, then, that the last verse in the book describes a restored city for Yhwh's people, a city which is named "Yhwh is There" (Ezek 48.35).

3. Ezekiel's depiction of the land

As one might expect from a book written to address the concerns of deportees, the land of Israel figures prominently in the arguments of the book of Ezekiel. Given the way in which the prophet talks about it, the reader might justifiably conclude that the land can actually be understood as a character in the story. It is referred to not only by the term "land [of Israel]," but also by the uniquely Ezekielian locution "mountains of Israel" (seventeen times). In this section, I will discuss four characterizations of the land: the land as offender, as aggressor, as victim, and as participant in the people's restoration.

a. The land as offender

By synecdoche, the inhabitants of places may be referred to by using the name of the place itself (e.g., "Jerusalem" for the inhabitants of Jerusalem). This takes an unusual form when Ezekiel accuses the "mountains of Israel" themselves for the illicit worship practices which the people are doing on the mountains (Ezek 6.1–7; cf. "eating on the mountains," 18.6, 11, 15; 22.9). Ezekiel is borrowing the language of Lev 26.30 for his statements in Ezek 6.1–7, which creates an incongruous result: the mountains that he is addressing have not only "high places, altars, incense altars, and idols," but also the "bones" (v. 5b) and "dwelling places" (v. 6) of the human referents of Lev 26. This incongruity was repaired by an insertion in MT Ezek 6.5a ("I will put the corpses of the sons of Israel before their idols"), which introduces an explicitly human referent also taken from Lev 26.30. The book goes even further in anthropomorphizing the land when it accuses the "mountains of Israel" of "causing your nation to stumble" (Ezek 36.15)—again, a reference to illicit worship practices on the mountains. The land itself is said to contain or possess "detestable things and abominations" (Ezek 11.18) that will be removed in the future. In other passages, the land is simply the locus of wicked activity: "the land is full of judicial murder, and the city is full of violence" (Ezek 7.23).

b. The land as aggressor

In Ezek 36.13, the "mountains of Israel" (cf. v. 1) are depicted as an aggressor: "They are saying to you, 'You devour humans, and you bereave your own nation!'" This passage is part of a larger argument in Ezek 36 that moves from problem (defilement of the land, deportation of its inhabitants) to solution (fertility of the land, restoration of its inhabitants). According to the priestly ideology of the book, the Israelites have defiled the land with their practices (Ezek 36.17–18), and have been exiled as a result (v. 19; cf. Lev 18.25–28). Verse 13 makes a similar argument, but anthropomorphizes the land to claim that it has actually eaten its own inhabitants and bereaved its nation of children. The latter locution is a modification of Ezek 5.17; 14.15, which states that "wild animals will bereave" the people as a punishment; this is an allusion to Lev 26.22. The former locution resembles Num 13.32, where those who returned from spying out the land of Canaan report that it is "a land that devours its inhabitants."

c. The land as victim

The land of Israel is depicted as a victim of three different parties in the book. First, it is a victim of the nations, who gloat over its devastation. Those who are singled out for their mockery of the land include Ammon (Ezek 25.3, 6), Edom (35.11–12, 15), and simply "the nations" (36.3, 4, 6). But the nations' hostility is not just expressed verbally; the book also accuses them of physically victimizing the land by "possessing" it, making it "desolate," "crushing" it, and "plundering" it (Ezek 35.10; 36.2–5). Second, the land has been victimized by the Israelites themselves: they "defiled" it with their bloodshed and idolatry (Ezek 36.17–18). As I have noted before, this is a particularly priestly conception, attested also in Lev 18.24–25 (which warns against practices ascribed to the Canaanites because these actually "defile" the land itself, causing it to vomit out its inhabitants) and Num 35.33–34 (which warns that bloodshed "pollutes" and "defiles" the land itself). In Ezek 24.7, the prophet borrows the priestly language of Lev 17.13 (mandating that shed animal blood be "poured out and covered with dirt") in order to accuse Israel of shedding *human* blood: they have not even attempted to hide it (by "pouring it out and covering it with dirt"), but have blatantly exposed it. Third, the land of Israel is described as victimized by Yhwh: by punishing its inhabitants, Yhwh has actually devastated the land. For example, Yhwh warns that he will "start a forest fire" to burn the land from south to north (Ezek 21.2-4 [ET Ezek 20.46-48]). In an oracle addressed to the "mountains of Israel," Yhwh speaks to the "mountains, hills, ravines, and valleys" and warns "I am bringing a sword upon you"; the result is that "the cities will be waste and the high places will be desolate" (Ezek 6.3, 6). This language of "desolation" (*šmm* and its cognates) and "waste" (*ḥrb* and its cognates) is used throughout the book (Ezek 6.14; 12.19-20; 15.8) to describe what Yhwh does to the land. Ezekiel claims that the land that is now a "waste" after the destruction (Ezek 33.27) will become even more "waste and desolate" (vv. 28-29) in order to punish those who remain in the land and lay claim to it (vv. 24-26). These locutions are derived from Lev 26.31-33, which is the source of other language used by Ezekiel to describe Yhwh's actions against the land. For example, in Ezek 14.12-21, Yhwh will take action against an initially unspecified "land" (revealed in v. 21 to be Israel) by "breaking its staff of bread," "cutting off humans and animals from it," sending "wild animals" who "bereave" the land so that it becomes "desolate," "bringing a sword on it," and "sending a plague against it"—all locutions taken from Lev 26.22, 25, 26.

d. The land as participant in the people's restoration

Part of the book's vision of hope is that the "waste and desolate" land of Israel will be restored so that the exiled people can return and live on it. In Ezek 11.18, the restored people themselves will "remove the detestable things and abominations" from the land. The restoration of land is presumed in Ezek 28.25-26, where the people are "living in safety" and "building houses and planting vineyards." It is also presumed in Ezek 34.13-14, where Yhwh will care for his people like a shepherd cares for his flock, feeding them in a "good pasture" on the "mountains of Israel." But it is in Ezek 34 and 36 that we see the most extravagant descriptions of a restored land. In Ezek 34.25–29, the restoration language is largely taken from material in Lev 26, and in some cases there are reversals of the ways in which the land was previously victimized: Yhwh will "remove wild animals from the land" (Ezek 34.25; cf. Lev 26.6; reversing Ezek 5.17; 14.15, 21; cf. Lev 26.22); the people will "live securely" (Ezek 34.25, 28; cf. Lev 25.18–19; 26.5); Yhwh will send "rain in its time" (Ezek 34.26; cf. Lev 26.4); "the tree of the field will yield its produce, and the land will yield its fruit" (Ezek 34.27; cf. Lev 26.4, 20); Yhwh will "break the bars of their yoke" so that they will not be "enslaved" (Ezek 34.27; cf. Lev 26.13); there will be "no one who terrifies" (Ezek 34.28; cf. Lev 26.6); there will be no famine (Ezek 34.29; reversing 5.12, 16–17; 7.15; 14.21); and the people will not experience the "insults of the nations" (Ezek 34.29, cf. 36.6, 15). The fate of the "waste and desolate" land described in Ezek 6.3, 6 is explicitly reversed in Ezek 36.4–6, and in the following verses (vv. 8–10, 33–36) its fertility is described in great detail. Yhwh himself speaks to the "mountains of Israel" and tells them, "I am for you, and I will turn to you.... I will treat you better than before" (Ezek 36.9, 11). The description of a restored land continues in Ezek 40–48, where (as I noted in Chapter 1) we see images of the water of life and trees of life used to depict fecundity and healing spreading throughout the land of Israel (Ezek 47.1–12). Finally, when Yhwh destroys Gog and his armies, the people will use the weapons of the dead for firewood rather than deforesting the land (Ezek 39.10), and will bury the slain so that the land may be "cleansed" (Ezek 39.12–15).

4. Ezekiel's depiction of the temple

If the book of Ezekiel argues that the presence of Yhwh is not constrained, and that it may be experienced even in exile, what is the importance of the temple? It is of course true that Ezekiel the prophet is described as a priest, and we might therefore expect him to express sentiments about the temple. But the statements about the temple in the book are not mere expressions of nostalgia for something that was lost. Rather, they represent yet another example of Ezekiel's attempts to solve the problems of the past and create a future beyond exile for his community.

a. The nature and function of the temple

The Jerusalem temple was understood as one place where Yhwh's presence could be localized: it was his "house," the place where he lived among his people and where they had access to him (Ezek 37.26-27). Insofar as Yhwh was conceived of as a king, the temple could be described as the place of his "throne" (Ezek 43.7). The temple was the earthly analogue of Yhwh's heavenly temple/palace, and its architecture embodied cosmic symbolism (Sweeney 2005: 141-42). Cosmic order (which included moral order) was maintained and celebrated at the temple when purification rituals were observed (Ezek 45.18-20) and when offerings were brought to Yhwh (Ezek 20.40). Moreover, the location of the temple in Jerusalem was linked to political realities; the choice of Zion as Yhwh's dwelling place was linked with traditions about the election of David (cf. Pss 78.68-70; 122.1-5; 132.10-18). As we will see below, Ezekiel creatively modifies some of these conceptions. Most notably, he reworks the relationship between the temple and the king, and omits any mention of Yhwh's heavenly throne in favor of a hope for his permanent presence in an earthly temple (Kasher 1998).

b. Correcting the damage

When the city of Jerusalem was sacked in 587 BCE, the temple was destroyed (cf. 2 Kgs 25.9, 13-17; Pss 74.3-7; 79.1). But from the perspective of Ezekiel, the crucial damage had occurred even before the physical destruction, a damage which is depicted in the guided tour of the "abominations" taking place in the temple (Ezek 8). The book describes the Jerusalem temple as being both profaned (*ḥll*; i.e., rendered common or non-holy) and defiled (*ṭmʾ*; i.e., rendered ritually unclean). According to Ezekiel, the temple was profaned by invading strangers (Ezek 7.21, 22; cf. 25.3), by Israel's practices (23.39; 44.7), and by Yhwh himself (24.21), to whom its destruction is ultimately attributed. It was defiled by Israel's abominable practices (Ezek 5.11; 23.38), and also by the slaughter of the citizens of Jerusalem within its precincts (9.7).

The loss of the temple and its cult would have had profound implications for how the exiles conceptualized their relationship to the deity. Any traditions of the election and inviolability of Zion would naturally have been shattered. And while the promise of Yhwh's presence in exile (Ezek 11.16) would have been a comfort, the lack of traditional conceptual structures (e.g., sacred space, sacred time) for accessing that presence would have presented a problem. How could the people present sacrifices and offerings in the absence of a ritually appropriate place? And even if a functional cult could be restored, Ezekiel believes that the people's offerings will not be acceptable until they themselves are transformed and back in the land. Without such a transformation, there would be nothing to prevent the repetition of past problems and the resulting damage to Yhwh's name (Ezek 20.39; 43.7-8). This explains why the two passages in Ezek 1–39 that look forward to a restored cult and Yhwh's permanent presence with his people (Ezek 20.40; 37.26-28) both emphasize the transformation and cleansing of the people (Ezek 20.43; 37.23).

While the hope for a transformed temple and cult is touched on briefly in these passages, they do not describe in detail what a transformed cult would look like. They simply hope for a day when proper offerings will be accepted in the land of Israel and Yhwh will dwell in the midst of his people forever. But given the abuses to the temple and cult described above—not to mention their destruction—it is clear that the implementation of a transformed cult would of necessity include changes with far-reaching consequences. And it is not surprising that the description of these consequences is left until the end of the book, until after the description of the people's transformation. Indeed, given Ezekiel's emphasis on permanent solutions, how could it be otherwise? Conversely, for Yhwh to be described as in the midst of his people would demonstrate that they have indeed been purified, and that the problem of the defiled temple has been remedied. The material in Ezek 40–48, then, is not a mere appendage to the book; it is practically demanded as the description of a solution to the problems mentioned earlier.

c. The function of Ezek 40–48 in the book

The material in Ezek 40–48 is presented as what is seen by and told to the prophet in a vision, in a guided tour of a temple compound on "a very high mountain" (Ezek 40.1-2), though this tour is occasionally interrupted. There are two significant inclusios in this material, the first bracketing chs. 40–42 by referencing the wall around the temple compound (Ezek 40.5 // 42.20), and the second bracketing chs. 40–48 as a whole by referencing the city on the mountain (Ezek 40.2 // 48.35). And while these chapters are composite and likely to contain later redactional supplementation, they are well-integrated into the book: we see the familiar first-person narration and dating convention (Ezek 40.1), the prophet is addressed as "son of man" (40.4; 43.7, 10, 18; 44.5; 47.6), and the earlier vision reports of Ezek 1–3 and 8–11 are referenced (43.2-4).

The vision moves from a description of the temple compound (Ezek 40–42, moving from outside inward) to a description of the land allotments on the mountain (45.1-8, for Yhwh and the priests, for the Levites, for the city, for the prince) to a description of the land (47.13-48.35, moving from its outer borders to its inner tribal land allotments to the city in the middle). These spatial descriptions are broken up by a vision of the Glory of Yhwh entering the sanctuary (Ezek 43), by regulations (largely concerning cult personnel and festival portions, Ezek 44–46), and by a description of the life-giving waters proceeding from the temple (Ezek 47.1-12). These units (which in some cases may at first glance seem quite disparate) are related to each other by their pronounced concern for how access to sacred space is controlled. For example, the temple compound is described in terms of its walls, gates, and courts, with particular emphasis on its outer and inner gates (Ezek 40–42). The description of the sanctuary as Yhwh's permanent dwelling contains a polemic against corrupted boundary conditions (43.7–9), and Yhwh's entry into the sanctuary creates new boundary conditions (44.1–3). The polemic against the Levites and the regulations for Levites and Zadokite priests are explicitly related to issues of access and boundary conditions (44.6–9, 13, 15–17, 19). The descriptions of the land and its allotments are obviously marked by the language of borders and boundaries (45.1–8; 47.13–48.35). Even the laws about festivals and sacrificial portions are described with reference to how the prince and people are allowed to enter and move about the temple court (45.2–3, 8–10, 12), and the flow of life-giving water proceeding from the temple is carefully mapped out (47.1–12). The significance of this emphasis on space will be discussed further below.

The genre of Ezek 40–48 is unmistakably that of a vision report: these chapters are explicitly introduced as a "vision" (Ezek 40:2; cf. 43:3), use terminology such as "I saw" (Ezek 41:8; 43:3; 44:3), "show/be shown" (Ezek 40:4), and "see with your eyes" (Ezek 40:4; 44:5), and are presented as a first-person report of what the prophet saw and heard. But as I noted in Chapter 1, this genre designation is somewhat complicated by the presence of four features that are not attested in earlier visionary literature: the presence of cosmic-mythic imagery, the presence of a heavenly interpreter/guide figure, the highly detailed description of sacred space, and the embedding of legal material. Each of these four innovations is relevant to Ezekiel's exilic audience.

The cosmic-mythic images include the "very high mountain" (Ezek 40.2) and the water of life and trees of life (47.1–12). These are employed to depict the temple as the locus of order, stability, life, and healing. As potent symbols of cosmic order, they challenge Ezekiel's audience to believe in a future in which they might again experience the presence of Yhwh in their midst.

The appearance of the heavenly interpreter/guide figure in Ezek 40–48 comes as a surprise because Yhwh himself filled this role in the earlier vision reports of the book (Ezek 8; 37). This is also how we see YHWH depicted in the vision reports in Jer 1 and Amos 7–9. So why the innovation? As Rimmon Kasher (1998: 194–96, 202) has argued, the fact that Ezek 43.1–9 presents YHWH as permanently in his sanctuary, never to depart (cf. 44.2), requires that another entity serve as a guide for Ezekiel the visionary. This is part of Ezekiel's argument that YHWH will reside among his people forever (Ezek 37.26, 28)—a hope for the future that goes significantly beyond his assessment of the current situation (Ezek 11.16), comforting though it may be.

The highly detailed description of sacred space in Ezek 40–48 is Ezekiel's response to past abuses to sanctity. Kalinda Rose Stevenson (1996: 19) notes that "the concern here is not the arrangement and construction of structures, but the spaces defined by the structures. From this perspective, separation of spaces is the real issue." We see this concern about space explicitly voiced in Ezek 42.20, where it is said that the function of the temple complex wall is to "make a separation between the holy and the common." We see it in the accusations that Israel violated sacred space and the sanctity of YHWH's name when they juxtaposed their own structures (royal funerary steles, associated with the cult of the dead?) next to the temple (Ezek 43.7–8), and allowed foreigners in the sanctuary (44.7). We see it in the fact that the temple complex has been separated from the city (40.2; 45.1–6) and from the prince's land allotment (45.7). We see it in the statement that Ezekiel is to describe the temple so that Israel may "measure the proportion" (43.10). We see the concern about space in the regulations governing movement and access, and in how these regulations differentiate between Zadokite priests, Levites, and laity (42.14; 44.2–3, 9, 13, 15; 46.2–3, 9–10). Finally, we see in these descriptions the principle of "graded holiness": namely, that there are adjacent zones of space that increase in sanctity. For example, the central land allotment 25,000 cubits by 20,000 cubits) is called "the holy allotment" (Ezek 48.10a, 13), but the smaller section of this in which the sanctuary is set is described as "most holy" (43:12; 45:3; 48.10b–12). But there are gradations in sanctity even within this area, between the inner and outer courts of the temple—gradations that require the priests to change clothes (44.17-19) when moving between them. These zones of increasing sanctity within the temple complex are set on three different levels and accessed by three sets of stairways: the first stairway is in the outer gates leading into the outer court (40.6, 22, 26), the second is in the inner gates leading into the inner court (40.31, 34, 37), and the third leads up to the sanctuary itself (40.49). The inner room of the sanctuary is, of course, the "most holy place" (41.4). These descriptions of space confront the reader as implicit accusations of past failings and as a vision of what holy temple service would ideally look like.

What can we say about the legal material embedded in Ezek 40-48? First, the material is obviously not a comprehensive law collection. A comparison to other legal corpora reveals many missing elements: the Decalogue is not embedded (as it is in Deuteronomy), nor is there anything analogous to the Decalogue; there are no laws regulating damages, slavery, or the treatment of the poor and needy; there are no laws that define crime or discuss its punishment; there are no laws about clean and unclean animals. Second, Ezekiel makes no attempt to provide rationales for the traditional observances (e.g., Sabbath; Passover) that he includes in his regulations; their meaning and importance are presumed (unlike what we see in Exod 23.15; 31.17; Lev 23.43; Deut 5.15; 16.1, 3). Third, the wording of many of the laws in Ezek 40-48 is similar to or even identical with the wording of certain laws in the Pentateuch: Ezek 44.17-19 (// Exod 28.42 + Lev 16.4, 23); Ezek 44.20 (// Lev 21.5); Ezek 44.21 (// Lev 10.9); Ezek 44.22 (// Lev 21.13-15); Ezek 44.23 (// Lev 10.10); Ezek 44.25 (// Lev 21.1-4); Ezek 44.28 (// Num 18.20); Ezek 44.29 (// Num 18.9, 11, 13, 14 + 15.21); Ezek 44.31 (// Lev 22.8); Ezek 46.7 (// Lev 5.11; 14.21, 22, 30-32; 27.8; Num 6.21); Ezek 47.22 (// Lev 19.34; 25.45-46). This should not come as a surprise; collections of laws in the biblical text often drew on earlier laws (cf. Deuteronomy's use of the Covenant Code) and grew by a process of supplementation (note the overlap between Lev 18 and 20, and the relationship of H to P). The literary dependence of Ezek 40-48 on earlier law collections is indicated, though it is probably the case that these legal collections were still in a process of growth and had not yet reached the form we now have in the Pentateuch. Fourth, the laws of Ezek 40–48 display some intriguing differences when compared to other law collections. To give just two examples: the purification ritual described in Ezek 45.18–20 is quite different from what we see in Lev 16, and the portions for the New Moon festival in Ezek 46.6–7 differ from what we see in Num 28.11–13.

If the laws of Ezek 40–48 are not a comprehensive attempt at legislation, if they are drawing on earlier law collections, and if they differ in some cases from these earlier laws, it would seem to be the case that the laws of Ezek 40–48 have been deliberately selected, and in some cases represent deliberate modifications. What then is the principle of selection and modification? According to Kasher (1998), it lies in Ezekiel's belief that Yhwh's proper place is in the sanctuary and that he will permanently reside there (Ezek 43.7). This belief is expressed in the following laws: the outer east gate shall be permanently shut because Yhwh has passed through it, never to leave again (44.1–2). There is no high priest, and no ritual that would require a high priest to enter the sanctuary, because the Glory of Yhwh is inside (43.4–5; see Exod 40.35; 1 Kgs 8.11, where the Glory prevents priestly access to the sanctuary). The purification ritual that used to take place in the inner sanctum is now moved outside to the altar in the inner court (Ezek 45.18–20). The temple has been emptied of all furniture (Ark; lampstand) requiring human maintenance; all that remains is a bare wooden altar/table (41.22), with no reference to burning incense or laying bread on it. And perhaps the restoration of the Ark would in any case have been superfluous or inappropriate given Yhwh's now-permanent presence, and the Ark's past associations with mobility (e.g., Num 10.33–36; Josh 3.3; 1 Sam 4.3–4, 11; 14.18). Another modification is that the altar of burnt offering must have steps (Ezek 43.17; *contra* Exod 20.26), which— according to Ezekiel's principle that space of greater sanctity is set higher than its surroundings—marks it as special. The concern for modesty prompting the law in Exod 20.26 is not an issue, because according to Ezekiel's vision the laity are no longer allowed to approach the altar (cf. Ezek 44.19; 46.3).

The other motivation for the selection and modification of earlier laws is Ezekiel's conviction that the sanctity of temple and temple service has been damaged. The laws of Ezek 40–48 are therefore fundamentally *responses* to past abuses. This explains the obsessive concern with sacred space and the emphasis on boundaries, borders, and the control of access (cf. Ganzel and Holtz 2014). It explains why Ezekiel accuses the princes of Israel of oppression and unjust appropriation (Ezek 45.8b-9), and surrounds this accusation with laws about land allotment (45.7–8a) and weights and measures (45.10–12). He accuses the people and kings of defiling the temple by the construction of funerary steles (43.7–9), and in response separates the sanctuary from the city and from royal land allotments (45.1–7). He accuses Israel of allowing foreigners to profane the temple by entering it (44.7–8), and accuses the Levites of "going astray after idols" (44.10, 12). It is difficult to determine what incident Ezekiel is referring to here (see the discussion in Cook 1995), but whatever the case, he responds to these abuses by excluding foreigners from the temple (44.9) and by restricting the Levites from "coming near to Yhwh to serve as priest, or coming near to my sacred donations, to the most holy things" (44.13). These latter two tasks are given to the Zadokite priests alone (44.15–16). While other law corpora make distinctions between priests of different status—for example, the more prominent priest must maintain his hair (Lev 21.10) and not marry a widow (Lev 21.14)— Ezekiel applies these stricter laws to all Zadokite priests (Ezek 44.20, 22, though they may marry the widow of a priest). Just as Ezekiel accused the priests earlier in the book of failing to differentiate between clean and unclean, sacred and profane (Ezek 22.26), he now repeats this language to remind them that this is their duty (Ezek 44.23).

The relationship between temple and state has also been reconfigured: the city is now separate from the temple and is not called "Jerusalem" (Ezek 40.2; 48.35), and the temple mount is not referred to as "Zion" (40.2). The role of the prince with respect to temple and cult is rigidly specified: the prince is no longer the patron of the temple building, but only of offerings (Ezek 45.17), and his movements in sacred space are limited and choreographed (44.3; 45.2, 8–10). These laws seem to represent an attempt to draw on certain advantages of royal sponsorship without the disadvantages and abuses of the past (Levenson 1976: 33, 57–69). And the nation itself has been spatially reconfigured: as Block (1998: 722–24) points out, the organization of tribal land in Ezek 47–48 not only reflects a realization of the hope for a unified north and south (cf. 37.15–22), but also "repudiates the pragmatically centralized administration of the monarchy" and is "based on a paradigm of tribal parity" (cf. 47.13–14)—all responses to problems in the past. To sum up: Ezekiel is responding to past abuses by collecting and shaping laws that increase and protect sanctity (Stevenson 1996: xxiv). He does this out of the conviction that Yhwh intends to permanently dwell in his sanctuary, among his people.

What then is the function of Ezek 40–48? One thing that it is not is an oracular prediction. This is ruled out by the genre, and by the conditional language in Ezek 43.11. And any attempt to determine what it is meant to accomplish must take the following features into account: on the one hand, we find the familiar priestly language of "observing and doing" (Ezek 43.11); on the other, we see no command to build the temple complex. There are some details that could be implemented if there were a temple (e.g., altar purification), but there are other details that would be impossible to implement (e.g., the very high mountain; the water of life; the trees of life). There are structures described that could in theory be built, but there is an absence of information (e.g., vertical dimensions) in the text that would allow it to serve as a blueprint for construction. There are some regulations that are realistic, such as the prescriptions for festivals; but other regulations seem to be purely idealistic, such as the redrawing of tribal boundaries, the regulations for the prince, and the apparent political autonomy of the land of Israel.

Not surprisingly, there is little agreement regarding the purpose of Ezek 40–48. Some have understood these chapters as a building plan with functional laws to be implemented. For example, Cooke (1936:

425) remarks that Ezekiel "is the most practical of reformers, and not only a prophet, but a priest, deeply concerned with the organization of religion in the community of the future. We can imagine him poring over architectural plans and regulations for worship, when he fell into an ecstasy . . ." Others believe these chapters to have a mixed function. Tuell (1996) argues that the earliest layer of Ezek 40–48 was a literary report of a heavenly ascent that functions as "verbal icon": Ezekiel describes his experience of the divine presence so that his community can vicariously experience Yhwh's presence apart from an earthly temple by reading a text. This vision report was later supplemented with practical legal material. Joyce (2007) argues that Ezek 40–42 alone is a report of a heavenly ascent, one in which the envisioned heavenly temple functions as a blueprint for a physical building and practical restoration program found in the subsequent chapters. According to Strong (2012: 203), Ezekiel's vision "was to serve as 1) a first installment of the future, earthly temple; and 2) as an archived document for theological study by the future community, not for the physical construction of a future temple, but for the theological foundation of a future community of faith organized around a temple." Still others believe that these chapters are not intended to serve as practical legislation, a blueprint, or a building plan. Kasher (1998: 194, 205) speaks of the "utopian world" of these chapters, and claims that "the temple is a finished creation of the Deity, and the Israelites most probably have no part in its erection." The intended effects of these chapters would therefore be social and psychological/spiritual in nature. Thus Stevenson (1996: 163) argues that these chapters are "territorial rhetoric, produced in the context of the Babylonian exile to restructure the society of Israel by asserting Yhwh's territorial claim as the only King of Israel." The point is not whether the laws of Ezek 40–48 could be implemented, or whether the temple complex could be built, but what kind of people could be created by reading and reflecting on these chapters. Such a function might be indicated by Ezek 43.10, which suggests that the description of the temple should produce shame in Ezekiel's audience. But whatever the proposal for the function of these

chapters, all of the authors mentioned above agree that Ezekiel is attempting to provide hope for his exilic community by envisioning future transformation.

Further reading

For a discussion of the ethics of Ezekiel, see Mein (2001b). For a discussion of how Israel and God are depicted in Ezekiel, see Odell and Strong (2000); Joyce and Rom-Shiloni (2015). For a survey of the major themes and issues in Ezek 40–48, see Joyce (2005).

4

From Problem to Solution

Milton's oft-quoted purpose for writing *Paradise Lost* was to "assert Eternal Providence, and justify the ways of God to men." As Henry McKeating (1993: 74–75) notes, this statement captures a good deal of what the book of Ezekiel is attempting to do. We have only to think of the repeated claims that "you/they will know that I am Yhwh," or the description of the motivation for Yhwh's actions as "for the sake of my name." But it is crucial to note the context in which these assertions and justifications occur. The book of Ezekiel is written for an audience that has undergone the trauma of forced deportation, and the prophet is simultaneously attempting to explain the exiles' condition and to envision hope for their future.

In the previous chapter, I compared Ezekiel's task to a juggling act in which the prophet had to explain the exile by convincing his contemporaries of their guilt, justify Yhwh's involvement in exile, prevent a despair that could lead to fatalism, decry the temptation to assimilate, and provide some reason for his audience to believe that they might survive as the people of Yhwh. To truly grasp the aims of the book, we must recognize its argumentative nature, and the degree to which it is attempting to solve the problems faced by the exiles. In this chapter I will discuss how the book of Ezekiel presents solutions to these problems. In some cases, the problems are explicitly presented as such and then addressed (e.g., the problem of Israel's exile; the problem of Israel's inability to obey). In other cases, the problems to be solved are addressed without being overtly stated as problems (e.g., the question of why the exile happened). I have divided these problems into two categories: problems that were experienced by the exiles, and problems that were caused by (or even inherent in) the exiles. As we can see, one of the challenges facing the prophet was the task of convincing his audience to adopt Yhwh's perspective on what constituted a problem to be solved.

1. Problems experienced by the people

a. Forced deportation from Israel and resettlement in Babylon

From the exiles' perspective, the most significant problem would undoubtedly have been their forced displacement from Israel and resettlement in Babylon. They would have experienced feelings of helplessness and shame, coupled with the loss of their former way of life, their social and kinship connections, and their religious institutions. They would have had no reason to believe that they would ever return, and despair at the inevitable loss of national identity would have made assimilation the logical course of action. What could explain why these things had happened to them? When faced with this kind of traumatic experience, humans demand answers—and if no answer is readily available, they will manufacture one (as the exiles are clearly doing in Ezek 18.2). Curiously, the question "Why did the exile occur?" or "Why has all this this happened to us?" is never explicitly raised in the book of Ezekiel (as it is in e.g. Deut 29.24–28; 1 Kgs 9.8–9; Jer 5.19; 13.22; 16.10–13; 22.8–9; Ps 74.1). Nevertheless, the problem of the exile—and the question of the rationale for the exile—are both dealt with in the book, and we see the prophet countering his contemporaries' attempts at explaining their condition with an explanation of his own. Ezekiel responds to the problem of exile with two strategies: first, he explains and justifies the exile; second, he offers hope for the end of exile.

Ezekiel lays the ground for his explanation by building an exilic perspective into the very structure of the book: the dating formulas that span the storyline are calculated from the deportation of 597 BCE (Ezek 1.2; 8.1; etc.). Moreover, the prophet Ezekiel is identified as an exile (Ezek 1.1; cf. "our exile," 33.21; 40.1), and he is commissioned to speak to his fellow-exiles (3.11; cf. 3.15; 11.25). The creation of an exilic perspective in which the prophet includes himself allows the exilic reader to more closely identify with the arguments of the book.

Places where the book of Ezekiel directly addresses the question of why the exile occurred include the following:

> ... I made them go far off among the nations, and I scattered them among the lands
>
> (Ezek 11.16a)

> Also, I swore to them in the wilderness to scatter them among the nations and to disperse them among the lands, because they did not do my ordinances, and they rejected my statutes and profaned my Sabbaths, and their eyes went after the idols of their ancestors.
>
> (Ezek 20.23–24)

> When the house of Israel was living in their land, they defiled it with their ways and their deeds ... so I poured out my wrath on them ... and I scattered them among the nations, and they were dispersed among the lands. According to their ways and their deeds I judged them.
>
> (Ezek 36.17–19)

> And the nations will know that the house of Israel went into exile because of their iniquity, because they acted unfaithfully against me; so I hid my face from them, and gave them into the hand of their enemies, and all of them fell by the sword.
>
> (Ezek 39.23; cf. vv. 24, 28).

According to the book, Israel was exiled by Yhwh as punishment for unfaithfulness.

These direct explanations of the exile are supported throughout the book by a pervasive attempt to link actions with consequences. This explains the book's heavy emphasis on causality, shown through the numerous occurrences of the word "because" (*y'n*; Ezek 5.7–8, 9, 11; 13.8; 15.8; 16.36–37; 20.15–16; 21.29 [ET v. 24]; 23.35; etc.). It explains the book's emphasis on equivalence in punishment, where Yhwh promises that he will (or did) punish the people "*according to* their/your ways" (Ezek 7.3, 8, 9; 18.30; 24.14; 33.20; 36.19; 39.24), or says that "I will deal with you *just as* you dealt with me" (16.59), or promises that "*just as* I entered into judgment with your ancestors ... so I will enter into judgment with you" (20.36). The linkage of sinful actions with punishment as a consequence explains the use of the idiom "I will place your ways upon your head" (Ezek 9.10; 11.21; 16.43; 17.17; 22.31). This linkage is also emphasized in Yhwh's response (Ezek 8.17-18) to the abominations in the temple described in Ezek 8.3-16, and in Yhwh's response to Ezekiel's question about the destruction of the city (Ezek 9.8-10).

Another way Ezekiel explains the exile by linking actions to consequences is in the way he uses earlier traditional material. The final chapter of the Holiness Code (Lev 17-26) promises blessing for covenant obedience (Lev 26.3-13; cf. v. 3, "if you walk in my statutes ...") and punishments for disobedience (Lev 26.14-39; cf. v. 14, "but if you do not obey me..."). When Ezekiel transforms the Holiness Code's laws into accusations and its conditional punishments into statements of judgment, he takes advantage of a known pattern that already linked actions with consequences and applies it to Israel's current situation. Thus the accusations of Ezek 5.5-7, 11 (which use the language of Lev 26.3, 14) are followed quite naturally by the judgments of Ezek 5.10-17 (which repeat the punishments of Lev 26.22, 25, 26, 29, 31-33). If the consequence of keeping Yhwh's statutes is "life" (Ezek 18.9; 20.11, 13; 33.15; taken from Lev 18.5), then the converse must also be true.

Ezekiel also creates a linkage of actions and consequences through the way he depicts Jerusalem. Ironically, some earlier commentators were skeptical of the possibility that a prophet living in Babylon would spend so much time addressing Jerusalem in his oracles. They tried to account for this feature of the book by theorizing that Ezekiel actually prophesied in Palestine rather than in Babylon—a theory which, after the rebuttals of Fohrer and Zimmerli, was quickly abandoned (cf. Mein 2001b: 44-48; Renz 1999: 27-38). So how should we explain this seeming obsession with the city of Jerusalem? It is not simply the case that the exiles in Babylon had an emotional attachment to their former city of residence, though they undoubtedly did; the prophet makes a reference to the kinship connections between the exiles and Jerusalemites, and refers to the temple as the "desire of their eyes and delight of their soul" (Ezek 24.21). Nor is Ezekiel's obsession with Jerusalem entirely due to the rhetoric of communal exclusion, in which the Jerusalemites and the exiles are each marginalizing the other and defining themselves as the sole people of Yhwh, the heirs of historic traditions, and the possessors of the land—though this was in fact occurring (cf. Ezek 11.14–21; 33.23–29). Rather, the primary function of the way Jerusalem is depicted in the book is to serve as a paradigm for the exiles and explain their condition.

Thomas Renz (1999: 93) has explained the numerous speeches addressing Jerusalem with reference to Ezekiel's rhetorical goals:

> First, the readers are identified with the Jerusalemites as part of a long history of rebellion against Yahweh.... Secondly, the readers are brought into the process of dissociating themselves from Jerusalem while at the same time realising their own rebelliousness ... It is thus a matter of making the exiles realise the nature of their association with the Jerusalemites and engaging them in a process of dissociation from the Jerusalemites at the same time.

The readers are invited to "identify with" Yhwh's judgment of Jerusalem, because this is a reflection on their own actions: "to accept Yahweh's verdict implies a judgement on the community's present attitudes and behavior" (Renz 1999: 41, 57, 131). While it is true that Ezekiel envisions complete destruction for Jerusalem and the possibility of hope for the exiles, the linkage of actions and consequences is the same for both communities. To explain the fall of Jerusalem as the consequence of rebellious actions is to explain the exiles' own condition as the consequences of their rebellious actions. After all, they are accused of the same sins—idolatry (Ezek 8; 14.1–3; 20.30, 39) and rebellion (Ezek 5.5–6; 12.2–3).

Ezekiel's attempt to explain the exile through the linkage of actions with consequences, then, explains why he spends so much time accusing

Jerusalem, judging Jerusalem, and justifying the fall of Jerusalem. It explains the compositional linkages in the book (Ezek 24.1–2, 24, 25–27; 33.21–22) that highlight the fall of the city. It explains why Ezekiel's performance of the siege of Jerusalem was a "sign for the house of Israel" (Ezek 4.3). This was not a sign about the mere fact of Jerusalem's imminent destruction, but as Renz (1999: 41) argues, a sign about its *significance*; the following interpretation (Ezek 5.5–8) of the sign act links the destruction of Jerusalem to the sins of its inhabitants. It explains why Ezekiel's fellow-exiles will "know that I am Yhwh" when the Jerusalemites are slain (Ezek 6.13), why Ezekiel tells his fellow-exiles (Ezek 11.25) his vision of the abominations in and destruction of the city (Ezek 8–10), and why Ezekiel is told to act out the impending deportation of Jerusalem's citizens as a "sign" for his rebellious contemporaries so that they might "see" (Ezek 12.1–11).

The linkage of Jerusalem's actions with the consequences of behavior is forcefully presented as a paradigm for the exiles in Ezek 14:

> Yet behold, survivors will be left over in it, sons and daughters who will be brought out; behold, they will go out to you, and you will see their ways and their deeds, and you will be comforted because of the disaster which I brought upon Jerusalem—namely, all which I brought upon it; and they will comfort you when you see their ways and their deeds, and you will know that not without cause did I do all which I did in it—utterance of Lord Yhwh.
>
> (Ezek 14.22–23)

These verses are clearly set off from the previous section (vv. 12–21), which forms a cohesive unit. But how are vv. 22–23 to be related to their context? The fact that these verses mention "survivors" is not a statement of hope or a reversal of the proclamation of complete disaster in the preceding section; rather, the "survivors" are a *result of* the disaster that has just been described. Nor are these survivors alive because of their righteousness; the preceding verses have just denied that there were any righteous Jerusalemites, going so far as to claim that even if Noah, Daniel, and Job were in the city, they could not save anyone. The survivors, then, serve only as witnesses to the disaster. But how are they a "comfort" to the exiles? As Block (1997: 451–52) observes, the "comfort" in question is the relief of the agonizing uncertainties the exiles would have experienced upon hearing the news of the fall of Yhwh's chosen city: was it a purely random event, or was there a deeper purpose at work? If it was Yhwh who destroyed his own city, was it really deserved? Ezekiel responds to these uncertainties by explaining why the city fell, forging an explicit causal connection between "the ways and deeds" of the Jerusalemites and "the disaster which [Yhwh] brought upon Jerusalem." But Ezekiel also justifies Yhwh's actions by claiming that they were not arbitrary and not undeserved: it was "not without cause" that he acted. The paradigmatic function of vv. 22–23 is thus created by the wordplay of the terms "comfort" (*nḥm*) and "without cause" (*ḥnm*).

But it is not enough to simply explain the reasons for the exile. Ezekiel must also offer his community hope for the future, and this is his second strategy for confronting their condition. In Ezek 11.13, the prophet himself voices the question that many of his contemporaries would have been asking: "Ah, Lord Yhwh! Will you bring the remnant of Israel to a complete end?" The answer that follows his question argues that hope lies with the exiles, and that Yhwh would transform them and restore them to the land. And in response to his contemporaries' despair ("Our bones have dried up, and our hope is lost; we are completely cut off," Ezek 37.11), the prophet offers a challenging vision of national restoration by the power of Yhwh's Spirit (Ezek 37.1–14; see Fox 1980). He flatly denies that assimilation is a viable option, and instead argues that Yhwh will assert his kingship and bring the people back as in the exodus from Egypt (Ezek 20.32–38). At numerous points, the book encourages its exilic and diaspora readers to believe that Yhwh will return them to the land (Ezek 11.17; 20.34, 40–43; 34.13; 36.8, 24, 28; 37.12, 14, 21; 39.27–28). The motive for this return is stated in Ezek 36.19–24; 39.25: the condition of exile is damaging to Yhwh's reputation, and he will act publically to glorify himself by bringing the exiles back.

b. Marginalization by the Jerusalemites

Another serious problem faced by the exiles was their marginalization by those who remained in the land (Rom-Shiloni 2013: 2, 139–97). According to earlier Holiness and Deuteronomic traditions (Lev 26.33; Deut 4.26–27), covenant unfaithfulness would result in scattering and death. The Jerusalemites interpreted this to mean that the exiles' displacement from the land implied the loss of covenant relationship with Yhwh. Conversely, the fact that some remained in the land after the deportations of 597 and 587 BCE implied to them that they alone were the people of Yhwh. This explains the Jerusalemites' statement to the exiles: "Go far off from Yhwh; this land has been given to us as a possession!" (Ezek 11.15). It also explains the use of patriarchal traditions by those who remained to claim that the land still belonged to them (Ezek 33.24). Ezekiel counters this marginalization first by assuring his fellow-exiles that Yhwh's presence has indeed been with them (Ezek 11.16), then by asserting that they would return to possess the land (vv. 17–20). For those who remained, however, Ezekiel envisions complete destruction (v. 21). Ezekiel also applies traditional material from the Holiness Code to his own time, arguing that those who do not live by Yhwh's statutes will experience judgment (Ezek 33.25–29; cf. Lev 18.20; 19.16, 26; 26.19, 22, 25, 31–32)—thereby suggesting that those who remained would *not* possess the land. And by describing the land as "desolate and waste" (e.g., Ezek 33.24, 27–29; 36.4; cf. Lev 26.31–33), he effectively depopulates it, making its hoped-for restoration available for the returning exiles alone.

c. Mockery by surrounding nations and ensuing shame

According to Ezekiel, Israel is experiencing shame and humiliation because the surrounding nations are mocking them for their exile and for the fall of Jerusalem (Ezek 16.56–57; 25.3, 6, 8; 35.12, 15a; 36.2–6). The book addresses this problem first by explicitly acknowledging it, then by arguing that Yhwh will punish the surrounding nations for their pride and mockery (Ezek 25.4–5, 7, 9–11; 35.11, 14, 15b; 36.7).

Israel's humiliation will be removed when Yhwh returns them to the land and provides permanent security and fertility (Ezek 28.24-26; 34.25-29; 36.1-15). Finally, the nations will come to know the truth about why Israel was exiled and restored (Ezek 36.36; 39.23-24, 27).

d. Devastation of the land of Israel

The Babylonian invasion would undoubtedly have devastated the land of Israel, but as the first generation of exiles had no reason to believe that they would return, it is difficult to say how problematic the condition of the land was for them. However, given that Ezekiel is trying to convince them that they will return to the land, he believes that the land's devastation is a problem to be solved. Yet this is to some extent a literary problem and solution: Ezekiel has argued that Yhwh's judgment on Israel resulted in the land becoming "waste" and "desolate" (e.g., Ezek 6.3, 6, 14; 12.19-20; 15.8; 33.24, 27-29; 36.4)—a judgment taken from Lev 26.31-33. The book solves the problem of the desolate land by arguing that in the future Yhwh will bring fertility to the land, resulting in rebuilt cities and plentiful crops (Ezek 34.25-31; 36.9-15, 29-30, 33-38)—solutions that are arrived at by reversing the Holiness Code's judgment language and by borrowing its language of blessing (Lev 26.4, 6, 9).

e. Destruction of the Jerusalem temple

Because of deeply entrenched traditions about the election and inviolability of Zion (cf. Mic 3.11b; Ps 46; 48.9 [ET v. 8]; 78.68-70), the destruction of the Jerusalem temple would likely have been a blow to Ezekiel's fellow-exiles. Ezekiel refers to its destruction and hints at the exiles' emotional attachment to the temple in Ezek 7.20-24; 24.21; 25.3. Given Ezekiel's priestly background, one might have imagined that he would have more to say about this; after all, we see poignant laments over the loss of the temple in other texts (e.g., Isa 64.9-11; Ps 74; 79; Lam 1.10; 2.6-7). But for Ezekiel, the temple has already been profaned and defiled by the people's actions, and his references to the temple's destruction are linked to this earlier problem (cf. Ezek 8–9). His hope for a restored cult and temple—a solution he envisions in Ezek 20.40; 37.26-28; 40–46—is therefore as much if not more a response to its defilement as it is to its destruction.

f. Downfall of the Judean monarchy

Another problem to which Ezekiel must respond is the downfall of the Judean monarchy. Just as the destruction of the Jerusalem temple was not merely the loss of a building but also a challenge to religious and political ideology, the downfall of the monarchy was not merely the loss of a king. Israelite notions of kingship were defined in terms of divine adoption and traditions about the election of David, and the downfall of the monarchy constituted a theological crisis (cf. Ps 89). Ezekiel laments the loss of the monarchy in general terms in the two poems in Ezek 19.1-9, 10-14. But he also refers to specific details: the status of King Jehoiachin as a political hostage, taken to Babylon with Ezekiel and his fellow-exiles (Ezek 1.2; 17.3-4, 12); King Zedekiah's foolish political decisions and the dreadful consequences (Ezek 12.8-14; 17.1-21; 21.30-32 [ET vv. 25-27]). The solution to the fallen monarchy is envisioned in Ezek 17.22-24 (in which it is argued that Yhwh, the God who performs reversals, will restore the monarchy) and in Ezek 34.23-24; 37.22, 24-25 (in which it is argued that Yhwh will raise up David to shepherd his people).

g. Historic division between northern and southern Israelite tribes

The reality of a historic division between northern and southern Israelite tribes is acknowledged at several points in the book (e.g., the references to Samaria and Jerusalem in Ezek 16; 23). But this hardly would have been an urgent issue for the exiles. So why does Ezekiel present it as a problem to be solved? It seems that Ezekiel's solution to the pressing problems of the day (the spiritual state of the people, their exilic condition, the loss of national identity) necessitated the solution of some historic problems as well. If there was to be a return and a restoration of national identity (Ezek 37.11-14), then this condition must be maintained. This is most easily accomplished by what is envisioned in Ezek 37.15-25—a single Davidic king ruling over a single nation, with harmony between Ephraim in the north and Judah in the south. The solution presented here fits the strategy of problem-solving elsewhere in the book of Ezekiel: it is not enough to simply remove a problem. Rather, the solution must prevent the problem from ever rising again.

h. Negligent leadership and oppression by the upper class

While Ezekiel sporadically refers to the problems posed by Israel's leaders (idolatry, claiming that Yhwh is not present to see, Ezek 8.10-12; "devising iniquity," 11.1-3; oathbreaking and disastrous political decisions, 17.1-21; bloodshed and dishonest gain, 22.6, 27), this topic is dealt with in a more sustained manner in Ezek 34. Here the "shepherds of Israel" are accused of feeding themselves and neglecting the flock (Ezek 34.2-8), and the "fat sheep" are accused of shoving others and trampling the pasture (Ezek 34.17-19, 21). The solution offered is that Yhwh himself (Ezek 34.11-16) will care for Israel as a shepherd cares for his flock. It appears that an editorial extension to this passage picked up the theme of the Davidic king from Ezek 37 and argued that Yhwh would care for his flock by appointing a Davidic shepherd as his agent (Ezek 34.23-24).

i. Threat of hostile nations

The hostile reaction of surrounding nations to the fall of Jerusalem is well-attested in the book of Ezekiel (Ezek 25.12, 15; 35.1-15; 36.5; cf. Obad 1.10-14). It is therefore not surprising that when the book holds out hope for the exiles' return, it specifies that they will "dwell securely"

(Ezek 28.24–26; 34.25, 28). But as we know from post-exilic writings, the exiles who returned to Israel from Babylon did not often experience the hoped-for security. On the contrary, they were just as much at the mercy of hostile neighbors and powerful empires as they were before (cf. Dan 8, 11; Ezr 4.7–24; Neh 4.7–8; 9.36–37). The material in Ezek 38–39, an editorial extension to the book, confronts this problem. These chapters argue that Yhwh will lure hostile nations (who are led by a mysterious figure named "Gog") into his land in order to make a final end to them, thereby guaranteeing permanent security for his people. Note that while the members of Gog's army (Ezek 38.2–6) bear the names of actual nations, they are employed in a purely schematic way here: they are very distant; they are located in the extreme north, south, and east; they are derived not from any specific historical situation or political condition, but from earlier texts. They therefore represent *all* foes of Israel.

2. Problems caused by and inherent in the people

a. Damage to Yhwh's name

While many of the problems listed above would have been readily acknowledged as such by Ezekiel's contemporaries, the prophet was faced with the challenge of convincing the exiles that their actions had created problems—and even that they themselves were a problem to be solved. One of the most serious problems identified in the book is the damage to the sanctity of Yhwh's name and threat to his reputation. Things that are said to "profane" Yhwh's name include: 1) the misrepresentation of Yhwh and usurpation of his role (Ezek 13.19); 2) the failure by priests to distinguish between clean and unclean, sacred and profane (Ezek 22.26); 3) illicit cult practices and the worship of other gods (Ezek 20.39; 43.7–8); 4) the Israelites' exilic condition, which causes other nations to doubt Yhwh's ability to care for his people (Ezek 36.20–23); and 5) the threat to the existence of Israel posed by hostile nations (Ezek 39.7). In some cases, the solution is judgment, which eliminates the damage to Yhwh's name along with the offender (e.g., Ezek 13.20-23, the women who threaten others; 22.31, the negligent priests; 39.1-6, the hostile nations). But in other cases, a more complex solution is required: Israel's pervasive unfaithfulness must be countered by spiritual transformation and a restored cult (Ezek 20.40-44; 43.7, 9). And the Israelites' exilic condition (which arouses disparaging comments by the nations) must be countered by a public return to the land and a spiritual transformation that solves the apostasy problem which incurred the exile in the first place (Ezek 36.21-32; 39.21-27).

This last argument deserves to be traced in greater detail. In Ezekiel's revisionist history lesson (Ezek 20), Yhwh's initial response to Israel's apostasy was a plan to completely destroy them—a response which he repeatedly abandoned because it would have caused the nations to doubt his ability to care for his people (Ezek 20.8-9, 13-14, 21-22). Yhwh's alternative to destroying his people was to exile them (Ezek 20.23). Ironically, the exile—which was initially presented as a solution in Ezek 20—has now itself become a problem; the Israelites' exilic condition is causing the very same damage to Yhwh's name (Ezek 36.16-20) that their complete destruction would have caused! And it is worth noting how the solution fits the problem: first, the emphasis on the global scope of the damage to Yhwh's reputation ("my holy name ... was profaned among the nations," Ezek 36.21) is provided with an equal emphasis on the global recognition of the solution (Ezek 36.23 "the nations will know that I am Yhwh ... when I show myself holy among you in their eyes"; cf. 20.41; 39.27). The very public damage to Yhwh's reputation is reversed when he returns Israel from exile, thereby publically vindicating his reputation. Second, the problem that caused the exile in the first place (the people's apostasy) is provided with a permanent and radical solution: an ontological transformation that guarantees obedience (Ezek 36.25-27).

b. Damage to sanctity of land and temple

A second problem caused by the people is the damage to the sanctity of the land and the temple. Because it is Yhwh's intention to live among his people, the matter of sacred space becomes an issue of crucial importance. Thus the book of Ezekiel repeatedly highlights the fact that the land of Israel has been defiled because of idolatry (Ezek 36.17–18), violence (Ezek 7.23; 8.17; 12.19), and bloodshed (Ezek 7.23; 9.9; 22.2–4, 6, 9, 12–13, 27; 23.37, 45; 24.6–9; 36.17–18). The solution to this problem has several components: first, the removal of the problem, which is described both in terms of the judgment and removal of the people living on the land (Ezek 7.24; 24.1–14; 36.18–19) and also in terms of the cleansing of the land (Ezek 11.18); and second, the prevention of any future threat to the land by transforming the people and returning them to the land (Ezek 36.24–45, 28–29). Thus the cleansing of the people goes hand in hand with the restoration of the land (Ezek 36.33–36). The damage to the sanctity of the temple is likewise discussed in detail; this damage is the result of idolatry and illicit worship practices (Ezek 5.11; 8.3–18; 23.38–39; 43.7–9; 44.6–8). Here too the solution has multiple components: first, the destruction of the temple and those who worship in it (Ezek 7.21–22; 9.6–7; 24.21); second, the transformation of the people who worship at the temple (Ezek 20.39–41; 37.23), the restoration of the cult (with safeguards to protect its sanctity, Ezek 40–48), and Yhwh's return to his sanctuary, to remain forever (Ezek 37.26–28; 43.7, 9).

c. Rebellious and unfaithful people

The damages mentioned in the previous two sections were caused by Israel's actions, and one might therefore conclude with good reason that Israel's actions are the problem to be solved. But what Ezekiel actually presents as the problem is the *nature* of the people who committed these actions. Ezekiel describes his contemporaries and their ancestors as "rebellious" (Ezek 2.3, 5, 7; 3.26; 5.6; 12.2–3, 9; 20.8; 24.3; 44.6), "unfaithful" (Ezek 14.13; 15.8; 20.27; 39.23, 26), and "stubborn" (Ezek 2.4; 3.7). They commit "abominations" (Ezek 5.9; 6.9, 11; 8.17; 12.16; 16.2; 20.4) and "do not walk in Yhwh's statutes and keep his ordinances" (Ezek 5.6–7; 11.12; 20.13, 21, 24; cf. Lev 18.4–5; 26.3, 14). Their specific offences include worship of other deities (Ezek 5.11; 6.3–6, 9; 8.3–17; 14.3; 16.16–21; 20.8, 30–32), making political alliances with other nations (16.26, 28–29; 17.15; 23.11–21; 29.16), violence and social injustice (7.23; 8.17; 9.9; 12.19; 22.2–13, 25–29; 33.25–26), false prophecy (13.1–10, 17, 22; 22.28), and cultic offences (20.13; 22.8, 26; 23.38).

Ezekiel diagnoses the problem behind these actions as (to use the terminology of Jacqueline Lapsley) the "lack of a moral self." His contemporaries have a "heart of stone" (Ezek 11.19; 36.26), they are unable to "remember" Yhwh's gracious acts in the past (16.22, 43), and they are unable to feel "shame" (16.52) for their actions. Yhwh's initial response is one of judgment: "the person who sins will die" (Ezek 18.20). This explains the extreme language of divine anger and punishment (Ezek 5.8; 8.18; 16.38, 43; 20.23–24; 24.14; 36.17–19). But this response, while just, will not solve the damage to Yhwh's reputation. And while Yhwh would be open to repentance if it occurred (Ezek 18.23), the book offers no reason to believe that Israel will be either willing or able to repent. According to Ezekiel, the only solution is for Yhwh to forcibly create an obedient people by transforming them. Thus he will remove their "heart of stone" and give them a "heart of flesh" and a "new spirit" (Ezek 11.19; 36.26), he will put his own Spirit within them (36.27) and cleanse them (36.25, 29, 33; 37.23), and he himself will atone for what they have done (16.63). Only then will they be able to "remember" and feel "shame" for what they had done (Ezek 16.61, 63; 20.43; 36.31); only then will they be able to obey (11.20; 36.27).

d. A damaged relationship

According to Ezekiel, Yhwh had initiated a relationship with Israel in the past, swearing to be their God and to bring them out of Egypt into another land (Ezek 20.5–6). The prophet elsewhere describes the beginning of this relationship in metaphorical terms as the rescue of a foundling child (Ezek 16.1–7) and as a marriage (16.8–14; 23.4). But this relationship has disintegrated: Ezekiel speaks of the failure of the marriage between Yhwh and Jerusalem, a failure due to Jerusalem's metaphorical "whoring" (that is, religious and political infidelity; cf. Ezek 16.15-34; 23.5, 11). His other accusations use relational language as well: Israel is "unfaithful" (Ezek 14.13; 15.8; 20.27; 39.23, 26), and the inhabitants of Jerusalem have "tossed Yhwh behind their back" (Ezek 23.35). Israel has "broken the covenant," and Yhwh will respond in kind (Ezek 16.59). The book describes the damaged relationship between Yhwh and Israel as a period when Yhwh is "hiding his face" from the people (Ezek 39.23, 24).

Ezekiel responds to the problem of the damaged relationship by arguing that Yhwh will create a new relationship with a transformed Israel in the future. To be sure, he claims that Yhwh is in some limited sense already committed to the exiles even in their current condition (Ezek 11.16), but the book presents a hope for a future relational dynamic that surpasses anything that Israel has experienced so far. Thus after accusing the people of "breaking the covenant" (Ezek 16.59), Yhwh claims that he will "establish an eternal covenant" (Ezek 16.60; 37.26)—that is, a covenant which cannot be broken. This is described as a "covenant of peace" (Ezek 34.25; 37.26), reflecting not only the guaranteed promises of fertility and peace that arise from the covenant (cf. 34.25-29; 37.24-25), but also the absence of covenant punishments (cf. Lev 26). The contrast between the past relationship and the envisioned future relationship is summed up in the statement "I will cause you to be inhabited as you were formerly, and I will treat you even better than in your former times" (Ezek 36.11). Finally, the traditional language of the covenant formula ("I will be your God, and you will be my people") is used to describe the restored and transformed relationship between Yhwh and Israel (Ezek 11.20; 34.30; 36.28; 37.23, 27).

e. Refusal to accept responsibility

As I argued in the previous chapter, it seems likely that the book of Ezekiel lacks certain words (love, compassion, etc.) because the prophet did not feel that these would be effective for the rhetorical setting in which he operated. Instead, the book of Ezekiel places great emphasis on assigning blame and on linking actions to consequences. This suggests that the prophet's contemporaries did not (or would not) acknowledge responsibility for the actions he claims have resulted in exile. One of the easiest ways to avoid responsibility is to blame someone else, and there are several indications in the book that this is occurring.

In Ezek 16.63 we see the curious statement that "there will never again be for you an opening of the mouth because of your humiliation"—a statement that Margaret Odell (1992) interprets as a reference to an unstated complaint by the exiles that Y{HWH} had failed them. According to Odell, the entire chapter functions as Ezekiel's argument that Y{HWH} had not failed *them*; rather, *they* have failed Y{HWH}, and in the future, they will never again be able to make such a complaint. If Odell's interpretation of the unusual expression in v. 63 is correct, it seems plausible that the people's complaint against Y{HWH} was a strategy to deflect blame and avoid responsibility.

Another place where the exiles are avoiding responsibility can be seen in the quotation of their words in Ezek 18.2: "The fathers have eaten sour grapes, and the children's teeth are set on edge!" Here the exiles are arguing that their condition is not a result of punishment for their own misdeeds; rather, they are suffering for the sins of their ancestors. Ezekiel responds with a lengthy and forceful argument that merit and blame cannot be passed on across generations:

> As I live—utterance of Lord Y{HWH}—you will no longer quote this proverb in Israel! ... The person who sins will die. A son will not bear the iniquity of the father, and a father will not bear the iniquity of the son; the righteousness of the righteous man will be upon him, and the wickedness of the wicked man will be upon him.
> (Ezek 18.3, 20)

But Ezekiel's audience will have none of this. They find it easier to believe that God punishes children for the misdeeds of their parents: "Why shouldn't the son bear the iniquity of the father?" (Ezek 18.19). To admit otherwise would mean that they must take responsibility for their own actions.

What of the words attributed to the exiles in Ezek 33.10: "Surely our transgressions and our sins are upon us, and we are rotting in them; how shall we live?" Is this not a confession of sin, perhaps even a statement of repentance? Are they not here accepting responsibility? On the contrary, this is not an expression of repentance, because Ezekiel finds it necessary to *argue* that Yhwh is open to repentance in the following verse (Ezek 33.11). Nor is it a confession of sin; the people are not addressing Yhwh, and show no remorse for having offended the deity (note the assessment of the people in vv. 31–32). Rather, what we read here is a locution taken from Lev 26.39 (already used in Ezek 4.17; 24.23) and placed in the people's mouths as an expression of despair. Whether the people have actually fallen into despair after Ezekiel's seemingly endless accusations is difficult to say; it is possible that he is creating a literary scenario in an attempt to prevent despair. Whatever the case, he attempts to counter despair, real or potential, by arguing that Yhwh is open to repentance. Of course, the issue of whether the people are willing or able to repent is another matter. The point here is that the problem lies not with Yhwh, but with the people.

Some have argued that Ezekiel is boldly inventing the doctrine of individual responsibility in chs. 18 and 33. The Talmud (*b. Mak.* 24a) records a rabbinic opinion that may have influenced this idea: "Moses said, 'visiting the iniquity of the fathers on the sons' [Exod 34.7]; Ezekiel came and overturned it, 'the person who sins, that person will die' [Ezek 18.4]." But as Paul Joyce (1989: 33–60, 2009: 23–26) has persuasively argued, Ezekiel did not invent this doctrine, and does not systematically deal with the issues of individual versus collective guilt and suffering. If, for example, we attribute to him the doctrine of individual responsibility, it is difficult to explain passages such as Ezek 21.8 [ET v. 3], which proclaims the death of all, both righteous and wicked, in Jerusalem. Moreover, we have evidence outside of the book of Ezekiel that there was a widespread controversy in ancient Israel about the transfer or non-transfer of guilt and punishment across generations. This controversy is reflected in texts such as Num 16.27–33; 26.11; Deut 24.16; 2 Kgs 14.5–6; Jer 31.29–30; Lam 5.7, and in the subtle differences between Exod 34.7; Num 14.18 and Exod 20.5; Deut 5.9; 7.10. So while Ezekiel takes part in this controversy (cf. Lev 26.39 vs. Ezek 24.23; *Tg. Onq.* Lev 26.39), he is not the originator. Finally, the emphasis on what looks like individual responsibility in Ezek 18.3–20 is due to the genre of the case law Ezekiel uses as an example—an example which he applies to an entire *generation* of exiles. Ezekiel's argument in ch. 18, then, is an attempt to counter his contemporaries' refusal to take responsibility, not to engage in abstract theological reflection.

So wherein lies Ezekiel's innovation, if he is not the inventor of the doctrine of individual responsibility? It is the doctrine that God deals with people "in the moment" (Schwartz 1994). In this scrupulous application of justice, Yhwh responds positively to the righteous and negatively to the wicked—and if they suddenly change, the change is immediately taken into account (Ezek 18.21–22, 24–29; 33.12–16). Thus neither past sin nor past righteousness has any bearing on the present. On the one hand, this means that Yhwh is always open to repentance (Ezek 18.23, 27–29, 30–32; 33.11, 14–16). On the other hand, it clearly struck Ezekiel's audience as astounding that Yhwh would not be influenced favorably by past righteousness, as is shown by their response: "The way of Yhwh is not right!" (Ezek 18.25, 29; 33.17, 20). Nevertheless, this model of how God deals with people plays an essential role in Ezekiel's rhetorical strategy. It explains why, when Ezekiel reviews Israel's history in ch. 20, he pointedly omits any mention of positive behavior in the past. By so doing, he denies his audience the chance to claim that Yhwh is indebted to them for past deeds of righteousness—which would constitute another attempt on the part of the exiles to avoid taking responsibility for their deeds. This is consistent with Ezekiel's argument that Yhwh is restoring Israel for his own sake alone, and not for their sake (Ezek 36.22, 32).

3. Conclusion: the purpose of the book of Ezekiel

The book of Ezekiel represents a response to the traumatic events of the sixth century BCE—the invasions of Judah by the Babylonians, the deportation of Judeans to Babylon, and the destruction of the city of Jerusalem and its temple. The prophet Ezekiel must explain to his fellow deportees why these events happened, and he does so by defining them as acts of judgment carried out by Yhwh himself. Ezekiel must then justify this judgment, which he does by linking actions to consequences: Israel has rebelled against God, and therefore deserves the punishment. The prophet describes his contemporaries as incorrigible, unwilling, and unable to repent, endlessly carrying out the same pattern of sinful behavior as their ancestors. His descriptions of the sin of and judgment on Jerusalem are therefore a commentary on the actions and condition of his fellow exiles. But it is not enough to explain the disaster; Ezekiel also seeks to arouse hope. If there is to be any future for Israel, it lies in the initiative of Yhwh, who will act to protect his reputation by gathering the exiles back to the land and transforming them so that they will be able to obey. The book of Ezekiel closes with a vision of a purified people living in a purified land, where the sanctity of the temple has been restored and where Yhwh lives among his people forever.

The book of Ezekiel is aimed at an exilic audience that has undergone forced deportation, but has not yet experienced the hope which the prophet insists lies in the future. As Thomas Renz (1999: 70) notes, "the exilic readers are in an intermediate stage between the Israel of the past to which an end was made in Jerusalem, and the Israel of the future to which a loyal heart and new spirit will be given." The book expresses the tension of this "intermediate stage" by admitting that God has been "hiding his face" (Ezek 39.23, 24), but claims that in the future he will "no longer hide his face" (39.29; cf. 36.9).

Did the prophet succeed in his rhetorical goals? We do not know precisely how the book's first readers responded to it, but it *was* copied and passed on for future generations—something that is difficult to explain if it had no effect on its readership. And the history of the book's interpretation shows us how it was received in the Second Temple period. A text known as the "Damascus Covenant" (CD), fragments of which were also discovered at Qumran (4Q266–273), sheds light on this matter. These texts reference the book of Ezekiel by acknowledging that God "hid his face" from Israel and "delivered them to the sword" because of their sins (CD-A 1.3–4; cf. Ezek 39.23–24). They reference the period of "390 years" mentioned in Ezek 4.9 as a "time of wrath" experienced by Israel (CD-A 1.5–6). But they also define the community for whom they were written in terms of the purified cult personnel envisioned in Ezek 44.15 (CD-A 3.18–4.4). It seems clear, then, that the book of Ezekiel succeeded in creating readers who accepted its judgments on their past and who embraced its hope for their future.

Further reading

For a discussion of the rhetorical goals of the book of Ezekiel, see Renz (1999).

Bibliography

Albertz, R. 2003. *Israel in Exile. The History and Literature of the Sixth Century* BCE. Translated by D. Green from *Die Exilszeit* (Stuttgart: Kohlhammer, 2001). Atlanta: SBL.

———. 2010. "How Radical Must the New Beginning Be? The Discussion between the Deutero-Isaiah and the Ezekiel School," in J. Middlemas, D. J. A. Clines, and E. K. Holt (eds.), *The Centre and the Periphery: A European Tribute to Walter Brueggemann*. Sheffield: Sheffield Phoenix Press, 7–21.

Becker, J. 1982. "Erwägungen zur ezechielischen Frage," in L. Ruppert, P. Weimar and E. Zenger (eds.), *Künder des Wortes: Beiträge zur Theologie der Propheten für J. Schreiner*. Würzburg: Echter, 137–49.

Block, D. I. 1997. *The Book of Ezekiel: Chapters 1–24*, NICOT. Grand Rapids: Eerdmans.

———. 1998. *The Book of Ezekiel: Chapters 25–48*, NICOT. Grand Rapids: Eerdmans.

Boadt, L. 1980. *Ezekiel's Oracles against Egypt: A Literary and Philological Study of Ezekiel 29–32*, BibOr, 37. Rome: Biblical Institute Press.

Bodi, D. 1991. *The Book of Ezekiel and the Poem of Erra*, OBO, 104. Göttingen: Vandenhoek & Ruprecht.

Bourguignon, E. (ed.). 1973. *Religion, Altered States of Consciousness, and Social Change*. Columbus: Ohio State University Press.

Broome, E. C. 1943. "Ezekiel's Abnormal Personality," *JBL* 65.3: 277–92.

Carley, K. W. 1975. *Ezekiel among the Prophets*. Naperville: Allenson.

Carr, D. 2005. *Writing on the Tablet of the Heart: Origins of Scripture and Literature*. Oxford: Oxford University Press.

Christensen, D. L. 1975. *Prophecy and War in Ancient Israel: Studies in the Oracles Against the Nations in Old Testament Prophecy*. Berkeley: BIBAL Press.

Clements, R. E. 1982. "The Ezekiel Tradition: Prophecy in a Time of Crisis," in R. J. Coggins, A. Phillips, and M. Knibb (eds.), *Israel's Prophetic Tradition: Essays in Honour of Peter Ackroyd*. Cambridge: Cambridge University Press, 119–36.

———. 1986. "The Chronology of Redaction in Ezekiel 1–24," in J. Lust (ed.), *Ezekiel and His Book: Textual and Literary Criticism and their Interrelation*, BETL, 74. Leuven: Leuven University Press, 283–94.

———. 1990. "The Prophet and His Editors," in D. J. A. Clines, S. E. Fowl, and S. E. Porter (eds.), *The Bible in Three Dimensions: Essays in Celebration of Forty Years of Biblical Studies in the University of Sheffield*, JSOTSup, 97. Sheffield: Sheffield Academic Press, 203–20.

Cook, S. L. 1995. "Innerbiblical Interpretation in Ezekiel 44 and the History of Israel's Priesthood," *JBL* 114.2: 193–208.

Cook, S. L. and Patton, C. L. (eds.) 2004. *Ezekiel's Hierarchical World: Wrestling with a Tiered Reality*, SBLSS, 31. Atlanta: SBL.

Cooke, G. A. 1936. *A Critical and Exegetical Commentary on the Book of Ezekiel*, ICC. Edinburgh: T&T Clark.

Crane, A. S. 2008. *Israel's Restoration: A Textual-Comparative Exploration of Ezekiel 36–39*, VTSup, 122. Leiden: Brill.

Crouch, C. L. 2011. "Ezekiel's Oracles against the Nations in Light of a Royal Ideology of Warfare," *JBL* 130.3: 473–92.

Darr, K. P. 1992. "Ezekiel's Justifications of God: Teaching Troubling Texts," *JSOT* 55: 97–117.

———. 1994. "Ezekiel among the Critics," *CR:BS* 2: 9–24.

———. 2001. "The Book of Ezekiel: Introduction, Commentary, and Reflections," in L. E. Keck (ed.), *New Interpreter's Bible*, vol. 6. Nashville: Abingdon, 1073–607.

Davis, E. F. 1989. *Swallowing the Scroll: Textuality and the Dynamics of Discourse in Ezekiel's Prophecy*, JSOTSup, 78. Sheffield: Sheffield Academic Press.

Day, P. L. 1995. "The Personification of Cities as Females in the Hebrew Bible: The Thesis of Aloysius Fitzgerald, F.S.C.," in F. Segovia and M. Tolbert (eds.), *Social Location and Biblical Interpretation in Global Perspective*, vol. 2. Minneapolis: Fortress, 283–302.

Driver, S. R. 1891. *An Introduction to the Literature of the Old Testament*. New York: Charles Scribner's Sons.

Filson, F. V. 1943. "The Omission of Ezekiel 12.26–28 and 36.23b-38 in Codex 967," *JBL* 62: 27–32.

Fishbane, M. 1985. *Biblical Interpretation in Ancient Israel*. Oxford: Oxford University Press.

Flanagan, J. 2009. "Papyrus 967 and the Text of Ezekiel: Parablepsis or an Original Text?," in C. A. Evans and H. D. Zacharias (eds.), *Jewish and Christian Scripture as Artifact and Canon*, LSTS, 70. New York: T&T Clark, 105–16.

Floyd, M. H. 2006. "The Production of Prophetic Books in the Early Second Temple Period," in M. H. Floyd and R. D. Haak (eds.), *Prophets, Prophecy, and Prophetic Texts in Second Temple Judaism*, LHBOTS, 427. New York: T&T Clark, 276–97.

Fohrer, G. 1968. *Introduction to the Old Testament*. Translated by D. Green from *Einleitung in das Alte Testament* (Heidelberg: Quelle & Meyer, 1965). Nashville: Abingdon.

———. 1983. 4d ed. *Exegese des Alten Testaments. Einführung in die Methodik*. Heidelberg: Quelle & Meyer.

Fox, M. V. 1980. "The Rhetoric of Ezekiel's Vision of the Valley of the Bones," *HUCA* 51: 1–15.

Friebel, K. G. 1999. *Jeremiah's and Ezekiel's Sign-Acts: Rhetorical Nonverbal Communication*, JSOTSup, 283. Sheffield: Sheffield Academic Press.

———. 2005. "The Decrees of Yahweh that are 'Not Good': Ezekiel 20:25–26," in R. L. Troxel, D. R. Magary, and K. G. Friebel (eds.), *Seeking Out the Wisdom of the Ancients: Essays Offered to Michael V. Fox on the Occasion of His Sixty-Fifth Birthday*. Winona Lake: Eisenbrauns, 21–36.

Frolov, S. 2012. "Judah Comes to Shiloh: Genesis 49:10bα, One More Time," *JBL* 131.3: 417–22.

Galambush, J. 1992. *Jerusalem in the Book of Ezekiel: The City as Yahweh's Wife*, SBLDS, 130. Atlanta: Scholars Press.

Ganzel, T. 2010. "Transformation of Pentateuchal Descriptions of Idolatry," in W. A. Tooman and M. A. Lyons (eds.), *Transforming Visions: Transformations of Text, Tradition, and Theology in Ezekiel*, PTMS, 127. Eugene: Wipf and Stock/Pickwick Press, 33–49.

Ganzel, T. and Holtz, S. E. 2014. "Ezekiel's Temple in Babylonian Context," *VT* 64: 211–26.

Garber Jr., D. G. 2004. "Traumatizing Ezekiel, the Exilic Prophet," in J. H. Ellens and W. G. Rollins (eds.), *Psychology and the Bible: A New Way to Read the Scriptures. Vol. 2: From Genesis to Apocalyptic Vision*. Westport: Praeger Press, 215–35.

———. 2011. "A Vocabulary of Trauma in the Exilic Writings," in B. E. Kelle, F. R. Ames, and J. L. Wright (eds.), *Interpreting Exile: Displacement and Deportation in Biblical and Modern Contexts*. Atlanta: Society of Biblical Literature, 309–21.

Garscha, J. 1974. *Studien zum Ezechielbuch: Eine redaktionskritische Untersuchung von Ez 1–39*, EH, 23. Bern: Herbert Lang / Frankfurt: Peter Lang.

Gese, H. 1957. *Der Verfassungsentwurf des Ezechiel (Kap. 40–48) traditionsgeschichtlich untersucht*, BHT, 25. Tübingen: J. C. B. Mohr (Paul Siebeck).

Glazov, G. Y. 2001. *The Bridling of the Tongue and the Opening of the Mouth in Biblical Prophecy*, JSOTSup, 311. Sheffield: Sheffield Academic Press.

Grayson, A. K. 2000. *Assyrian and Babylonian Chronicles*. Winona Lake: Eisenbrauns.

Greenberg, M. 1983. *Ezekiel 1–20. A New Translation with Introduction and Commentary*, AB, 22. New York: Doubleday.

———. 1984. "The Design and Themes of Ezekiel's Program of Restoration," *Interpretation* 38: 181–208.

———. 1986. "What are Valid Criteria For Determining Inauthentic Matter in Ezekiel?," in J. Lust (ed.), *Ezekiel and His Book: Textual and Literary Criticism and their Interrelation*, BETL, 74. Leuven: Leuven University Press, 123–35.

———. 1997. *Ezekiel 21–37. A New Translation with Introduction and Commentary*, AB, 22A. New York: Doubleday.

Gunkel, H. 1987. "The Prophets as Writers and Poets," in D. L. Petersen (ed.), *Prophecy in Israel: Search for an Identity*. Translated by J. L. Schaaf from "Die Propheten als Schriftsteller und Dichter," in *Die Propheten* (Göttingen: Vandenhoeck & Ruprecht, 1923), 34–70. Philadelphia: Fortress Press, 22–73.

———. 2003. "The Literature of Ancient Israel," in T. J. Sandoval and C. Mandolfo (eds.), *Relating to the Text: Interdisciplinary and Form-Critical Insights on the Bible*. Translated by A. Siedlecki from "Die Israelitische Literatur," in P. Hinneberg (ed.), *Kultur der Gegenwart. Ihre Entwicklungen und ihre Ziele*, I/vii (1906; Leipzig, 1925, 2d ed.), 51–112. New York: T&T Clark, 26–83.

Habel, N. 1965. "The Form and Significance of the Call Narratives," *ZAW* 77.3: 297–323.

Halperin, D. J. 1976. "The Exegetical Character of Ezek x 9–17," *VT* 26: 129–41.

———. 1993. *Seeking Ezekiel: Text and Psychology*. University Park: Pennsylvania State University Press.

Haran, M. 1979. "The Law Code of Ezekiel XL–XLVIII and its Relation to the Priestly School," *HUCA* 50: 45–71.

———. 2005. "Observations on Ezekiel as a Book Prophet," in R. L. Troxel, K. G. Friebel, and D. R. Magary (eds.), *Seeking Out the Wisdom of the Ancients: Essays offered to honor Michael V. Fox on the occasion of his sixty-fifth birthday*. Winona Lake: Eisenbrauns, 3–19.

Herrmann, S. 1965. *Die prophetischen Heilserwartungen im Alten Testament: Ursprung und Gestaltwandel*, BWANT, 85. Stuttgart: Kohlhammer.

Hölscher, G. 1924. *Hesekiel, der Dichter und das Buch: Eine literarkritische Untersuchung*, BZAW, 39. Giessen: Töpelmann.

Jong, M. J. de. 2007. "Ezekiel as a Literary Figure and the Quest for the Historical Prophet," in H. J. de Jonge and J. Tromp (eds.), *The Book of Ezekiel and Its Influence*. Aldershot: Ashgate, 1–16.

Joyce, P. M. 1989. *Divine Initiative and Human Response in Ezekiel*, JSOTSup, 51. Sheffield: JSOT Press.

———. 1996. "Dislocation and Adaptation in the Exilic Age and After," in J. Barton and D. J. Reimer (eds.), *After the Exile: Essays in Honour of Rex Mason*. Macon: Mercer University Press, 45–58.

———. 2005. "Temple and Worship in Ezekiel 40–48," in John Day (ed.), *Temple and Worship in Biblical Israel. Proceedings of the Oxford Old Testament Seminar*, LHBOTS, 422. New York: T&T Clark, 145–63.

———. 2007. "Ezekiel 40–42: The Earliest 'Heavenly Ascent' Narrative?" in H. J. De Jonge and J. Tromp (eds.), *The Book of Ezekiel and Its Influence*. Aldershot: Ashgate, 17–41.

———. 2009. *Ezekiel: A Commentary*. New York: T&T Clark.

Joyce, P. M. and Rom-Shiloni, D. (eds.) 2015. *The God Ezekiel Creates*. London: Bloomsbury T&T Clark.

Kasher, R. 1998. "Anthropomorphism, Holiness and Cult: A New Look at Ezek 40–48," *ZAW* 110: 192–208.

Keel-Leu, O. 1977. *Jahwe-Visionen und Siegelkunst. Eeine neue Deutung der Majestätsschilderungen in Jes 6, Ez 1 und 10 und Sach 4*, SBS, 84/85. Stuttgart: Katholisches Bibelwerk.

Kelle, B. E. 2008. "Wartime Rhetoric: Prophetic Metaphorization of Cities as Female," in B. E. Kelle and F. R. Ames (eds.), *Writing and Reading War: Rhetoric, Gender, and Ethics in Biblical and Modern Contexts*. Atlanta: SBL, 95–111.

———. 2013. *Ezekiel. A Commentary in the Wesleyan Tradition*. NBBC. Kansas City: Beacon Hill Press.

———. 2014. "The Phenomenon of Israelite Prophecy in Contemporary Scholarship," *CBR* 12.3: 275–320.

Klein, A. 2008. *Schriftauslegung im Ezechielbuch: Redaktionsgeschichtliche Untersuchungen zu Ez 34–39*, BZAW, 391. Berlin: Walter de Gruyter.

———. 2010. "Prophecy Continued: Reflections on Innerbiblical Exegesis in the Book of Ezekiel," *VT* 60: 571–82.

Konkel, M. 2001. *Architektonik des Heiligen: Studien zur zweiten Tempelvision Ezechiels (Ez 40–48)*, BBB, 129. Berlin: Philo.

Kutsko, J. 2000. *Between Heaven and Earth: Divine Presence and Absence in the Book of Ezekiel*. Winona Lake: Eisenbrauns.

Lapsley, J. E. 2000. *Can These Bones Live? The Problem of the Moral Self in the Book of Ezekiel*, BZAW, 301. New York: de Gruyter.

Levenson, J. D. 1976. *Theology of the Program of Restoration of Ezekiel 40–48*, HSM, 10. Missoula: Scholars Press.

Levitt Kohn, R. 2002. *A New Heart and a New Soul: Ezekiel, the Exile and the Torah*, JSOTSup, 358. Sheffield: Sheffield Academic Press.

——. 2003. "Ezekiel at the Turn of the Century," *CBR* 2.1: 9–31.

Lewis, I. M. 1989. *Ecstatic Religion: A Study of Shamanism and Spirit Possession*, 2d ed. Routledge: London and New York.

Lilly, I. E. 2012. *Two Books of Ezekiel: Papyrus 967 and the Masoretic Text as Variant Literary Editions*, VTSup, 150. Leiden: Brill.

Lipschits, O. 2005. *The Fall and Rise of Jerusalem: Judah under Babylonian Rule*. Winona Lake: Eisenbrauns.

Long, B. O. 1976. "Reports of Visions among the Prophets," *JBL* 95.3: 353–65.

Ludwig, A.M. 1969. "Altered States of Consciousness," in C. Tart (ed.), *Altered States of Consciousness*. New York: John Wiley & Sons, 9–22.

Lust, J. 1981. "Ezekiel 36–40 in the Oldest Greek Manuscript," *CBQ* 43: 517–33.

——. 2003. "Major Divergences between LXX and MT in Ezekiel," in A. Schenker (ed.), *The Earliest Text of the Hebrew Bible: The Relationship between the Masoretic Text and the Hebrew Base of the Septuagint Reconsidered*, SBLSCS, 52. Atlanta: SBL, 83–92.

Lyons, M. A. 2007. "Marking Innerbiblical Allusion in the Book of Ezekiel," *Biblica* 88.2: 245–50.

——. 2009. *From Law to Prophecy: Ezekiel's Use of the Holiness Code*, LHBOTS, 507. New York: T&T Clark.

——. 2014. "Envisioning Restoration: Innovations in Ezekiel 40–48," in L.-S. Tiemeyer and E. Hayes (eds.), *'I Lifted My Eyes and Saw': Reading Dream and Vision Reports in the Hebrew Bible*. New York: Bloomsbury T&T Clark.

Mackie, T. P. 2014. "Expanding Ezekiel: The Hermeneutics of Scribal Addition in the Ancient Text Witnesses of the Book of Ezekiel," FRLANT, 257. Göttingen: Vandenhoek & Ruprecht.

Mayfield, T. 2010. *Literary Structure and Setting in Ezekiel*, FAT, 2/43. Tübingen: Mohr Siebeck.

McKeating, H. 1993. *Ezekiel*. Sheffield: Sheffield Academic Press.

McNamara, P. 2009. *The Neuroscience of Religious Experience*. Cambridge: Cambridge University Press.

Mein, A. 2001a. "Ezekiel as a Priest in Exile," in J. C. De Moor (ed.), *The Elusive Prophet: The Prophet as a Historical Person, Literary Character, and Anonymous Artist*. Leiden: Brill, 199–213.

———. 2001b. *Ezekiel and the Ethics of Exile*. Oxford: Oxford University Press.

Moran, W. L. 1958. "Genesis 49,10 and its use in Ezekiel 21,32," *Biblica* 39: 405–25.

Moughtin-Mumby, S. 2008. *Sexual and Marital Metaphors in Hosea, Jeremiah, Isaiah, and Ezekiel*. Oxford: Oxford University Press.

Mowinckel, S. 1934. "The 'Spirit' and the 'Word' in the Pre-Exilic Reforming Prophets," *JBL* 53.3: 199–227.

Newsom, C. A. 1984. "A Maker of Metaphors—Ezekiel's Oracles Against Tyre," *Interpretation* 38: 151–64.

Niditch, S. 1983. *The Symbolic Vision in Biblical Tradition*, HSM, 30. Chico: Scholars Press.

Nihan, C. 2007. *From Priestly Torah to Pentateuch. A Study in the Composition of the Book of Leviticus*, FAT, 2/25. Tübingen: Mohr Siebeck.

Nissinen, M. 2000. "Spoken, Written, Quoted, and Invented: Orality and Writtenness in Ancient Near Eastern Prophecy," in E. Ben Zvi and M. H. Floyd (eds.), *Writings and Speech in Israelite and Ancient Near Eastern Prophecy*, SBLSS, 10. Atlanta: SBL, 235–71.

———. 2003. *Prophets and Prophecy in the Ancient Near East*. Atlanta: SBL.

———. 2004. "What is Prophecy?," in J. Kaltner and L. Stulman (eds.), *Inspired Speech: Prophecy in the Ancient Near East. Essays in Honour of Herbert B. Huffmon*, New York: T&T Clark, 17–37.

———. 2005. "How Prophecy Became Literature," *SJOT* 19.2: 153–72.

Odell, M. S. 1992. "The Inversion of Shame and Forgiveness in Ezekiel 16.59–63," *JSOT* 56: 101–12.

Odell, M. S. and Strong, J. T. (eds.). 2000. *The Book of Ezekiel: Theological and Anthropological Perspectives*, SBLSS, 9. Atlanta: SBL

Olley, J. W. 2011. "Trajectories of Ezekiel: Part 1," *CBR* 9.2: 137–70.

Overholt, T. W. 1989. *Channels of Prophecy: The Social Dynamics of Prophetic Activity*. Minneapolis: Fortress.

Patton, C. L. 2000. ' "Should Our Sister be Treated Like a Whore?' A Response to Feminist Critiques of Ezekiel 23," in M. S. Odell and J. T. Strong (eds.), *The Book of Ezekiel: Theological and Anthropological Perspectives*, SBLSS, 9. Atlanta: SBL, 221–38.

———. 2004. "Priest, Prophet, and Exile: Ezekiel as a Literary Construct," in S. L. Cook and C. L. Patton (eds.), *Ezekiel's Hierarchical World: Wrestling with a Tiered Reality*, SBLSS, 31. Atlanta: SBL, 73–89

Pohlmann, K.-F. 1996. *Das Buch Hesekiel (Ezechiel). Kapitel 1–19*, ATD, 22/1. Göttingen: Vandenhoeck & Ruprecht.

—— (mit einem Beitrag von T. A. Rudnig). 2001. *Das Buch Hesekiel (Ezechiel). Kapitel 20–48*, ATD, 22/2. Göttingen: Vandenhoeck & Ruprecht.

——. 2006. "Forschung am Ezechielbuch 1969–2004 (I–III)," *TR* 71: 60–90; 164–91; 265–309.

Price-Williams, D. and Hughes, D. J. 1994. "Shamanism and Altered States of Consciousness," *Anthropology of Consciousness* 5.2: 1–15.

Raabe, P. R. 2010. "Transforming the International *status quo*: Ezekiel's Oracles against the Nations," in W. A. Tooman and M. A. Lyons (eds.), *Transforming Visions: Transformations of Text, Traditions, and Theology in Ezekiel*, PTMS, 127. Eugene: Wipf and Stock/Pickwick Press.

Raitt, T. M. 1977. *A Theology of Exile: Judgment/Deliverance in Jeremiah and Ezekiel*. Philadelphia: Fortress Press.

Rendtorff, R. 1991. *The Old Testament: An Introduction*. Translated by J. Bowden from *Das Alte Testament: Eine Einfürung* (Neukirchen-Vluyn: Neukirchener Verlag, 1983). Philadelphia: Fortress Press.

Renz, T. 1999. *The Rhetorical Function of the Book of Ezekiel*, VTSup, 76. Leiden: Brill.

Reuss, E. 1876. *La Bible. Traduction Nouvelle avec Introductions et Commentaires. Ancien Testament—Deuxième Partie. Les Prophètes*, vol. 2. Paris: Sandoz et Fischbacher.

Robson, J. 2006. *Word And Spirit in Ezekiel*, LHBOTS, 447. New York: T&T Clark.

Rollston, C. A. 2010. *Writing and Literacy in the World of Ancient Israel: Epigraphic Evidence from the Iron Age*. Atlanta: SBL.

Rom-Shiloni, D. 2005. Facing Destruction and Exile: Inner-Biblical Exegesis in Jeremiah and Ezekiel," *ZAW* 117: 189–205.

——. 2013. *Exclusive Inclusivity: Identity Conflicts Between the Exiles and the People Who Remained (6th-5th Centuries BCE)*, LHBOTS, 543. New York: Bloomsbury T&T Clark.

Schöpflin, K. 2002. *Theologie als Biographie im Ezechielbuch: Ein Beitrag zur Konzeption alttestamentlicher Prophetie*, FAT, 36. Tübingen: Mohr Siebeck.

——. 2005. "The Composition of Metaphorical Oracles within the Book of Ezekiel," *VT* 55.1: 101–20.

Schwartz, B. J. 1994. "Repentance and Determinism in Ezekiel," in *Proceedings of the Eleventh World Congress of Jewish Studies: The Bible and its World*. Jerusalem: World Union of Jewish Studies, 123–30.

———. 2000. "Ezekiel's Dim View of Israel's Restoration," in M. S. Odell and J. T. Strong (eds.), *The Book of Ezekiel: Theological and Anthropological Perspectives*, SBLSS, 9. Atlanta: SBL, 43–67.

Sherlock, C. 1983. "Ezekiel's Dumbness," *ExpTim* 94: 296–98.

Smith-Christopher, D. L. 2002. "Ezekiel in Abu Ghraib: Rereading Ezekiel 16:37–39 in the Context of Imperial Conquest," in S. L. Cook and C. L. Patton (eds.), *Ezekiel's Hierarchical World: Wrestling with a Tiered Reality*, SBLSS, 31. Atlanta: SBL, 141–58.

———. 2011. "Reading War and Trauma: Suggestions toward a Social-Psychological Exegesis of Exile and War in Biblical Texts," in B. E. Kelle, F. R. Ames, and J. L. Wright (eds.), *Interpreting Exile: Displacement and Deportation in Biblical and Modern Contexts*. Atlanta: SBL, 253–74.

Steiner, R. C. 2010. "Poetic Forms in the Masoretic Vocalization and Three Difficult Phrases in Jacob's Blessing: יתר שאת (Gen 49:3), יצועי עלה (49:4), and יבא שילה (49:10)," *JBL* 129.2: 219–26.

———. 2013. "Four Inner-Biblical Interpretations of Genesis 49:10: On the Lexical and Syntactic Ambiguities of עד as Reflected in the Prophecies of Nathan, Ahijah, Ezekiel, and Zechariah," *JBL* 132.1: 33–60.

Stevenson, K. R. 1996. *The Vision of Transformation: The Territorial Rhetoric of Ezekiel 40–48*, SBLDS, 154. Atlanta: Scholars Press.

Stökl, J. 2012. *Prophecy in the Ancient Near East: A Philological and Sociological Comparison*, CHANE, 56. Leiden: Brill.

———. 2013. "The מתנבאות in Ezekiel 13 Reconsidered," *JBL* 132.1: 61–76.

Strine, C. A. 2012. "The Role of Repentance in the Book of Ezekiel: A Second Chance for the Second Generation," *JTS* 63.2: 467–91.

Strine, C. A. and Crouch, C. L. 2013. "Yhwh's Battle against Chaos in Ezekiel: The Transformation of Judahite Mythology for a New Situation," *JBL* 132.4: 883–903.

Stromberg, J. 2008. "Observations on Inner-Scriptural Scribal Expansion in MT Ezekiel," *VT* 58: 68–86.

Strong, J. T. 2012. "Grounding Ezekiel's Heavenly Ascent: A Defense of Ezek 40–48 as a Program for Restoration," *SJOT* 26.2: 192–211.

Sweeney, M. A. 2005. "Ezekiel: Zadokite Priest and Visionary Prophet of the Exile," in M. A. Sweeney, *Form and Intertextuality in Prophetic and Apocalyptic Literature*, FAT, 45. Tübingen: Mohr Siebeck, 125–43.

Tiemeyer, L.-S. 2006. "God's Hidden Compassion," *TynBul* 57.2: 191–213.

Tooman, W. A. 2009. "Ezekiel's Radical Challenge to Inviolability," *ZAW* 121.4: 498–514.

———. 2011. *Gog of Magog: Reuse of Scripture and Compositional Technique in Ezekiel 38–39*, FAT, 2/52. Tübingen: Mohr Siebeck.

Toorn, K. van der. 2000. "From the Oral to the Written: The Case of Old Babylonian Prophecy," in E. Ben Zvi and M. H. Floyd (eds.), *Writings and Speech in Israelite and Ancient Near Eastern Prophecy*, SBLSS, 10. Atlanta: SBL, 219–34.

———. 2007. *Scribal Culture and the Making of the Hebrew Bible*. Cambridge: Harvard University Press.

Torrey, C. C. 1930. *Pseudo-Ezekiel and the Original Prophecy*, Yale Oriental Series, Researches, 18. New Haven: Yale University Press.

Tov, E. 2012. 3d ed. *Textual Criticism of the Hebrew Bible*. Minneapolis: Fortress.

Tuell, S. S. 1992. *The Law of the Temple in Ezekiel 40–48*, HSM, 49. Atlanta: Scholars Press.

———. 1996. "Ezekiel 40–42 as Verbal Icon," *CBQ* 58: 649–64.

Wellhausen, J. 1885. *Prolegomena to the History of Israel*. Translated by J. Sutherland Black and Allan Menzies. Edinburgh: A. & C. Black.

Wilson, R. R. 1972. "An Interpretation of Ezekiel's Dumbness," *VT* 22: 91–104.

———. 1978. "Early Israelite Prophecy," *Interpretation* 38.3: 3–16.

———. 1979. "Prophecy and Ecstasy: A Reexamination," *JBL* 98.3: 321–37.

———. 1980. *Prophecy and Society in Ancient Israel*. Philadelphia: Fortress.

———. 1984. "Prophecy in Crisis: The Call of Ezekiel," *Interpretation* 38: 117–30.

Wood, A. 2008. *Of Wings and Wheels: A Synthetic Study of the Biblical Cherubim*, BZAW, 385. Berlin: de Gruyter.

Zimmerli, W. 1965. "The Special Form- and Traditio-Historical Character of Ezekiel's Prophecy," *VT* 15.4: 515–27.

———. 1979. *Ezekiel 1*, Hermeneia. Translated by R. E. Clements from *Ezechiel 1, I. Teilband* (BKAT 13/1; Neukirchen-Vluyn: Neukirchener Verlag, 1969). Philadelphia: Fortress.

———. 1983. *Ezekiel 2*, Hermeneia. Translated by J. D. Martin from *Ezechiel 2, II. Teilband* (BKAT 13/2; Neukirchen-Vluyn: Neukirchener Verlag, 1969). Philadelphia: Fortress.

———. 1995. "From Prophetic Word to Prophetic Book," in R. P. Gordon (ed.), *The Place is Too Small for Us: The Israelite Prophets in Recent Scholarship*. Translated by A. Köstenberger from "Vom Prophetenwort zum Prophetenbuch," *ThLZ* 104 (1979): 481–96. Winona Lake: Eisenbrauns, 419–42.

Index of Scriptural References

Genesis
2.9–14   40
6.5   136
10   69
18–19   99
18.20   100
49.1   102
49.1–28   102
49.8–12   102–3
49.9–11   103
49.10   102–3
49.28   103

Exodus
3.4–9   27
3.10   27
3.11   27
3.12   27
4.1   27
4.2–9   27
4.10   27
4.11–12   27
4.13   27
4.14–16   27
6.7   33
7.5   33
7.17   33
8.18   33
10.2   33
13.12–13   146
14.4   33
16.10   147
20.5   183
20.24–26   19
20.26   160
22.22–24   100
23.15   159
24.9–10   38
24.16–17   147
25.18–19   39

25.22   39
28.15–21   100
28.42   100, 159
31.13   100
31.17   159
32.10   143
32.10–14   139
33.18–23   147
34.7   182–3
35.30–35   136
40.34   147
40.35   160

Leviticus
5.11   100, 159
7.18   18
9.23   147
10.9   100, 159
10.10   100, 109, 159
14.21   100, 159
14.22   100, 159
14.30–32   100, 159
16   160
16.4   100, 159
16.23   100, 159
17–26   36, 110, 168
17.13   151
18   159
18.4–5   20, 36, 112, 178
18.5   111, 112, 124, 146, 168
18.7   111, 124
18.7–9   20
18.9   111, 124
18.15   20, 111, 124
18.17   111, 124
18.19   20, 111, 112, 124
18.20   111, 112, 124, 172
18.24–25   151

18.24–28   19
18.25–28   151
18.26–30   125
19.3   20, 111, 124
19.7–8   18
19.8   20
19.13   20, 111, 124
19.16   20, 111, 124, 172
19.26   172
19.30   111, 124
19.34   100, 159
20   159
20.9   111, 124
20.9–11   20
20.10   111, 112
20.11   111
20.12   111
20.17   111
20.23   125
20.25   100, 109
21.1–4   100, 159
21.5   100, 159
21.10   161
21.13–15   100, 159
21.14   161
22.2–16   108
22.8   18, 100, 159
22.15   111, 124
22.26   100
23.43   159
25.8–22   80
25.9   81
25.10   81
25.18–19   153
25.25–28   110
25.36   20, 111, 112, 124
25.43   110
25.45–46   159
25.46   110
25.53   110

25.45-46   100
26   95, 111, 133, 134,
   153, 180
26.3   111, 138, 168, 178
26.3-13   112, 133, 168
26.4   111, 112, 153, 173
26.4-6   20, 134
26.5   68, 112, 153
26.6   112, 153, 173
26.9   173
26.12   112, 134
26.12-13   20
26.13   112, 134, 153
26.14   111, 168, 178
26.14-39   133, 168
26.18   133
26.19   31, 172
26.20   153
26.21-38   41
26.22   31, 95, 111, 119,
   151-3, 168, 172
26.23   111
26.23-24   133
26.25   31, 119, 152,
   168, 172
26.25-26   111
26.26   111, 119, 152,
   168
26.27-28   133
26.29   168
26.30   72, 74, 150
26.31-33   152, 168,
   172, 173
26.33   31, 44, 111, 119,
   135, 172
26.39   182, 183
26.40-42   133
26.44   133
27.8   100, 159
27.32   100

Numbers
4   23
4.1-3   18
4.23   18
4.30   18
5.14   136
6.21   100, 159
10.33-36   160
13.32   151
14.10   147
14.11-19   139
14.18   183
14.24   136
15.21   100, 159
16.19   147
16.27-33   182
18.9   100, 159
18.11   100, 159
18.13   100, 159
18.14   100, 159
18.20   100, 159
24.7   3
24.7-9   102
24.14   102
24.17   102
26.11   182
28.11-13   160
35.33-34   19, 151

Deuteronomy
4   104
4.17-18   72
4.23   104
4.25   104
4.25-28   133
4.26-27   172
4.27   104
4.28   103-4
4.29-30   133
4.34   103-4
5.9   183
5.15   104, 159
7.10   183
7.19   104
11.2   104
12.2   94, 101
12.31   123
16.1   159
16.3   159
24.16   182
26.8   104
28   133
28.1   138
28.15   104, 138
28.30   68
28.36   104
28.64   104
28.64-65   104
29.16   72, 104
29.24-28   166
30.1   133
30.2   133
30.3-8   133
31.16-18   133
31.20-21   133
31.29   133
33.2   40

Joshua
3.3   160

Judges
6.11-17   27

1 Samuel
1.8   136
4.3-4   160
4.4   39
4.11   160
14.18   160
25.36-37   136

2 Samuel
5.2   122

1 Kings
3.9   136
6.23-28   148, 149
8.11   160
8.42   104
8.46-50   133
9.8-9   166
14.23   94, 102
15.30   94

21.22   94
22.10–12   29

2 Kings
3.9   118
3.26–27   123
10.18   147
14.5–6   182
16.4   94, 102
17.10   94, 102
17.17   123
17.31   123
19.18   104
22.3   23
23.11   123
23.26   94
25.1   22, 23, 78
25.9   154
25.13–17   154
25.6–7   95

1 Chronicles
12.39   135
28.18   4

2 Chronicles
6.32   104
30.12   135

Ezra
4.7–24   176

Nehemiah
4.7–8   176
9.26–31   55
9.29   111
9.36–37   176

Job
17.13–16   39
20.7   35
24.24   147

Psalms
18.11–13   39

46   148, 173
46.5   40
48.2–3   40
48.9   176
49.13–15   39
68.17–19   40
74   173
74.1   166
74.3–7   154
78.68–70   154, 173
79   173
79.1   154
79.1–4   69
86.11   135
88.4–7   39
88.11–13   39
89   174
99.1   39
105.16   111
122.1–5   154
132.10–18   154
136.12   104
143.10   136

Proverbs
18.15   136

Ecclesiastes
12.7   136

Isaiah
1.10–17   52
1.21   46
2.2–4   42
2.4   103
3.25–26   46
5.14   39
6   28, 38
6.1   78
6.1–10   27
8.1–4   78
8.2   60
8.16   60
10.3   69
10.6–7   69

10.7   136
10.12–14   31
11.1–5   42, 136
11.6–9   41
11.10   42
12.1   37
14   4, 39
14–21   29
14.9–11   39
14.15   39
14.28   78
16.6   31
19.19–25   42
20.1–6   124
23   29
25.6–8   42
30.1–5   124
31.1–3   124
32.15–20   137
34.6–7   69
36.6   100
37.19   104
40–55   141
40.1   37
40.1–2   141
40.9–28   141
41.1–4   141
41.8–18   141
43.1   141
43.5   141
43.25   144
44.2   141
44.22   141
44.24–28   141
48.9   144
48.11   144
49.6   42
49.13   37
49.18   45
49.19–22   46
50.1   46
56.6–8   42
60.3–9   42
60.4   46
62.5   45

63.11   122
64.9-11   173
65.14   136
65.21   68
66.10-11   46

Jeremiah
1   28, 158
1.4-16   27
1.7-8   101
1.9   101
1.17-19   27, 101
2.2   45
2.14-19   124
2.20   46
2.20-25   124
2.33   46
2.36-37   124
3.1-10   46
3.1-13   124
3.6   102
3.6-10   101
3.8   46, 118
3.12   126
3.13   102
3.17   42
3.20   46
4.1-2   126
5.7-8   46
5.19   166
6.14   101
6.22   69
6.22-23   69
6.23   69
7.1-7   126
7.1-12   50
7.1-15   49
7.16   143
7.30-31   123
7.31   145
8.11   101
9.19-20   27
11.6   60
11.14   143
12.7   148

13.22   166
14.11-12   143
14.12   41
14.14-15   101
14.18   41
15.1-3   101
15.2-3   41
15.16   73, 101
16.1-9   101
16.10-13   166
17.2-3   102
18.1-2   60
18.18   101
18.21   41
19.4-5   123
21.1-7   50
21.5   104
21.7   41
21.9   41
21.11-12   50
22.8-9   166
22.10-12   94
23.1-5   124
23.1-6   101
24   28
25.1   78
26.4   76
28.1   78
29.1-3   101
29.1-7   11
29.15   101
29.24-29   101
30.3   76
31.4-5   76
31.13   37
31.28   76
31.29-30   101, 182
31.31-34   134
32.1   78
32.21   104
32.37-40   101
32.39   135
32.40   134
33.6-12   101
35.7   68

36.9   78
39.1   22
42.10   76
46-51   29
48.17   27
48.47   42
49.6   42
49.30-33   69
49.39   42

Lamentations
1.10   173
2.6-7   173
2.21-22   46
5.7   182

Ezekiel
1   4, 24, 38, 75, 148
1-2   149
1-3   16, 18, 21, 156
1-24   20, 21, 81, 82
1-33   20, 801-39   155
1.1   17, 18, 22, 23, 28,
   66, 78, 84, 85, 166
1.1-3   9, 10
1.1-28   27
1.1-3.14   28, 84
1.2   22, 23, 78, 166, 174
1.2-3   24, 66
1.3   17, 18, 66, 84, 85
1.4   4, 28, 66
1.4-21   84
1.5   38
1.7   38
1.24   73, 84, 85
1.26   38, 84
1.26-27   84
1.27   38, 148
1.28   16, 28, 84, 85, 147
2.1-2   27
2.2   16, 28, 73, 84, 85
2.3   121, 126, 178
2.3-4   27
2.3-5   13
2.3-8   25

Index of Scriptural References

2.4 8, 16, 54, 126, 136, 178
2.5 8, 16, 54, 127, 178
2.5–8 121, 126
2.6 28
2.7 16, 54, 178
2.8 27
2.8–3.3 28, 101, 144
2.10 82
3 86, 87
3.1 16, 54, 73, 99
3.11 16, 167
3.12 16, 28, 85
3.14 16, 17, 26–8, 73, 85, 136
3.15 53, 86, 167
3.16 86
3.16–21 8, 27, 85, 86
3.17 54, 86
3.17–21 25, 90
3.18–19 86
3.18–21 127
3.20–21 86
3.22 84, 86
3.22–27 28, 84
3.23 84, 147
3.24 16, 28, 84, 85, 87, 88, 136
3.24–25 88
3.24–27 87
3.25 87
3.25–27 88
3.26 87, 88, 121, 143, 178
3.26–27 16, 78, 87, 88, 144
3.27 87, 121
3.4 16, 54, 101
3.7 13, 25, 86, 121, 126, 127, 136, 178
3.7–9 9
3.8–9 28, 101
3.9 86, 121, 126
4–5 29, 55, 56, 60
4–24 21

4.1–2 60
4.1–3 41, 82
4.3 29, 170
4.4–5 29, 61
4.4–6 118
4.6 61
4.9 1, 61, 185
4.9–11 41, 60
4.12 29, 35
4.12–15 61
4.13 19, 29
4.14 18, 26
4.15 35
4.16 111
4.16–17 41, 61
4.17 182
5.1–2 29, 61, 82, 110, 119
5.1–4 61
5.2 41, 44
5.3 29
5.3–4 61
5.5 29, 61
5.5–6 120, 169
5.5–7 168
5.5–8 170
5.6 121, 124, 126, 178
5.6–7 178
5.7 36, 80, 121, 124
5.7–8 167
5.8 33, 140, 179
5.8–11 119
5.9 34, 80, 121, 167, 178
5.10 41
5.10–17 168
5.11 19, 34, 36, 80, 121–3, 127, 143, 155, 167, 168, 178, 179
5.11–12 10
5.12 41, 44, 61, 110, 111, 119
5.13 33, 37, 109
5.14–15 11, 41
5.15 67

5.16 41, 111
5.17 31, 41, 95, 111, 151, 153
6.1 33
6.1–7 74, 150
6.2–3 74
6.2–7 95
6.3 31, 152, 153, 173
6.3–6 123, 179
6.4 19, 74
6.4–6 35, 122
6.5 19, 74, 150
6.6 72, 150, 152, 153, 173
6.8 135
6.8–10 120
6.9 121, 135, 137, 144, 178, 179
6.9–10 141
6.10 80, 29, 54, 120, 178
6.11–12 41, 119
6.12 33, 109–11
6.13 19, 36, 94, 95, 101, 123, 170
6.14 41, 152, 173
7 73
7.1–4 144
7.3 121, 126, 168
7.3–4 142
7.4 33, 121, 127, 143
7.8 33, 105, 109, 126, 168
7.9 119, 126, 127, 143, 168
7.11 122
7.12–13 110
7.13 127
7.15 41, 110, 119
7.16 41, 120
7.18 11
7.19 73
7.20 122
7.20–21 26
7.20–24 10, 173

7.21 36, 126, 155	9.6–7 19, 178	155, 158, 167, 172, 180
7.21–22 19, 178	9.7 36, 155	
7.22 36, 155	9.8 26, 33, 83, 93, 105, 147, 149	11.17 12, 76, 96, 135, 140, 147, 171
7.23 122, 150, 178, 179		
7.24 126, 178	9.8–10 126, 168	11.17-1 119
7.26 101, 110	9.9 26, 118, 122, 142, 147, 149, 178, 179	11.17–18 41
7.27 109, 110, 126		11.17–20 132, 134, 172
8 9, 120, 123, 154, 158, 169	9.9–10 83	11.17–21 21, 82, 83
	9.10 85, 119, 127, 143, 168	11.18 20, 122, 138, 150, 152, 178
8–9 174		
8–10 170	10 4, 38	11.19 127, 130, 134, 135, 136, 179
8–11 25, 40, 53, 148, 156	10–11 24	
	10.1 38, 84	11.19–20 76, 128, 140
8.1–11.25 28, 84	10.2 148, 149	11.20 36, 76, 116, 126, 134, 135, 179, 180
8.1 16, 22, 23, 28, 84, 118, 166	10.3 148	
	10.4 148	11.21 109, 119, 121, 122, 135, 168, 172
8.2 28, 84, 148	10.5 73, 84, 148	
8.3 17, 28, 84, 85, 122	10.7 148, 149	11.22–23 148
8.3–16 168	10.9–22 84	11.23 85, 149
8.3–17 179	10.12 74	11.24 17, 28
8.3–18 178	10.14 4, 74	11.25 28, 53, 54, 167, 170
8.4 28, 84, 147, 148	10.15 38, 84, 148	
8.5 122, 123	10.18 148	12.1–6 41
8.6 28, 34, 35, 96, 118, 121, 147	10.18–19 148	12.1–11 170
	10.19 85	12.1–12 29
8.9 121	10.20 38, 84	12.1–13 94
8.10 72, 122, 123	10.22 84	12.2 94, 121
8.10–12 118, 175	11 120, 135	12.2–3 120, 126, 169, 178
8.11 71	11.1 17, 28, 148	
8.12 26, 34, 35, 122, 142, 147, 149	11.1–3 175	12.3 94, 121
	11.1–11 12	12.4 94
8.13 121	11.1–12 82, 119	12.5 94
8.14 123	11.3 26, 34, 43, 119	12.6 29, 94
8.15 34, 35, 121	11.5 120	12.7 54, 94
8.16 123	11.6–7 43, 122	12.8–14 174
8.17 34, 35, 118, 121, 122, 178, 179	11.7–11 44	12.9 26, 29, 34, 54, 120, 121, 178
	11.8 31	
8.17–18 168	11.12 36, 139, 178	12.11 29
8.18 92, 119, 127, 143, 144, 179	11.13 26, 83, 93, 147, 171	12.12 94
		12.13 94
9.1 92	11.14–21 83, 147, 169	12.15 31, 135
9.1–7 149	11.15 11, 12, 26, 83, 96, 119, 120, 147, 172	12.16 41, 120, 178
9.3 148, 149		12.17–20 29
9.5 127	11.16 18, 83, 96, 119, 125, 135, 144, 147–9,	12.19 118, 122, 178, 179
9.5–7 119		

Index of Scriptural References

12.19–20   152, 173
12.20   41
12.21–14.10   89
12.21–25   88
12.21–28   55
12.22   26, 34
12.25   121
12.26–28   88
12.27   26, 34
13   89, 109
13.1–10   179
13.1–16   55, 123
13.2   89, 90, 101
13.2–16   89
13.5   109
13.6   26, 34, 89, 90, 109
13.6–8   101
13.7   34, 89, 90, 109
13.8   34, 80, 89, 167
13.9   89
13.9–10   115
13.10   26, 34, 90, 101, 109
13.10–15   109
13.15   33, 109
13.17   89, 179
13.17–23   89, 123
13.18   34
13.18–23   54
13.19   36, 89, 176
13.20–23   177
13.21   144
13.22   80, 90, 179
13.23   89, 144
14   132
14.1   9, 54
14.1–3   120, 169
14.1–5   122
14.1–10   83
14.3   135, 179
14.3–7   122
14.4–5   132
14.4–6   16
14.6   13, 37, 129
14.9–10   145

14.10–11   132
14.11   19, 21, 36, 82, 83, 116
14.12–21   41, 101, 119, 152, 170
14.13   31, 111, 121, 178, 180
14.13–14   87
14.13–21   111, 127
14.15   95, 111, 151, 153
14.17   31
14.19   31, 33, 105
14.21   31, 110, 149, 152, 153
14.22   37, 125
14.22–23   120, 170, 171
14.23   37, 126
15   42, 44
15.1–6   41
15.2–4   34
15.8   121, 152, 167, 173, 178, 180
16   37, 43, 44, 46, 52, 92, 100, 101, 116, 117, 120, 121, 124, 130, 135, 137, 145, 174
16.1–7   179
16.1–14   125
16.2   45, 178
16.3   100, 124
16.6   145
16.6–7   144
16.8   47
16.8–14   45, 144, 179
16.15   124
16.15–17   124
16.15–34   46, 180
16.16–21   179
16.16–25   124
16.17   122
16.19   36
16.20   34, 45, 46, 124
16.20–21   123, 146
16.22   124, 137, 179
16.24–25   44

16.25   46, 124
16.26   46, 124, 125, 179
16.27   124
16.28   46, 124
16.28–29   125, 179
16.28–34   124
16.29   46
16.31–34   137
16.32   124
16.33–34   125
16.36   35, 46, 80, 123, 146
16.36–37   167
16.37   126
16.37–42   47
16.38   122, 179
16.38–39   46
16.41   43
16.42   33
16.43   80, 109, 137, 168, 179
16.44   125
16.44–45   124
16.44–52   116, 125
16.46   116
16.49–50   100
16.52   137, 179
16.53–55   116
16.54   37, 137
16.55   45, 46
16.56   34
16.56–57   172
16.57   66, 68
16.59   92, 116, 121, 127, 142, 168, 180
16.59–63   46
16.60   134, 137, 144, 180
16.60–61   128
16.60–63   21, 54, 82
16.61   117, 137, 179
16.62   139
16.62–63   128
16.63   19, 87, 88, 137, 138, 179, 181

17   43, 44, 92, 123
17.1   97
17.1–7   41
17.1–10   41, 97
17.1–21   12, 174, 175
17.2   97
17.3   97
17.3–4   174
17.3–10   54
17.4   97
17.5   97
17.5–6   97
17.8   97
17.9   34, 97
17.10   34, 97
17.11–21   10, 97
17.12   34, 35, 121, 174
17.15   34, 124, 179
17.15–18   123
17.16   35, 92
17.16–17   82
17.17   41, 168
17.18   92
17.19   92, 123
17.20   41
17.21   41, 97
17.22   97
17.22–24   21, 40, 41, 54, 82, 97, 138, 174
17.23   97
17.24   97
18   18, 37, 52, 86, 112, 142, 182, 183
18.1–4   101
18.2   26, 34, 166, 181
18.3   181
18.3–20   183
18.4   182
18.5–13   20
18.6   20, 36, 95, 112, 150
18.8   112
18.9   36, 112, 168
18.11   36, 95, 112, 150
18.13   34, 112
18.15   36, 95, 112, 150
18.17   36, 112
18.19   26, 34, 54, 181
18.20   179, 181
18.21   112
18.21–22   86, 183
18.23   34, 179, 183
18.24   34, 86
18.24–29   183
18.25   26, 34, 54, 183
18.27–29   183
18.29   26, 34, 183
18.30   13, 37, 168
18.30–32   129, 130, 183
18.32   13, 37, 144
19   10, 27, 43, 90, 103, 109
19.1   90
19.1–9   24, 41, 174
19.2   90, 103
19.2–3   90
19.2–9   59, 90
19.3   103, 109
19.4   90
19.4–5   90
19.5   103
19.6   103, 109
19.6–7   90
19.7   109
19.8–9   90
19.9   12
19.10   90, 103, 109
19.10–11   90
19.10–14   24, 41, 59, 90, 174
19.11   103
19.12   43
19.12–14   90
19.14   43
19.14   90, 103
20   25, 37, 52, 93, 104, 116, 125, 129, 130, 134, 135, 177, 183
20.1   9, 16, 22, 23, 54, 118
20.1–4   42
20.3   34, 118
20.4   34, 35, 178
20.5   116
20.5–6   125, 179
20.5–10   100
20.5–28   100
20.6   145
20.7   19, 36, 122
20.7–8   83, 122
20.8   33, 105, 109, 121, 122, 125, 127, 178, 179
20.8–9   139, 177
20.9   33, 36, 139, 140
20.10–29   127
20.11   36, 111, 124, 146, 168
20.12   100
20.13   19, 20, 33, 36, 105, 109, 111, 121, 123, 124, 126, 146, 168, 178, 179
20.13–14   139, 177
20.14   33, 36, 139, 140
20.15–16   167
20.16   19, 20, 36, 83, 123
20.18   19, 36
20.19   36
20.21   19, 20, 33, 36, 105, 109, 111, 121, 123, 124, 146, 178
20.21–22   139, 177
20.22   33, 36, 139, 140
20.23   31, 135, 177
20.23–24   167, 179
20.24   19, 20, 36, 83, 123, 178
20.25   111, 145
20.25–26   145
20.26   19, 36, 123, 145, 146
20.27   121, 178, 180
20.27–29   94

Index of Scriptural References

20.28   36, 94, 101
20.28–29   123
20.28–32   83
20.29   93, 94
20.30   19, 34, 36, 120, 122, 125, 127, 169
20.30–32   179
20.31   19, 34, 36, 120, 123, 146
20.32   26, 34, 83, 104
20.32–34   103, 104, 140
20.32–38   171
20.33   33, 104, 105, 140
20.33–38   21, 82, 83
20.34   33, 76, 104, 105, 135, 171
20.34–38   12, 132, 105
20.36   105, 168
20.37   100
20.38   19
20.39   33, 36, 120, 123, 125, 127, 135, 140, 155, 169, 176
20.39–40   20
20.39–41   178
20.39–44   21, 82, 83, 127
20.40   36, 37, 58, 97, 138, 154, 155, 174
20.40–41   70, 74
20.40–43   132, 171
20.40–44   177
20.41   33, 36, 68, 76, 139, 140, 177
20.41–42   12, 135
20.43   19, 76, 137, 155, 179
20.44   33, 139
21.2–4   152
21.3   41, 90, 97
21.4   32
21.5   9, 13, 26, 44, 54, 127
21.7   82
21.8   91, 182

21.9   90
21.10   32
21.11   54
21.11–12   29
21.13–18   93
21.14–15   93
21.17   29, 54, 115
21.19   29, 54
21.22   33, 54
21.23–25   10
21.23–27   40
21.24–27   29
21.25   118
21.27   41
21.29   80, 167
21.30   118
21.30–31   103
21.30–32   12, 174
21.32   102, 103
21.33   93
21.33–37   30, 93
21.36   33
22   106, 108, 109
22.1   106
22.1–12   106
22.1–16   26
22.2   34, 35
22.2–3   82
22.2–4   122, 178
22.2–13   179
22.3   19, 36, 108, 122
22.4   11, 19, 36, 72
22.6   108, 122, 175, 178
22.6–12   36
22.7   108, 122
22.7–12   20, 111, 124
22.8   19, 36, 108, 123, 179
22.9   95, 108, 122, 123, 150, 178
22.10–11   122
22.11   19, 36
22.12   108, 122
22.12–13   122, 178
22.13   54, 108, 122

22.13–16   106
22.14   34, 135
22.15   19, 31
22.16   33, 36
22.17   106
22.17–22   26, 106
22.19   80
22.20–22   42
22.21   108
22.22   33, 105
22.23   106
22.23–31   106
22.25   108, 109
22.25–28   108
22.25–29   179
22.25–31   106
22.26   19, 36, 100, 108, 109, 123, 161, 176, 179
22.27   108, 109, 122, 175, 178
22.28   34, 108, 109, 109, 123, 179
22.29   108, 122
22.30   87, 109, 144
22.31   33, 108, 109, 168, 177
23   37, 43, 44, 46, 101, 117, 120, 124, 137, 174
23.1–21   46
23.3   46, 124
23.4   45, 47, 67, 179
23.5   124, 180
23.5–7   125
23.5–21   124
23.7   19, 36, 124
23.8   124
23.9–10   117
23.11   124, 180
23.11–18   117
23.11–21   179
23.12   69
23.13   19, 36
23.14   124

23.14–17   12
23.16–17   125
23.19   124, 137
23.20   137
23.20–21   46
23.21   124
23.22   82, 126
23.22–26   41
23.24   69
23.25   43, 46
23.25–26   47
23.27   124
23.28–29   47
23.30   19, 36
23.31   117
23.32–34   25, 117
23.35   142, 167, 180
23.36   34, 35
23.37   122–4, 146, 178
23.38   19, 36, 123, 155, 179
23.38–39   178
23.39   19, 36, 122, 123, 146, 155
23.40–44   46, 137
23.45   122, 178
23.46–47   47
23.47   43
23.48   67
24   44, 88
24–25   79
24.1   22, 23, 78, 89
24.1–2   78, 79, 82, 88, 170
24.1–14   10, 178
24.2   58
24.3   121, 178
24.3–13   43
24.3–14   79
24.6   82
24.6–9   122, 178
24.7   79, 151
24.12–14   79
24.13   33, 142
24.14   119, 126, 127, 144, 168, 179
24.15–18   9
24.15–23   101
24.15–24   29, 45, 79, 93
24.16   79, 93
24.18   9, 54
24.19   26, 29, 54
24.20   54
24.21   10, 19, 31, 36, 79, 93, 125, 149, 155, 169, 173, 178
24.21–24   79
24.23   29, 182, 183
24.24   29, 170
24.25   79, 88, 93
24.25–26   34, 79, 82, 87, 93, 170
24.26   87, 88
24.27   29, 88
25   30
25–27   78
25–32   20, 21, 30, 68, 81, 82
25–48   82
25.1–7   12, 79
25.1–28.33   89
25.2–7   11
25.3   10, 11, 19, 30, 34, 36, 41, 79, 82, 118, 151, 155, 172, 173
25.4–5   172
25.5   31
25.6   30, 79, 151, 172
25.7   31, 172
25.8   11, 30, 34, 79, 172
25.8–11   79
25.9–11   172
25.11   31
25.12   30, 31, 79, 175
25.12–14   67, 79, 92
25.13   31
25.14   31
25.15   30, 79, 175
25.15–17   67, 79
25.17   1, 31, 139

26   45
26–27   44
26–28   24, 30, 89
26.1   22–4, 89
26.1–14   24, 55, 59
26.2   30, 34, 82
26.4–5   45
26.6   31
26.7   12
26.7–9   41
26.7–14   23
26.9   31
26.9–12   41
26.12   45
26.14   45
26.15   34
26.16   31
26.16–18   26
26.17–18   27
26.20   39, 93
26.21   93
27   41, 45, 69
27.2   34
27.3   31, 93
27.4   45
27.4–9   45
27.10–25   45
27.15   12
27.17   118
27.26   45
27.26–27   45
27.32   26, 27, 34
27.34   45
27.36   93
28   4, 5
28.1–10   91
28.2   34, 39, 91
28.2–6   31
28.5   91
28.6–10   39
28.7   36, 91
28.8   39
28.9   34
28.11–19   91, 99
28.12   93

Index of Scriptural References

28.12–13   100
28.12–19   27
28.16   31, 36, 91
28.17   31, 91
28.18   31, 91
28.19   93
28.20   67
28.20–23   67
28.21   67
28.22   31, 33, 139
28.22–23   68
28.24   21, 67, 68, 82, 135
28.24–26   32, 89, 138, 173, 176
28.25   31, 33, 135, 139, 140
28.25–26   21, 67, 68, 82, 152
28.26   68
29–32   24, 30, 89
29.1   22, 23, 24, 89
29.1–32.32   89
29.3   31, 34, 39, 41
29.4   69
29.5   69, 93
29.6–7   12, 31, 100, 124
29.8   31
29.9   34
29.12   31
29.13–16   42
29.16   124, 179
29.17   22, 23, 89
29.17–20   24, 41, 55, 59, 78, 89
29.18   10, 45
29.18–20   12
29.21   21, 82, 87, 88
30.1   89
30.6   31
30.15   33, 105
30.18   31
30.20   22, 23, 89
30.21   10
30.23   31

30.24–25   12
30.26   31
31   39, 44
31.1   22, 23, 89
31.1–18   41
31.2   34, 100
31.2–9   31
31.3–17   100
31.10   31
31.11–14   31
31.14–18   39
31.16   37
31.17   93
31.18   34, 93, 100
32.1   22–4, 89
32.2   31, 39
32.4   93
32.7–8   39
32.17   22, 23, 89
32.18–32   39, 93
32.19   34, 93
32.20–26   93
32.21   39, 93
32.24–30   93
32.28–32   93
32.31   37
32.32   93
33   21, 37, 82, 86–8, 182
33–39   21
33–48   20, 81, 82
33.1–6   41
33.1–9   8, 85, 86
33.2–6   86
33.7   86
33.7–9   86
33.8–9   86
33.10   26, 87, 130, 182
33.10–11   129
33.10–20   86
33.11   13, 37, 144, 182, 183
33.11–20   87
33.12–16   183
33.14–16   183

33.15   20, 111, 112, 168
33.17   26, 34, 54, 183
33.20   26, 34, 168, 183
33.21   10, 23, 24, 78, 87, 89, 166
33.21–22   78, 79, 82, 87–9, 144, 170
33.22   88
33.23–29   12, 169
33.24   26, 34, 82, 99, 119, 172, 173
33.24–26   152
33.25   34, 122
33.25–26   179
33.25–29   172
33.26   34
33.27   110, 111, 119, 152
33.27–29   172, 173
33.28   31
33.28–29   152
33.29   41
33.30   26
33.30–31   13
33.30–32   9, 13, 54, 128
33.31   128
33.31–32   182
33.32   128
33.33   8, 16
34   2, 42, 98, 110, 124, 135, 138, 153, 175
34–37   21
34–48   20
34.1–9   144
34.1–10   98
34.1–16   2, 101
34.1–22   138
34.1–23   41
34.1–24   59
34.2   34
34.2–3   98
34.2–6   122
34.2–8   175

34.4   98, 110
34.4–5   2
34.5–6   98
34.6   98
34.10   2, 98, 144
34.10–16   144
34.11–12   98
34.11–16   98, 175
34.12   58, 74, 98
34.12–15   98
34.13   76, 135, 171
34.13–14   152
34.13–15   98
34.16   98
34.17   2
34.17–19   144, 175
34.17–21   122
34.17–22   98
34.18   34
34.21   175
34.22   135, 144
34.23   2, 98, 101
34.23–24   42, 59, 98, 174, 175
34.25   41, 68, 112, 137, 138, 153, 176, 180
34.25–28   134
34.25–29   41, 153, 173, 180
34.25–30   2, 20, 112
34.25–31   144, 173
34.26   37, 110, 112, 153
34.26–27   138
34.27   68, 76, 112, 153
34.27–28   138
34.28   68, 112, 135, 153, 176
34.29   76, 135, 137, 138, 153
34.30   112, 134, 180
34.31   41
35   21, 30, 82, 83, 92
35.1   91
35.1–15   12, 92, 175
35.1–36.15   41, 91

35.2   91
35.2–15   11, 91
35.3   91, 92
35.4   91, 92
35.5   82, 91
35.7   91, 92
35.8   91, 92
35.9   91, 92
35.10   26, 31, 34, 92, 117, 149, 151
35.11   92, 172
35.11–12   151
35.12   34, 82, 91, 92, 149, 172
35.14   91, 92, 172
35.15   30, 82, 91, 92, 151, 172
36   42, 76, 83, 91, 135, 138, 139, 151, 153
36.1   61, 91, 95, 151
36.1–15   61, 91, 92, 173
36.2   34, 61, 92
36.2–5   151
36.2–6   172
36.3   62, 91, 92, 151
36.3–4   11
36.3–5   61
36.4   91, 92, 95, 151, 172, 173
36.4–6   153
36.5   31, 61, 92, 175
36.6   11, 30, 61, 91, 92, 151, 153
36.6–7   137
36.7   172
36.8   91, 95, 171
36.8–10   153
36.8–12   41
36.9   153, 184
36.9–11   138
36.9–15   173
36.10   58, 62, 91, 92
36.11   153, 180
36.12   62, 92, 135
36.12–13   95

36.12–14   41, 95
36.12–15   95
36.13   34, 151
36.14   95, 135
36.14–15   95
36.15   11, 95, 135, 137, 150, 153
36.16   91
36.16–19   10
36.16–20   177
36.16–23   75
36.16–24   135
36.17–18   19, 151, 178
36.17–19   167, 179
36.17–20   132
36.18   33, 36, 41, 105, 122
36.18–19   178
36.19   31, 135, 151, 168
36.19–20   139
36.19–24   171
36.20   33, 34, 36
36.20–21   140
36.20–22   19
36.20–23   33, 176
36.21   33, 36, 129, 139, 177
36.21–32   177
36.22   33, 36, 76, 129, 139, 183
36.22–36   134
36.23   20, 33, 36, 68, 75, 76, 139, 140, 177
36.23–24   139
36.23–38   75, 76
36.24   76, 135, 171
36.24–27   128, 132
36.24–28   101
36.24–45   178
36.25   20, 138, 179
36.25–27   177
36.25–37   2
36.26   127, 134, 136, 179
36.26–27   76

Index of Scriptural References

36.27   36, 134–6, 140, 179
36.28   76, 171, 180
36.28–29   178
36.29   20, 76, 138, 179
36.29–30   138, 173
36.30   135
36.31   76, 137, 179
36.32   76, 129, 137, 139, 183
36.33   2, 20, 179
36.33–36   76, 153, 178
36.33–38   41, 101, 138, 173
36.34–38   144
36.36   76, 130, 173
36.37–38   41
36.38   75
37   76, 98, 117, 135, 146, 158, 175
37.1   28, 84
37.1–14   28, 84, 138, 171
37.2   84
37.3   26
37.8   28
37.10   85
37.11   26, 34, 58, 171
37.11–14   175
37.12   12, 135, 171
37.14   69, 76, 132, 136, 171
37.15–22   29, 117, 138, 162
37.15–25   175
37.16   58
37.16–17   29
37.17   117
37.18   26, 29
37.18–19   117
37.20   58
37.20–22   117
37.21   135, 171
37.21–23   132
37.22   35, 42, 135, 174

37.23   19, 20, 36, 76, 116, 122, 134, 135, 138, 155, 178–80
37.24   35, 36, 42, 138
37.24–25   98, 174, 180
37.25   68
37.25–28   134
37.26   134, 137, 158, 180
37.26–27   154
37.26–28   138, 149, 155, 174, 178
37.27   3, 116, 140, 180
37.27–28   20, 70
37.28   158
37.29   135
38–39   3, 21, 25, 54, 58, 69, 76, 140, 176
38.1   69
38.2   69
38.2–6   176
38.4   69
38.5–6   69
38.6   69
38.8   69
38.8–13   69
38.11   26, 34
38.13   34
38.14   34, 69
38.15   69
38.16   33, 69, 139, 140
38.17   34, 69
38.23   33, 139, 140
39   69
39.1–6   177
39.4   69
39.6   69
39.7   33, 36, 139, 140, 176
39.10   153
39.12   20
39.12–15   153
39.13   140
39.14–16   20
39.17   69

39.21–22   140
39.21–27   177
39.23   121, 167, 178, 180, 184
39.23–24   142, 173, 185
39.24   167, 168, 180, 184
39.25   33, 58, 74, 139, 144, 171
39.26   121, 138, 178, 180
39.27   33, 68, 135, 139, 140, 173, 177
39.27–28   171
39.28   58, 74, 167
39.29   69, 184
40–42   156, 157, 163
40–43   70
40–46   174
40–48   2, 18, 19, 21, 24, 25, 28, 35, 36, 53, 70, 100, 123, 153, 156–63, 178
40.1   18, 23, 28, 69, 78, 80, 81, 85, 166
40.1–2   156
40.1–48.35   28, 84, 85
40.2   17, 28, 37, 40, 85, 156–8, 161
40.2–3   3
40.4   28, 156, 157
40.5   156
40.6   159
40.22   159
40.26   159
40.31   159
40.34   159
40.37   159
40.45–46   70
40.49   159
41.4   159
41.8   28, 157
41.22   160
42.14   158
42.20   156, 158

43   156
43–44   36
43.1–2   148
43.1–9   158
43.1–12   20
43.2   85
43.2–4   147, 156
43.3   4, 28, 75, 85, 149, 157
43.4   85
43.4–5   148, 160
43.5   28, 85
43.7   33, 35, 36, 85, 135, 138, 149, 154, 156, 160, 177, 178
43.7–8   19, 155, 158, 176
43.7–9   20, 123, 157, 161, 178
43.8   33, 36
43.9   85, 96, 138, 149, 177, 178
43.10   156, 158, 163
43.10–11   137
43.11   58, 162
43.12   18, 158
43.17   160
43.18   18, 156
43.18–27   18
43.19–25   18
44–46   156
44.1–2   160
44.1–3   157
44.2   158
44.2–3   158
44.3   28, 157, 162
44.5   28, 156, 157
44.6   121, 178
44.6–8   178
44.6–9   157
44.6–31   20
44.7   19, 36, 155, 158
44.7–8   161
44.8   108
44.9   158, 161
44.10   96, 161
44.12   161
44.13   70, 108, 157, 158, 161
44.15   3, 158, 185
44.15–16   161
44.15–17   157
44.17–19   100, 159
44.17–31   20
44.19   157, 161
44.20   100, 159, 161
44.21   100, 159
44.22   100, 159, 161
44.23   100, 159, 161
44.25   36, 100, 159
44.28   100, 159
44.29   100, 159
44.31   100, 159
45.1–6   158
45.1–7   161
45.1–8   156, 157
45.2   162
45.2–3   157
45.3   158
45.7   158
45.8–9   161
45.8–10   157, 162
45.9   122
45.10–12   161
45.12   157
45.17   162
45.18–20   154, 160
46.2–3   158
46.3   161
46.6–7   160
46.7   100, 159
46.9–10   158
46.17   81
47   42, 117
47–48   20, 41, 162
47.1   3
47.1–12   20, 40, 144, 153, 156, 157
47.6   156
47.12   3, 40–2
47.13–14   162
47.13–48.35   156, 157
47.22   100, 159
48.10   158
48.10–12   158
48.13   158
48.15–16
48.35   149, 156, 161

Daniel
5.4   104
5.14   136
5.23   104
7–8   28
8   176
9.1–19   55
11   176

Hosea
1.2   46, 124
1.9   127
2.4   46
2.10–15   124
2.21–22   46
4.12–13   46
4.13   102
7.11–13   124
8.9–10   124
11.1–4   125
12.2   124

Joel
3.1   137
3.1–2   69
4.10   103

Amos
1   29
1.4   69
1.7   69
1.10   69
2.9–11   125
4.1–3   12, 51, 52
4.13   51

5.1–2 27	*Micah*	2.1 78
5.8–9 51	1.16 46	2.10 78
5.11 68	3.11 148, 173	2.11–13 18
6.4–7 51		2.20 78
7–9 28, 158	*Habakkuk*	
7.1 3	2.2–3 78	*Zechariah*
7.1–8 143		1–6 28
7.10–13 49	*Zephaniah*	1.1 24, 66, 78
8.1–2 143	1.13 68	
9.5–6 51	1.14–18 73	1.4 128
9.7–10 12	2 29	1.7 78
9.8–10 51	3.1 108	1.15 147
9.11–15 12, 51	3.3–5 106–8	4.6–7 136
9.14 68	3.4 108	7.1 78
9.14–15 12	3.8 106–8	8.20–23 42
		9.9–10 42
Obadiah	*Haggai*	10.2–3 2
1.10–14 30–1, 175	1.1 24, 66, 78	11 2
1.12 30	1.15 78	11.16 2

Index of Authors

Albertz, R.   11, 48, 53, 57, 59, 60, 141
Becker, J.   56
Block, D. I.   32, 58, 75, 89, 117, 145, 148, 162, 171
Boadt, L.   39
Bodi, D.   12, 148
Bourguignon, E.   17
Broome, E. C.   15

Carley, K. W.   17
Carr, D.   50
Christensen, D. L.   29
Clements, R. E.   52, 62
Cook, S. L.   18, 161
Cooke, G. A.   59, 69, 77, 145, 162–3
Crane, A. S.   76
Crouch, C. L.   39–40

Darr, K. P.   20, 48, 58, 113
Davis, E. F.   58, 85
Day, P. L.   45
Driver, S. R.   53, 110

Filson, F. V.   75
Fishbane, M.   106
Flanagan, J.   77
Floyd, M. H.   51–2
Fohrer, G.   20, 59, 63
Fox, M. V.   146, 171
Friebel, K. G.   29, 56, 118, 145
Frolov, S.   102

Galambush, J.   45
Ganzel, T.   103, 105, 161
Garber Jr., D. G.   11
Garscha, J.   64
Gese, H.   70
Glazov, G. Y.   88
Grayson, A. K.   48

Greenberg, M.   9, 38, 58–9, 70, 88–9, 130, 145, 148
Gunkel, H.   50, 52, 58, 60

Habel, N.   27
Halperin, D. J.   15, 75
Haran, M.   58, 70
Herrmann, S.   64
Hölscher, G.   57, 64, 77
Holtz, S. E.   161
Hughes, D. J.   17

Jong, M. J. de.   8
Joyce, P. M.   65, 131, 139, 147, 163–4, 182

Kasher, R.   154, 158, 160, 163
Keel-Leu, O.   38
Kelle, B. E.   45, 48
Klein, A.   99, 113
Konkel, M.   70
Kutsko, J.   12, 147

Lapsley, J. E.   131, 136–7
Levenson, J. D.   40, 70, 162
Levitt Kohn, R.   103, 105, 113
Lewis, I. M.   17
Lilly, I. E.   76
Lipschits, O.   48
Long, B. O.   28
Ludwig, A. M.   17
Lust, J.   76
Lyons, M. A.   28, 108, 110

Mackie, T. P.   74
Mayfield, T.   21, 78–9
McKeating, H.   14, 165
McNamara, P.   17
Mein, A.   18, 164, 168
Moran, W. L.   102

Moughtin-Mumby, S. 46
Mowinckel, S. 14

Newsom, C. A. 44
Niditch, S. 28
Nihan, C. 110
Nissinen, M. 15–16, 50–1

Odell, M. S. 164, 181
Olley, J. W. 113
Overholt, T. W. 16

Patton, C. L. 8, 18, 48
Pohlmann, K.-F. 20, 57, 113
Price-Williams, D. 17

Raabe, P. R. 31
Raitt, T. M. 34, 130
Rendtorff, R. 64
Renz, T. 12–13, 23, 32, 80–2, 120, 132, 168–70, 184–5
Reuss, E. 53
Robson, J. 130
Rollston, C. A. 50
Rom-Shiloni, D. 103, 118, 125, 164, 172

Schöpflin, K. 42, 48
Schwartz, B. J. 132, 140, 183
Sherlock, C. 88
Smith-Christopher, D. L. 11
Steiner, R. C. 102
Stevenson, K. R. 158, 162–3
Stökl, J. 16, 90
Strine, C. A. 39–40, 132
Stromberg, J. 71
Strong, J. T. 163–4
Sweeney, M. A. 18, 154

Tiemeyer, L.-S. 143
Tooman, W. A. 69–70, 148
Toorn, K. van der 50–1
Torrey, C. C. 56
Tov, E. 71
Tuell, S. S. 70, 163

Wellhausen, J. 110
Wilson, R. R. 14, 16, 38, 88
Wood, A. 38

Zimmerli, W. 20, 32, 52, 59–62, 77–8, 80–1, 88, 91–2, 99, 110, 145

www.ingramcontent.com/pod-product-compliance
Lightning Source LLC
Chambersburg PA
CBHW050138240426
43673CB00043B/1716